Praise for the book

'A hero without heroics – what a life, what a story. Hassen Ebrahim successfully set up MK units and underground ANC cells in Soweto, Lenasia and elsewhere, and then put down his AK 47s and limpet mines, and picked up his computer to become the soft-spoken, ever genial executive director of the Constitutional Assembly that drafted our Constitution. He later became a pioneer user of IT in the public administration and finally went on to share the South African experience of constitution-making as a UN expert in half a dozen war-torn societies. Phew! What a book.' – Albie Sachs, former Justice of the Constitutional Court

'This book is a welcome contribution to South African history, of one of the ANC's most prolific and successful politico-military machineries. It is important for our knowledge of the African National Congress to understand the role these machineries played and the sacrifices the cadres made preceding the negotiation of the political transition that took place in South Africa. It is no surprise that so many of these brave and outstanding operatives got to play such an important role in the building of a democratic South Africa.' – Sue Rabkin, Political Military Committee (PMC), Lusaka.

'Getting to know and work with Hassen as a fellow former MK cadre during the days of South Africa's constitution-making from 1994–96 was a rare pleasure. This book is an important contribution to the history of our liberation struggle and takes us on a journey of someone who has travelled a remarkable journey from the bushes of Angola, to the World Trade Centre and finally the adoption of our Constitution, one of our new democracy's greatest achievements.' – Marion Sparg, former Deputy Executive Director, Constitutional Assembly.

'Hassen alias "George" Ebrahim is a former member of uMkhonto WeSizwe who may only be known to many as a lawyer who studied at Edinburgh and the University of Botswana and worked for the Constituent Assembly during the drafting of the constitution. Hassen was a student by day and an ANC operative by night. His discipline and passion for ITC at an early stage gave the ANC underground machinery in Botswana delightful depth in mobilising for a People's War to end apartheid.' – Thabang Makwetla, Deputy Minister of Defence and Military Veterans

From Marabastad to Mogadishu
The Journey of an ANC Soldier

Hassen Ebrahim

With the kind assistance of the Ahmed Kathrada Foundation for marketing and publicity.

First published by Jacana Media (Pty) Ltd in 2019

10 Orange Street
Sunnyside
Auckland Park 2092
South Africa
+2711 628 3200
www.jacana.co.za

© Hassen Ebrahim, 2019

All rights reserved.

ISBN 978-1-4314-2901-1

Cover design by publicide
Design and layout by Shawn Paikin
Editing by Lara Jacob
Proofreading by Nkhensani Manabe
Set in Ehrhardt 11.5/15.5pt
Printed by ABC Press, Cape Town
Job no. 003648

See a complete list of Jacana titles at www.jacana.co.za

Contents

Foreword: At heart, a public servant vii
Preface xv

I	Mayhem in Mogadishu	1
II	Origins	7
III	Emerging Political Consciousness	15
IV	Entering the Fold	25
V	Going into Exile	47
VI	Exile: New Beginnings	59
VII	Changing Conditions of Struggle	87
VIII	The Kabwe Generation	99
IX	Stepping Up – In Full Flight	147
X	Finding a Political Solution	153
XI	Closing of a Chapter	157
XII	Kabwe Machinery's Closure	167
XIII	My Homecoming	169
XIV	Negotiating Peace	177
XV	Negotiating the Constitution	193
XVI	Joining Justice	213
XVII	Starting a New Life	229
XVIII	Working Internationally	237
XIX	Somalia Revisited	251
XX	Time to Come Home	253

Endnotes 255

FOREWORD

At heart, a public servant

This is a most welcome addition to the growing – albeit rather slow-growing – body of literature that helps us understand where we come from and how we are going about reconfiguring our country.

Hassen Ebrahim is one of those many seldom-heard-of foot-soldiers of the 1976 generation who joined the underground and was linked to the ANC structures operating from Botswana. He has been at the coal face of so many facets of South Africa's march to freedom. He was there during the times when involvement in the struggle against apartheid carried the risk of death; he was involved in our negotiated transition to democracy; he was the chief executive of the elected Constitutional Assembly which wrote and adopted our Constitution; thereafter and until 2007 he served in the Department of Justice.

During the early period in the underground he recruited Rocklyn Williams, who was a conscript in the apartheid army based at the Voortrekkerhoogte military headquarters with access to the telecommunications facilities. Rocklyn and Hassen worked together to convey to their Botswana contacts, Marius and Jenny Schoon, copies of all telexes coming in to the headquarters of the South African Defence Force (SADF). Marius and Jenny passed it on to the Revolutionary Council of the ANC based in Lusaka, who in turn used it with growing effectiveness in its political and military planning as well as counter-intelligence and security measures.[1]

At a certain stage, when the authorities began questioning Rocklyn it was decided that Hassen leave the country for his own safety as well as in order to contain whatever fall-out may result from the questioning. Hassen was then based in Botswana as part of the ANC Internal Political and Reconstruction Department (IPRD) charged with the task of organising the ANC underground, assisting with mass mobilisation and distribution of propaganda, as well as the development of MK within South Africa.

As it happened, the apartheid security apparatus had not tumbled onto Rocklyn's clandestine work and he remained in South Africa. He was subsequently re-activated as part of MK's military intelligence, in which role he performed with distinction.

Botswana was a tough place from which to operate. All work of the ANC, MK, SACP and SACTU from Botswana faced monitoring by the Botswana police (some of whom were working cahoots with the apartheid security force [2]), as well as the risk of kidnapping and death during raids by the apartheid security forces. Many innocent Botswana citizens were killed during these operations.

Botswana was vulnerable to the economic and military pressures by apartheid South Africa even after it became an independent state in 1965. It however sought to steer a tricky path in which it tried to close one eye to the activities of the South African liberation movement provided that the movement was discreet in the way in which it conducted its work, while at the same time confining many South African and Namibian refugees to a camp in Dukwe in the far north of Botswana.

As a cover to hide his work for the underground and to legitimise his stay in Botswana, Hassen enrolled as a student of law at the University of Botswana and eventually qualified through the University of Edinburgh with an LL.B degree.

During the day he was an upright, law-abiding, law-practising attorney in a legal firm in Gaborone, while most of his nights were devoted to underground work. How he and Barbara managed to birth and nurture two children under such a consuming schedule and during such fraught times remains a puzzle for me!

Let the book speak for the work that Hassen and his comrades did and with what measure of success. Suffice to note here that what stands out when one reads the first-hand testimonies and biographies of those who participated in the struggle to end apartheid is the varied life experiences from which liberation combatants were drawn.

Apartheid wrought devastation on the lives of every black person – every person of colour – irrespective of the person's wealth or station in life. This enormous pool of life experiences enriched the liberation movements with individuals who spared neither limb nor life in the pursuit of freedom, individuals whose contribution ought to be celebrated as part of the warp and weave of our nation-in-the-making. Each of them, whatever the positions they held in the structures of the organisations, helped shape the struggle, while they in turn were moulded by the struggle.

Hassen made a special imprint on my radar when around 1978 he recruited Rocklyn Williams. It seemed to me that here was a young black man who understood, perhaps instinctively, the tactical and strategic imperative that while keeping our focus on the primary task of organising and mobilising the oppressed and exploited into action, we should chip away at and weaken the white monolith that had been nurtured under institutionalised racism.

The recruitment of Rocklyn was not only invaluable in its own right. It sharpened the awareness in the IPRD that it was becoming possible to do systematic political work among the white community and that this was an area of work not restricted only to the gathering of intelligence for military purposes. Equally it reinforced the view that political work among the white community and the white armed forces was not a task to be left solely to members of the white community to perform among their own community.

Prosecuting the struggle was based on a clear strategic and tactical understanding, as Walter Sisulu put it that:

> (O)bjectively we, as the oppressed people, possess by our overwhelming majority a strategic advantage over the enemy, an advantage that guarantees the victory of our revolution. ... (But) for any revolution to succeed, it is essential to pare away the

strength of the enemy and to pin it down to the narrowest limits. Revolutions triumph not on the basis of absolute strength but on revolutionaries gaining a position of relative superiority over the enemy. ... Every reduction of the enemy's strength has a much greater effect than absolute numbers. At this level there are two aspects to weakening the enemy – that of winning sections onto the side of the revolution and that of neutralizing sections of the enemy camp. To achieve both we have to take account of the fact that white supremacy benefits all sections of the whites. This means that we have to look more closely at the structure of their societies and the different forces and currents of thought among them to devise appropriate tactics.[3]

That was the firm guideline in all our work in relation to the four pillars of struggle. Such an understanding of the imperatives of conducting the struggle is not something with which a freedom fighter is born. It usually comes through battle-hardening (which bears with it many scars) and a continual striving to understand the nature of the struggle being waged. I was intrigued to get to know more about this young Muslim man from Marabastad who found his way to befriend a white conscript in the apartheid army.

Ever since we became a constitutional democracy, the ANC, supported by its allies COSATU, the SACP and SANCO, has been the governing party. In this period while its membership has been growing, its reach into the different classes and strata in our society seems to have been narrowing. One would have expected the movement, with the vantage of occupying the seat of political power, to broaden as well as deepen it influence.

Instead of this happening through a growing trade union movement based on the principle of 'one industry, one union' and 'one country, one trade union federation,' we have been experiencing a fracturing of unions and a proliferation of union federations.

The black middle class that has grown substantially during the post-apartheid dispensation has been drifting away from the ANC.

People of mixed racial origin, the so-called coloureds, and those of

Indian extraction, who were active in the mass democratic movement of the 1980s, have became inactive and hesitant to identify with the ANC.

Instead of the religious sector developing on the unity of the interdenominational faiths that was so visible in the 1980s, instead of that unity reaching across and drawing in the independent churches, we find the latter being courted by the ANC while it seems to be at loggerheads with the churches and faiths that were integral to the mass democratic movement.

Save for a few odd fruitless efforts to eat into the white constituency through opportunistically co-opting some of re-imaged National Party leaders, there has been no real progress in drawing in sections of this community into sharing the goal of transformation and reconstruction.

The net effect has been that the constituency of the ANC has been narrowing and it has become more dependent on the rural sector.

This does not bode well: neither for the ANC, nor the country. The beach-head the ANC came to occupy through the achievement of democracy was supposed to be exploited to the full by systematically reconstructing our society pivoted on its commitment to the poor and the exploited. At the same time the promotion of the interests of the poverty-stricken and the workers was to be done in such a way to reinforce the view that such reconstruction of our economy and society was also in the interest of other classes and strata in our country. Along this path the interest of the poor and the workers would become the bedrock of the national interest, a shared interest, of the nation as a whole.

With many of the impediments to organising and mobilising removed through the achievement of democracy and with the opportunity to bring real and demonstrable change to countless lives, it is necessary to reflect on the ANC's experience over the past 25 years and find the appropriate tactics and strategy to deepen its reach into its core constituencies and expand its reach beyond them.

In the democratic era the ANC has been in a more advantageous position than it was under apartheid. Yet it was able to lead the process of uniting the people during the struggle to overthrow apartheid, when repression was rampant.

This memoir by Hassen Ebrahim, helps us interrogate that past, appreciate the knowledge and skills we developed both in the struggle to overthrow apartheid and the pursuit post-1994 of a programme of reconstruction and nation-building.

Since 2011 Hassen has been working mainly outside South Africa, more out of necessity than choice, on projects many of which have been associated with the United Nations and in relation to countries emerging from bitter conflicts. Along this trajectory he has been engaged in Zimbabwe, Somalia, Liberia, Sierra Leone, Libya, Yemen, the Philippines and is currently completing a contract in Somalia. That is an enormous storehouse of experience.

However, he confesses that '(T)his is not really what I wanted even if I enjoyed the work greatly.' There remains in him a yearning for a less peripatetic and a less fractured life, a life that encompasses a family, and above all a life grounded on public service within South Africa, the engine room of making life better for all. Marabastad may be no more. Hassen remains a Marabastad boy.

It is painful to learn of this yearning. At the close of his book he confesses that

> while I have enjoyed being an international public servant and working for the United Nations in different developing countries, it is my fervent hope that I would have the privilege of returning home to serve the people of South Africa. At heart, I am a public servant and don't know any other life. I have deeply regretted that I was not able to serve the people of the country whose freedom I fought for. I have therefore set myself the goal of finding a way of coming back home and working in the public sector.

He ends, ever the optimist, with the hope: 'Fortunately, the change of leadership in the country has created new possibilities and much hope. One can only hope that the public sector would be less toxic than it was before and more open. Home is where I want to be.'

From Marabastad to Mogadishu is an easy read, free of bitterness and victimhood, though at times one wishes he would delve deeper into events and expand on his insights. Read it carefully, thoughtfully, sensitively, because such memoirs help us look at ourselves and ask ourselves difficult questions.

Like Nazism, apartheid was an abomination. Building a caring and a humane society on the dehumanisation wrought by apartheid will not happen by default. There is no escape from history. There are always lessons buried in our past that help us not to repeat our mistakes, to make course-corrections that are normal to a historic journey such as ours and to chart a future in which our children will not have to scratch among the ashes is search of signs of the promise of a better life.

Some of those lessons are to be found in the stories of foot-soldiers like Hassen who have devoted their entire lives to the service of the people.

Mac Maharaj
17 February 2019
Durban

Preface

I dedicate this book to the memory of Prakash Napier, Yusuf Akhalwaya, Gary, Rocklyn Mark Williams (Rocky), Freddy Nephawe, Strike Bila, Ephraim Motlalepule Nkoe and Paul Sefularo. I was privileged to work with each of these very special people. They were cadres who served our country with distinction and played an important role in the success of the Kabwe Machinery (which I discuss in some detail later).

I would like to, however, make special mention of the role played by Prakash, Yusuf and Jameel Chand of the Ahmed Timol Unit. These young soldiers were members of one of the most successful MK units that were founded and based inside the country. Prakash and Yusuf lost their lives in the early hours of 12 December 1989 on the eve of the ANC's unbanning and just as we were to start negotiating an end to our conflict and the birth of our democracy. This was also the first MK unit that I helped establish, train, arm and deploy. Their lives will always remind me of the price that many young people paid for the freedom we enjoy today. This dedication is therefore my commitment to continue working for the ideals for which they fought and to make sure that they have not died in vain. It is my hope that our memory of these great patriots will sustain us in our efforts to continue the struggle for a better life for all South Africans.

My eight wonderful grandchildren – Lily, Imaan, Mohammed, Yusuf, Zaeem, Zahraa, Sabreen and Ameera – have become an equally important reason for me to continue to work to make this country a better place. These beautiful young people continue to offer me love in abundance and give me hope each time I see them.

※

This book is the result of the nagging pressure from Nava Pillay and Neeshan (Shan) Balton to write it and I am very grateful to them because there are several reasons why I needed to do it.

The struggle against apartheid gave meaning to my life and I am extremely fortunate for the opportunity I had to play a role in our liberation. This struggle produced some of Africa's finest leaders and I was privileged to work with many of them, all of them empowering experiences that made me realise my self-worth. I also had the rare privilege of being part of several of our country's defining moments, not least of all the birth of our constitutional democracy. However, an even more important part of this experience is the good fortune I had to be the commander of a politico-military machinery, which performed an outstanding role in our struggle for freedom.

This book offers me an opportunity to pay tribute to those leaders, combatants and operatives with whom I worked, and some who paid the ultimate sacrifice. It is an honour to share some of these experiences. The approach adopted in this book is therefore more that of a political memoir.

My journey

My journey starts in a dusty location called Marabastad, which is a short distance from the centre of Pretoria, now known as Tshwane. Like many others of the 1976 generation, I was driven by a sense of justice, left the country in search of the African National Congress (ANC), and after a few short years of work in the ANC's underground, was asked to go into exile. After spending some years in the ANC's Forward Areas building an underground machinery, I returned home in 1991 to help re-establish the ANC's legal structures that elected its first leadership inside the country. I then participated in and supported the process of negotiating both the interim and final constitutions, and even got elected to the first democratically elected government. I spent the next ten years in the Department of Justice and Constitutional Development helping to build institutions critical to our constitutional democracy. Once I left public service, I spent most of my time as an international public servant, working mainly for the United Nations. In this capacity, I had the opportunity to engage with leaders in several countries as a constitutional expert.

The late Reginald September (Uncle Reg), a stalwart and veteran of our struggle, used to say that the struggle for freedom is like a long train journey. Along the way, many would get on or off the train as it passed through the different stations of struggle. People will board at different times and many of those who started on the journey may not be on the train when it reaches its destination. Uncle Reg used to joke that his final destination was returning to Cape Town, which was both his home and the seat of Parliament.

Over time, my understanding of what the destination of my journey should be has changed. I started with the idea that our objective in the struggle was political freedom as represented by the right to vote and the right to belong to any political organisation that one wished. I learnt along the way that however desirable political freedom was, it would amount to little if it did not include equality in all its forms. Now that we have won the right to vote and adopted one of the most advanced constitutions in the world, we must embark on the next stage of our journey – to make sure that the new democratic state becomes an effective instrument for socio-economic change.

Seeking closure

My resistance to writing my story also withered once I came to accept my obligation to give an account of my journey. Part of this obligation is to record our experience, for if we don't, we risk losing it. I learnt that we have a duty to inform, and perhaps educate, if not inspire, the next generation to continue the struggle that we embarked upon and improve on, if not correct, what we have done. We must stand ready to pass the baton over to the new generation of leaders because the struggle is far from over.

There is also another more important reason that I feel compelled to write this history. When we were unbanned in 1990, the ANC was obliged to immediately throw all its energy into preparing to establish itself as a legal organisation and enter negotiations. In doing so, the ANC failed to bring closure to its underground units and operatives who risked their lives to bring about our political freedom. These units represented the ANC and gave leadership on the ground but were not recognised by the ANC when the legal structures were established. It was as if they did not exist.

Our underground units were accountable and reported to the National Executive Committee of the ANC though the Politico-Military Council, but we were never asked to submit our closing reports. The underground machinery just stopped functioning and we were forgotten. For me, this account is the submission of my closing report. It is also my attempt, albeit more than 25 years late, to pay tribute, show my respect and recognise the contribution of the heroes and heroines that I worked with. Many cadres selflessly gave up their youth, time, families, and even their lives, to answer our call to enlist into the world of the underground.

To each of them, I say that history should never forget your contribution and I, for my part, remain indebted.

Many comrades and friends who played critical roles in the struggle were disillusioned when the ANC lost its way during the Zuma years and the political freedom that we won was seemingly not at all what they had hoped for. This history is therefore a restatement of why so many of us became involved in the struggle. This is also why I have decided that apathy and withdrawal are not the answer – even if there is good reason to feel disillusioned by bad leadership, lack of governance, accountability and corruption. If anything, they call for more determined effort to fight. The objectives for which I fought remain and that is what I continue to be loyal to.

The struggle must continue. Aluta continua!

Preface

The underground

There are some preliminary issues that I want to address from the outset. The first relates to the use of the term 'underground' and the second to the underground machinery referred to in this book.

The term 'underground' has been used in various contexts and given unique interpretations by many writers. My use of the term is based on the interpretation given by the ANC during the early 1980s, when it defined its overall approach to the struggle as the four pillars: mass mobilisation, armed operations, underground organisation and international solidarity work. Generally, the term 'underground work' is understood to be activity deliberately carried out in a clandestine manner. However, not all underground work was illegal. During the period leading up to the banning of the ANC, the repressive nature of apartheid regime forced activists into adopting underground methods of conducting struggle. The ANC had to consider this possibility especially after the banning of the Communist Party in 1950. Mandela who authored the famous M-Plan was already banned and could not attend the very same conference that adopted it in 1953. Again, during the 1980s, many United Democratic Front (UDF), civil society and union activists were forced to adopt underground methods of struggle even if their activities were not illegal.

But the underground work carried out by operatives of the ANC was illegal because it was a banned organisation. The importance of this is that not all underground work was carried out by ANC people exclusively and that not all ANC people during the period leading up to 1990 were active in the underground. Many, but not all, people committed to the ANC were active in the underground. Supporting the ANC and doing work in the underground as members of the organisation were not the same thing. To avoid any confusion, the term 'underground' used in this book specifically refers to that work carried out by units and individual operatives of the ANC.

The second, and perhaps more important, clarification is that the underground units referred to in this book are specifically those units that I was responsible for or worked with. Since the culture and discipline of ANC operatives in different underground machineries was not necessarily the same, it is not appropriate to make generalisations of them.

I also had to remind myself that this piece of work is my political memoir and not a history of the underground, and therefore not a complete history or exhaustive list of all the units or operatives active under my command. I have had to focus on specific units and people who played an important role and made an impact on my life's experiences. I have generally recorded the activities of only those units that I have knowledge of or have been able to interview, and where it was possible, to verify the facts. I have resisted the temptation to speculate. In some instances, I was also able to rely on records of that period.

I must however encourage scholars and comrades to record their experiences in greater detail than I have been able to do in this account.

The Kabwe Machinery

For ease of reference, I chose to refer to the collection of underground structures that I was responsible for as the Kabwe Machinery. I would like to explain this nomenclature because this reference was not used before the writing of this account.

The term 'machinery' has generally been accepted to mean a network of units that operated under a single command structure in a coherent manner. While each of the units may have operated in total secrecy and without knowledge of the other units in the machinery, they would collectively be accountable to a single command structure. This term also suggests a synchronous operation of the different units that were not related to each other horizontally.

I chose to refer to the collection of units that were accountable to me as the Kabwe Machinery because they were established after and guided by the resolutions of the Kabwe conference of 1985, which are dealt with later. I also decided that it was better, for purposes of this account, to use a name to refer to the machinery rather than refer to it in personal terms.

Another dilemma I faced while writing was the level of detail that I ought to include on the history of the Kabwe Machinery. While the book is a political biography, it is also intended as a tribute to the people I worked with. I decided to focus only on units I established in three specific areas – Soweto, Lenasia and Pretoria – because it provides for a unique study of the underground during the latter part of the 1980s and explains the leadership role they played in their respective areas.

Finally, the focus of this book is solely from my personal perspective rather than those of the members of the Kabwe Machinery. While I collaborated with many of the comrades that I worked with in writing this book, I must however assume sole responsibility for any errors or omissions made. It is also my fervent hope that the comrades who were responsible for the various units in this machinery would record the history of their units because there is much to learn from their experiences.

Beyond political freedom

Many believed that the destination of Uncle Reg's train was the political freedom we attained in 1994. For me, this was insufficient. As significant as the right to vote and the adoption of one of the world's most progressive constitutions may be, the struggle is far from over.

The crises that both the ANC and its government faced (especially during the years under President Zuma's leadership) calls for the transformation of our state, the economy and the political party. There are important challenges that call for solutions. Now is not the time to be complacent. Fortunately, the struggle no longer entails the extraordinary human sacrifices that our generation, and those before us, were forced to endure. More immediate, though, is our struggle against racism, which is far from over. Racism is still rife and we are yet to resolve the national question.

I will always proudly retain the values I had as an ANC cadre and will continue to work for peace and justice even if it is outside South Africa. For several years, I was forced to do work internationally, mainly for the United Nations. The work I did was in the mediation of peace, constitution making, the management of transitions and governance. In this, I have always relied on what I learnt as a member of the ANC.

Recording history

South Africans of Indian origin have a proud history of struggle. Recording this history is important because we have a duty to inspire the participation of future generations in the collective struggle of South Africans of all races for a better life. The Pretoria Indian community, of which I am a part, has been perceived of as little more than a conservative group of affluent traders. This narrative is not accurate because it ignores the great contributions and sacrifices made by so many members of this community towards the political freedom that we enjoy today. This book is therefore also a tribute to that contribution.

The delay in the recording of this account is regretted because it comes at some cost. As I retrace my journey, I learnt that one's memory can be a most unreliable companion that is not always faithful. As human beings, we are inclined to shape our memories in the form that we would most like to believe. I have tried to deal with this weakness in several ways. I carried out detailed research of both the media and other historical accounts as well by interviewing people.[4] In doing this, I realised that many comrades in the Machinery also suffered from my very weakness. I therefore tried to keep to a narrative or set of facts that I could confirm. An example of this is the number of military operations mentioned are only those that I have been able to verify.

This book would not have been possible without the kind help of Harsha Dayal, Razia Saleh, Fazila Saleh, Ebrahim Ghoor, Maya Sooka and a number of other kind people who assisted me in various different ways to get this project completed. I remain indebted to them for their kind support. A special word of appreciation is also due to Sue Rabkin, Barbara Hogan and Shan Balton for reviewing the draft and offering their comments and wise counsel. I had great difficulty in finding an appropriate title for the book. It was Shan that suggested that it be *From Marabastad to Mogadishu*. I thought it was most appropriate.

I need to further express my gratitude to Barbara Hogan and the Bertha Foundation for their kind support in making this book possible.

Life in exile was not easy. During those tough and testing years, I had the great fortune to benefit from the kindness and generosity of several people. First among these are my cousin Solly and his wife Hajoo (Hajira) who are now both deceased. Without any hesitation, and at great risk, they took care of me when I needed it most. I found the same wonderful human spirit in the Bhoola family, particularly a most generous lady who I had come to refer to as 'Mummy Bhoola' because she became a second mother to me. I got to know Mummy Bhoola through her brother-in-law Ismail Bhoola, who was an exiled lawyer living in Botswana, and with whom I was friendly. The kindness and generosity of Mummy Bhoola, who offered me food and a home to stay when I needed one, made everything easier for me.

I need to pay tribute to my family. My parents were beyond wonderful. They gave me support and love in abundance and were always kind and gentle. My life was made infinitely more bearable despite the hardships imposed on me. I don't have any memory of the deprivations that my family faced because I can only remember how we managed, not how we struggled. My parents never allowed me to see or feel the difficulties they experienced to survive or eke out a living. I never thought of our family as being poor, yet we were. We always seemed to manage, were content and never felt short of anything. This attitude to life gave me the strength to endure the hardships of exile and living under constant threat.

I regret that I learnt the true value of my parents so late in life. I was so determined to get on with my life and the struggle that I failed to pay much attention to their selflessness and dedication. On reflection, I would not have been able to achieve anything much without their very quiet and gentle support. The truth is that the great successes that I refer to in this record came at an immeasurable cost to my family, and one that I am not very proud of.

My family, particularly my father, mother, first wife Barbara and my children – Ruby and Yusuf, suffered greatly because of my involvement in the struggle. I placed the struggle above them and failed in many of my responsibilities. This is a pain that I will continue to endure. It is therefore critical that I acknowledge with total humility and pay tribute to the enormous sacrifices that they made. I also sincerely apologise for the hurt and harm caused to each of them.

Despite my failures, I have been most fortunate. Ruby, my first born and wonderful daughter, will always be one of my heroes. Despite the challenges she has faced, I have never heard her complain of anything. Ruby has also blessed me with the first of my wonderful grandchildren, Lily.

My grounding in life continues to come from my son, Yusuf. He is as wonderful a teacher as you can find and who has allowed me to understand myself so much better. In many ways, he continues to be a mirror reflecting an image of me. I have learnt to understand myself much better because of him.

Marrying Soraya changed my life. With her, I started rediscovering the joys of having a family. Her love, support, endless patience and kindness beyond measure has made life infinitely more pleasant. Life's blessings never seem to cease. Marrying Soraya meant that I have the pleasure of my family being extended by three more wonderful sons, Aadil, Zaahid and Luqmaan. Not long after my marriage, Aadil married and has since blessed us with four grandchildren. Zahid and Luqmaan also followed suit, and Alhamdulillah, I am now able to experience the boundless joys (and a few challenges) of having eight grandchildren (Lily, Imaan, Mohammed, Yusuf, Zaeem, Zahraa, Sabreen and Ameera). My family truly does make me feel complete. Seeing them enjoy the freedoms that we fought for gives the struggle the most meaning to me.

I

Mayhem in Mogadishu

There is an incredible bang followed by a dull sound. The house rocks. The ground and everything on it shakes. Our ears ring and much of what I hear following this is muffled in a strange kind of a way. The air is thick with smoke and an acrid smell of sulphur and diesel immediately attacks the senses in a most disorienting way. The security personnel immediately spring to action with their AKs at the ready in total bewilderment and start scurrying about in all directions. After those few first moments, they immediately take up position to guard the entrance to the home.

Before I can regain my composure, there is a burst of gunfire from automatic weapons in the immediate vicinity of the house. This is followed by shorter volleys and is interspersed by smaller explosions from grenades lobbed in different directions. There is total pandemonium, but it is soon obvious that the aggressors are positioned on the other side of the perimeter wall of the house. The guards move us to the basement of the old house. From the angry exchange of gunfire, it is clear that both sides are using AKs and PKMs – a mixture of both light and medium machine guns.

This is Mogadishu in Somalia. The attack started at about 18h45 on 8 July 2014 just as evening was beginning to set in. It was shortly after we broke our fast during the month of Ramadan. Our sugar levels were just beginning to return to normal and energy levels were starting to climb. Al Shabaab was delivering on a promise to launch their fiercest attacks during this most holy month on the Islamic calendar.

My first instinct was to identify where the attack was coming from and assess what our vulnerabilities were. Despite the guards' instructions, I push past them at the entrance of the house and insist on making my own assessment of the threat. As I peek through the doorway, I can see the tracer bullets flying up and down the road, which runs along the north-east perimeter wall of our compound. The wall is about three metres high and 30 metres away from our house, and so not impossible to be scaled. Should this happen, we would be in serious trouble, as our only defence would be breached. The first explosion had been a car bomb at the entrance checkpoint to the compound known as Villa Somalia, which accommodates the official residences of the president, prime minister and speaker of Somalia's Federal Parliament. Fortunately, the explosion did not cause our perimeter wall to collapse.

Since September 2012, I have been spending a lot of time in Somalia. Over the next two years, there were at least seven car bombs and more skirmishes than I care to remember that took place in close proximity to Villa Somalia where I lived. This was, however, the closest attack. It was also one of the deadliest.

Very soon I realised that I had left my body armour[5] and helmet, together with my two-way radio and cell phone, in my house next door. I wasn't allowed to carry a weapon and this made me feel vulnerable. With some few poorly armed soldiers on guard duty with limited ammunition, our ability to fend off an attack was limited. After a brief consultation with the commanders on duty, we were able to make some sense of what was happening.

The house I was in was the official residence of the speaker of the Somali Federal Parliament. As a mediation expert for the United Nations providing strategic advice to the Somali government and the Speaker, I was given special permission to be stationed at the Speaker's residence.[6] The house is located at the entrance of Villa Somalia and the security check point is located just outside its western wall on the road to the presidential palace, which runs along the north-western wall of the speaker's house.

From what information we had, the driver of a car had acted suspiciously at the checkpoint. Obviously nervous, after an exchange of words with the security personnel, the driver alighted the vehicle and remotely detonated the bomb. The car was packed with a large quantity of high-grade military explosives sufficient to cause extensive damage to infrastructure.

The standard modus operandi of Al Shabaab is to use a car bomb to initiate the launch of an attack. Car bombs are usually set off at the entrance of a building to neutralise the security there, kill as many of the guards as possible, sow maximum confusion and allow for the perimeter to be breached sufficiently by heavily armed units waiting in the wings.

It later became clear that the original intention was to get the car as close to the president's residence as possible before launching the attack. The nervous reaction of the driver at an earlier checkpoint scuttled their plans and the attackers, who in this instance were already able to make their way into the Villa Somalia complex because they were using standard issue uniforms, were forced to launch their attack prematurely. This explained the explosion and exchange of gunfire outside the speaker's house instead of it being closer to the president's residence.

With my blood-sugar levels restored and the ensuing adrenalin rush, I was fully alert. It is obvious to me now that the training I received 35 years ago as an ANC solider in the jungles of Angola was not in vain. My instincts as a soldier kicked in. I knew what I had to do and did so without panic. Fifteen minutes into the battle, it became clear that the conflict had extended along the southern wall as well. We were trapped because our exit points were where the action was. To make matters worse, darkness had now descended, and poor visibility made our ability to defend ourselves more difficult.

There were about 50 people of various ages, including some very young and old people, trapped in the house with me. We were also not sure about the number of insurgents involved in the attack. All we could go by was the intensity of the gunfire; and this was ferocious. What I feared most was the breach of the perimeter wall; by my estimate, we would be able to defend ourselves for no more than fifteen minutes before we ran out of ammunition.

An hour into the attack, we started receiving calls from the office of the UN's Special Representative to the Secretary-General, Nick Kay, enquiring about my safety and whether it was necessary to send in an extraction team. I apologised for not having my radio and mobile with me but declined the offer. There was no way I was about to retreat alone without the safety of the speaker and the others in the house also being secured. Fortunately, the attack was over a short while later.

What amazed me is just how quickly things returned to normal. Within a short space of time after the attack, everyone in the house continued as if nothing had happened. This was bizarre, but I have seen this on each subsequent occasion. Somalia has taught me a lot about human resilience. Somalis are so used to the possibility of attacks, the sound of gunfire and explosions, that they merely continued work or their meetings as if nothing had happened. Having lived and worked in war zones, I have become all too aware that we too could be victims of the violent conflict. Despite this, the violence of an attack is a shock to the system because you never quite believe that you will be attacked until it happens. Knowing that it is possible is very different to experiencing it.

In the days that followed, the UN offered to withdraw me even if for a break. I declined this offer too. I am not sure why, but I felt that I had a job to do and I was going to see it through. The experience did however force me into thinking about the meaning of life and what I wanted out of it. When I think about this, I naturally cast my mind back to Sharpeville Stadium on the morning of 10 December 1996.

This was on this day that Nelson Mandela signed our constitution into law. On that day, just before I led Madiba out to the podium, I asked him to sign my personal copy of the Constitution. He obliged with the usual disarming smile and warmth. He even took his time about it. And for good measure, he generously signed it in two places as if to reassure me that he was happy to do so. This was the first signed copy of South Africa's constitution – and it was mine. Soon after this, Madiba went on to sign the copy for the official record in the presence of a few thousand people who had come to witness the event. There is no greater honour that I could possibly receive. When I remind myself of this, I know that my life was worth living.

Looking back at this event, I feel assured that my commitment to the struggle for political freedom was not in vain. In fact, it was an honour to participate and a privilege for which I am grateful. In times of political turmoil and turbulence, this is the event to which I turn my mind and remind myself that it was all worthwhile. I was given an opportunity to participate in the making of our country's history. More than that, I helped prepare the birth certificate of the new democratic order in South Africa. What more can I ask for? I also feel compelled to honour the great revolutionaries and freedom fighters that I had the privilege to live and work with, particularly those in the Kabwe Machinery.

However, I am getting ahead of myself.

II

Origins

My journey begins in Marabastad, Pretoria. My family history is not particularly special or dissimilar to many other families of Indian origin. Family legend has it that Dada (my paternal grandfather), also Hassen Ebrahim, came to South Africa on board a ship of 'passenger' Indians.[7] Dada was however unlike most of the other 'passengers'; penniless, he did not have the money for his passage and was a stowaway. An illiterate young man in his early-20s, widowed and divorced once each by this time, Dada set out on his journey with little more than the few clothing items he carried and sheer determination.

Dada came from Sonvadi village in the state of Gujarat in India.[8] I could find no record of the exact date of his arrival or the reasons why he would leave these 'fields of gold' as a penniless young man to come to South Africa. Circumstantial information however suggests that it would have been in or about 1910. My research also revealed that there was terrible famine and many succumbed to plague in India at the end of the 19th century. This only served to add to the suffering already brought on by the hardship of colonial rule. The general view is that Dada was forced to leave India because of poverty. His situation must have been quite desperate because he came to South Africa as an illegal immigrant and without any papers to prove his identity.

I am told that Dada disembarked in the dark of night to avoid detection. There was no one to receive him or he knew in South Africa. With no one to call upon for any help, it must have been quite a daunting time for him. Another possible reason for his journey could have been the promise held by the discovery of gold in South Africa, which would explain why he, as with many other 'passenger' Indians, made his way to the Transvaal as soon as he could rather than try to make a life for himself in Durban. As soon as he disembarked, Dada offered his services as a cook to Indian families living in Natal, but as soon as he could, Dada headed for the Transvaal. Apparently, he worked and walked all the way from Durban and finally made it to 'Asiatic Bazaar', which was adjacent to the area now known as Marabastad in Pretoria.

Putting down roots in Pretoria

Pretoria was no easier than Natal. Like the British in Natal, the Afrikaners in the Transvaal were not too excited about Indian migrants settling in territory under their control. The first group came around 1865 after gaining their freedom at the end of their five-year period of indenture on the sugar cane plantations in Natal. Ironically, many Indians empathised with the Boers in their struggle against the colonialists because of their experience of British colonialism. The Afrikaners however were oblivious to this reality.

As in Natal, the success of the Indian trader did not win them any favours with the Afrikaners. By 1911 the estimated Indian population in Pretoria was about 11,004. The Afrikaners, who were agitated by this reality, produced more legislation that prohibited Indians from becoming citizens or owning property in the Transvaal. In addition, any Indian wishing to trade was compelled to pay a registration fee of £25, an enormous sum for any struggling entrepreneur.

Determined to make life more difficult for black people, the Afrikaners government established three adjacent ghettoes limited to a few streets. These ghettoes were located close to town, making it easy for workers to get to work in the morning and return in the evening as they were not allowed to live there. The formal name used to describe the area was 'Asiatic Bazaar' and it was located between Marabastad in the north and the Cape location to the south. A street separated each area – Barber Street in the north separated Marabastad from the

Asiatic Bazaar and three streets to the south was Grand Street, which separated Asiatic Bazaar from the Cape location. The Apies River, which ran north to south, formed the eastern boundary of the three ghettos. Across the river was a settlement of poor whites who were employed in the public service and utilities.

We grew up referring to Asiatic Bazaar as 'the Location', but in more recent years, it generally came to be known as 'Marabastad'. to the whites, the area was disparagingly referred to as the 'Coolie location'. Asiatic Bazaar was a community of small general dealer shops and tailors, and the fruit market for which the area became very popular. To eke out a living, Dada started work as a cook for some Indian families and performed various menial tasks. However, with hard work Dada soon established himself as a fruit vendor, selling mainly bananas – hence the nickname 'Hassen Banana'. Over time, he prospered. More confident now, he wanted to settle down.

Family legend has it that he was encouraged by a friend to propose marriage to a widowed mother of one child whom he had never seen. Dada faced two challenges. The first was that both mother and child were still in India and the marriage proposal would therefore have to be in writing. The second challenge was that he was illiterate. The proposal was written on his behalf. He must have been totally astonished to learn that my grandmother, or 'Dadi', agreed. Her husband died during the plague in India. I am not sure of the details, but she managed to travel to South Africa and eventually married Dada.

By all accounts, Dada was a stern but good man; poor but always generous and charitable. He had a family of four sons and five daughters. My father, Ismail Hassen Ebrahim, was the third son. Being part of a large family, my father left school to start working at a young age because there was no apparent value in formal education. Education was for those who could afford it. Born in 1938, my father was for most of his life a man of modest means. Life was a struggle. Nothing came easy. He was always seen as the black sheep of the family and was very conscious of this. It was not uncommon for wealthier ones to quietly snigger, jibe or tell an unkind joke about him.

My father, or 'Papa' as we called him, worked extremely hard and was determined to make a success of his life. My brother Raffique was born from his first marriage. This marriage did not last, and Papa was convinced a year after his divorce to marry again. He married my mother, Zubeida Rajah, who was 18 years old at the time and hailed from Ventersdorp in the Transvaal. Mum came from a poor rural family that were not accustomed to any of the ways of urban life. She was always content with the simple things in life.

I inherited Dada's name because I was the first grandson to be born after he passed on in 1956. I was born in 1957 in Ventersdorp and my sister, Hajira, came two years later. Work was scarce and conditions pitiful. After losing his job in a shoe shop, Papa got my mother to spend the last of the money she had (as part of her dowry) on ingredients required to make samosas, which he then sold by going house to house in the location. This humble business provided Papa with the income he needed to look after us.

Growing up in the location

Location was a very small area with no room for expansion because it was boxed in on all sides. After almost three generations, Location became a slum. It was less than one square kilometre and remained so for the next 70 years when we were all forcibly removed, mainly to Laudium. Initially, the houses were all simple structures made of wood and corrugated iron. Over time, despite the fact that we could not own land, some of the homes were rebuilt as solid brick structures, especially the shops.

For many years, the roads were all corrugated tracks, except for two tarred roads, Boom Street and Blood Street. The system of land tenure was peculiar. The intention was to discourage people of Indian origin from striking roots. This, however, did not stop the community from taking pride in their dwellings.[9] Despite the oppressive laws and living conditions, Location was extremely vibrant and a place I will always remember very fondly. People were happy there. It was truly a melting pot of different cultures, races and religions. This is where we learnt to respect diversity. We lived amongst Africans, coloureds and a few Chinese families. There was a real sense of community. My father was always very proud of the fact that he knew the families of all the children in the location. Despite the hardship suffered, this is where we learnt the social and cultural values that we still hold dear today. It was more than the passing of cups of sugar over fences. People looked out for one another. The conditions we lived under obliged us to not only tolerate other races, religions and cultures, but to respect them. Because we grew up in each other's homes, we learnt about and enjoyed participating in each other's religious and cultural festivals.

While the Afrikaners across the Apies River were favoured by a system of job reservation, we had to work hard to eke out a living. People lived humbly and prided themselves in their honesty and the quality of services delivered. Traders, especially in our fruit market, thrived and attracted customers from far and wide. People found a way of getting around the oppressive laws that dictated the hours of business and who we could serve.[10] Often, we were expected to pay a bribe by those enforcing the law when the requirements of conducting business were not strictly adhered to. If people needed something, they paid for it. It was normal to offer a little 'gift', or more commonly a 'discount' for something in the shop. It was normal to take some samosas along even when you went to the bank for a loan or to apply for a driver's or trader's licence. Corruption was institutionalised and nobody gave it much thought.

I had a happy childhood in the location. We played in the streets because there was nowhere else to do so. There were no parks and not many trees. The roads were narrow and the buildings old. Our houses were small, and our yards were crammed spaces with no gardens. Cars were parked on the pavements because few had garages. There were several shebeens including one just opposite the road from us. Every weekend we had to contend with loud music till late and drunks sometimes passed out on the pavements. Marabastad was after all the home of the famed marabi music. Despite the brutality of apartheid, our culture and the spirit of the people remained vibrant. People continued to find ways of celebrating and enjoying life.

A walk down the road would expose you to the distinctive smell from coal-burning stoves. You could tell when a delicious meal was being prepared or served. A very common smell was the burning of incense or *agharbati*. I can still taste the sweet cinnamon-flavoured syrup from the *koeksisters* that Tamatjie used to sell from her basket going door to door. During winter, many would keep their houses warm using coal-burning steel drums called *bowlas*. The houses were so close to each other, we always heard what music, radio station or argument was taking place. Naturally, there were no secrets in the location. Everyone knew what was going on. In part, we relied on that. People depended on each other and sought advice, help and the odd cup of sugar or rice from one another. Since my grandfather's time, we had in our house one of the few safes in the location. This meant that family and friends would deposit their valuables with us for safekeeping. Location was a colourful community of poor people united by their common will not only to survive in the face of adversity, but to do well in spite of it.

Our streets were generally safe. The only violent crimes were the occasional brawl between drunken patrons returning from a shebeen or a fight between rival gangs. Much to the despair of our parents, free time was often spent sneaking out to the Apies River for a swim. We often played hide and seek in the streets and hid between the wrecks of cars on pavements. A race around the block was always fun. We played soccer, cricket and other simpler games in the streets. Bicycle rims and cars made of wire were our toys. Those more creative built wooden go-karts, which we raced down the streets. When it rained, the streets of gravel became streams, which flowed down Mogul street towards the Apies river providing for much fun. The only time one played indoors was when using a board game of sorts. Monopoly was a favourite in our home. Card games were frowned upon. Competition during play was always tough.

The used bicycles my father bought us to share brought us much joy. Watching Sundowns play was a major weekend attraction and school was a ten-minute walk. While my father was an avid reader, we did not grow up with any encouragement to read. I cannot remember an interest in visiting our library either. I do however remember taking some interest in the comics that my father so fondly collected in his earlier years. These were about the great classics and they were particularly good. In general, because I found it so hard to study or remain calm for too long, the streets of Location proved to be a great release and place to be. I was also away from the attention of the elders and avoided annoying them too much.

For much of his life, my father battled to earn a living. He ran a small home business selling the samosas that my mother made and the mango pickle that she packed into meal-sized containers. Over time, he employed a few workers but still operated from home. Each evening, and sometimes early in the morning, we would load the van that my father drove to deliver the goods. He paddled his trade in the industrial areas of Pretoria and Johannesburg, mainly to Portuguese-owned cafés that served African workers. During the holiday times, I would go along to help him off-load the goods.

The hero in our home was my mother. I have yet to meet someone with her work ethic. In her quiet way, she kept the family together in the most difficult of times, often working until the early hours of the morning in a very small unventilated room frying the samosas for sale the next day. She never complained. While some of our richer relatives would pass the odd remark, for Mummy there was no alternative but to persevere. No matter how late she worked, Mummy was always up early enough to ensure that a fresh pot of curry was prepared for breakfast. The aroma of this food is something I grew to love and enjoy. A big meal for breakfast was sufficient nourishment to sustain my father through the day, his favourite being mince and roti. I was however partial to her mutton curry.

Listening to the radio was an important part of family life – sometimes annoyingly so because my father insisted on playing it so loud. He wired speakers throughout the house to make sure that he did not miss a thing. This is obviously where I developed a keen interest in current affairs and political developments. While I was too young in the 1960s to understand political developments, it was nonetheless dramatic enough to get a sense that something important was afoot and made me curious. Listening to the news was sacred time. No one was allowed to make any noise.

Forced removals

The uprooting and forced removal of entire communities was one of the more cruel aspects of apartheid policy. These removals spanned between 1940 and 1970, affecting first the African people, then the coloured and later people of Indian origin. The African people were moved to Atteridgeville and Mamelodi, the coloureds to Eersterust and those of Indian origin to Laudium. This policy was speeded up when the National Party came into power in 1948. Two years after they came into power, the National Party passed the dreaded Group Areas Act.

Laudium was established in 1960 and set aside for the Indians in Pretoria as a residential area. It was 12km away from the city centre. This was the beginning of the total segregation between the races in Pretoria. Government hoped to make Marabastad a commercial centre by declaring it an industrial area. The attraction to move to Laudium was that Indians were for the first time allowed to own land in Pretoria. Whereas the location was overcrowded and had few amenities, in Laudium people could own houses and have gardens. It even had open public spaces and boasted the promise of parks. Council-built houses were offered as an incentive to those who could not afford to build their own. Despite this, people resisted the removals because it was forced on them and they were hesitant to move away from their places of work, which would add to the cost of living.

This marked the end of an extremely vibrant and colourful community life. We were one of the last families to move from Marabastad. As people were forced out of their houses, the government destroyed these buildings to prevent anyone from occupying them. One of the unfortunate results of this was that all manner of rodents and insects would then make their way to the remaining houses. This was a serious problem because our dogs and cats made a sport of catching the rodents overnight and we would wake most mornings to encounter the remains of the night's activity in our yard.

III

Emerging Political Consciousness

A happy upbringing

Ours was a happy home. We were used to modest means and lived accordingly. Despite this, my father insisted on taking us annually on holiday. A regular holiday and affordable destination was Maputo (or Lorenço Marques as it was then called) because we lived with family friends.

My father was a typical patriarch, almost always stern as though it was required of him. I used to think of him as difficult, but he was not. I admired his determination to make a better life for us than he had. He dedicated his life to this. Helping out in the family business was part of growing up. Over time, I became an expert in the art of folding samosas, packing and plastic-wrapping them in polystyrene trays for easy distribution. In my early teens, I eagerly learnt to drive by reversing my father's van so that it was ready to be loaded in the morning or unpacked at the end of the day. Occasionally, I would also get to drive the van around the corner to the filling station.

My father finally relented and agreed to move to Laudium in 1972. We rented an apartment in a block of flats, which was one of 11 blocks making up the council-owned Bangladesh Flats. Ironically, these flats were more spacious than our house in Marabastad. It was also new, and the area was not as congested as we were used to. There was even some lawn around our block. This was most welcome. We lived there for nearly three years after which my father secured a piece of land to build our house. I cannot remember my father being happier. Planning our new house became a family affair and we would often spend hours around the kitchen table drawing plans of what we thought our house should look like. These were happy times. Papa finally got to build the house of his dreams when he could barely afford it.

My father was largely self-educated. He enjoyed reading. Going through the Sunday newspapers was an important part of the week. He was also opinionated and knowledgeable about a wide range of subjects including politics and history, which he enjoyed talking about to anyone who would listen. I naturally took an interest in these matters too.

In 1974, when I was in matric new regulations had us write our matric exams under the auspices of a separate 'Indian Education' department instead of the common provincial Transvaal Education Department (TED). No one in my class was excited about receiving an 'Indian Education' matric because it was regarded as inferior. Some of the students decided to leave school to study through correspondence and then write the Joint Matriculation Board exams, which were regarded more prestigious. My confidence was bolstered by the fact that my best friend agreed that we would study and write the exam together.

I went home that day and boldly informed my parents what we intended to do. They were not impressed especially because I had just started performing better after receiving extra tuition, which they so willingly paid for. This was the first time in my life that I took a major decision and was determined to go through with it. It was my first real fight for what I thought was correct. My parents finally relented. The next day I went to school with a huge grin, feeling quite proud of my victory.

I strode into my classroom, handed in my text books and announced my departure, I noticed that my best friend was in uniform and still seated in his usual place. He had reneged on our agreement and decided to remain in school without bothering to inform me. I was too proud to reverse my decision. I registered for a correspondence course, but had to study on my own and without the discipline of a class and a teacher to guide me. I was so ill prepared, I can't even remember having sat for the exams. I made my first big stand in life and failed – quite miserably so.

I was so embarrassed at my failure that I decided to give up my education and to persuade my father to work for him in the business. He refused and insisted that I go back to school. To make my point, I complained that I had lost so much ground that, if I went back to school, it would be better to go to the grade preceding matric. To my astonishment, my father called my bluff. So, I went back to standard nine and I was now in class with students two years younger than me. How much more awkward could it get? This was the cost of my arrogance.

It was not long before I started bunking school. Each morning, I got dressed in my school uniform and left the house, bag in hand. I usually waited at a convenient point to watch my parents leave for work and returned home. By sheer chance I met up with a friend who was preparing to write his matric at the end of the year through the Joint Matriculation Board. Without telling my parents, I registered and started studying along with him. This gave me the confidence I needed. To make sure that we succeeded, we worked extremely hard and studied all the past exam papers and finally wrote our exams at the end of the year.

At this time, I also started taking a deeper interest in religion. Our madrasa, which lasted for only during my early schooling years, did no more than teach us to read the Koran, learn about Islamic history and perform the rituals. These were not places of intellectual stimulation. I was eager to know more than this. I was looking for the intellectual tools to make sense of our life experiences and environment, and this stimulation came from literature outside my formal education. I developed a keen sense of justice and the importance of the struggle to improve oneself and the environment around us. I participated in charity work and religious propagation. This we did mainly in the surrounding African townships and rural areas. This was an important learning experience which made me aware of the living conditions of many black people and the injustices of apartheid.

Having sat for my matric exams, I convinced my parents in December 1975 that I deserved a holiday in the Cape. The holiday did not cost me much because I travelled with a friend and lived with his family. In return, all I had to do was help with the driving. As was usual, I made collect-calls to my parents just to let them know that I was alright. On one such call my father informed me that he received official-looking mail addressed to me. Because he was curious, he had opened it only to discover that it was notification that I had passed my matric examinations with a university exemption. I was not sure if my father was pleased that I had passed or upset that I had deceived them. Without further conversation, I was instructed to return home immediately. My father booked me on a flight, which was my first experience on a plane.

Westville university

When I got home, I was told to get ready to go to Westville university, the only university that people of Indian origin could gain admission to. I protested. Like my friends, I too felt that Westville was an apartheid 'bush' college and its qualifications did not carry much weight. I insisted that my father send me to a foreign university if at all. My father was determined, did his research and knew exactly what he was going to do. A couple of days later, I was bundled into our car and taken to Durban for admission to Westville university. This was in early February 1976.

Leaving home was almost uneventful if not for my mother's sadness. She wept inconsolably and found our separation very hard. I would often think of this when I considered my later separation from home, which proved to be infinitely more traumatic. My mother never spoke of this latter experience, but the scars are still evident.

I registered for the 'Big Four' (zoology, botany, physics and chemistry) along with several hundred other students – all of us hoping to become doctors. This was the big fad amongst young people of Indian origin. Pharmacy, accounting or law were less popular.

Admission into medical school was so limited that only about 10% of the class would succeed. This meant that competition was tough, and you would only really succeed if you were to perform exceptionally well. This was going to be really hard work.

Going to university was a big step and it was time to grow up. Lectures were difficult and for the better part unintelligible. The pace of learning was incredible, with no spoon-feeding like in school. You either made it or dropped out. I could never get my mind around all those classifications in zoology and botany. None of the subjects were easy and my performance was miserable.

There were however many distractions, both social and political. I was young and took advantage of my new freedom. Durban was extremely vibrant with much happening politically. This is when I was first introduced to the Black Consciousness Movement. I also took an interest in the many debates, especially the Students Representative Council elections. It wasn't long before the country was engulfed in the June 1976 uprisings. Student marches and protest meetings became my daily bread and I was in the thick of things. Lectures were boycotted, university life disrupted, and it was not long before there was no point in continuing with my course work for the year. I returned home and swore never to return to a 'bush college'.

My father was quite logical in his response to my new-found militancy. He assured me that he would have long sent me to the best universities in the world if only he could afford it. I was clearly rebelling without much of a cause. The rest of 1976 was spent at home carefully observing developments around the country, but not taking part in any activities. Laudium was unaffected by the turmoil taking place in the rest of South Africa. During this time, I helped my father in his business and assisted with the building of our house which we completed by the end of 1976.

Wits university

Early in 1977, my father heard from friends that Wits university was admitting students of Indian origin if registering for a major not catered for at a 'bush' college. This would qualify as an exemption to attend a 'white' university like Wits. My parents could not have been more pleased. My father hurriedly borrowed the money for my university registration and textbooks, even raising some extra to buy me a new car to travel to university. I bought trendy clothes and was given an attaché case to go with it because my father wanted me to look like a professional. I felt every bit like a king but looked like a real nerd and even had a hairstyle to go with it. Fortunately for me, this appearance did not last too long. To maintain the car, I took paying passengers who were fellow students.

I registered once again for subjects that would allow me admission into medical school, which was a default position rather than a clearly thought-out decision. I had no academic ambitions and was not sure what I wanted to do with my life. I had no career guidance and none of this was really discussed at home either. I was therefore just going through the motions. Little did I know just how important 1977 was to become in changing my life.

I got involved in everything other than my studies. Student life was extremely exciting and Wits was politically alive. The Black Students Society (BSS) was one of the first structures I came across and participated in their activities. There were also lots of workshops and seminars, which gave me my first taste of Marxist philosophy. The great thing about Wits University was the access to political literature. I enjoyed reading *Work in Progress* and other insightful journals and papers. The university libraries were a real treasure trove. It opened up a whole new world for me.

The development of my ideological perspective and a vision of what a just society could be like was a real thrill. I spent a lot of time exploring socialist ideas and discovered with great interest how people from other countries dealt with their struggles. Fortunately, the successes and challenges of the struggle against colonialism in southern Africa were most topical. I took a keen interest in the politics of liberation. The victories in Angola and Mozambique were an inspiration and the ongoing conflicts in Namibia and Zimbabwe were studied and analysed. At this time, many young white students were confronted with the prospect of conscription and needed to know how to deal with it. Also very topical was the discussion on PW Botha's Total Onslaught and the 'winning hearts and minds' or the WHAM strategies.

The liberation of Mozambique and Angola gave us a great deal of hope. Liberation was no longer a theory. It was real and it was happening in our neighbourhood. This experience gave us an opportunity to visualise what freedom could be and the struggle required to attain it. Nothing could be more exciting than this.

It was not long before some of the harsher realities of our struggle began to strike home; and it took place not far from the university campus where we studied. On the 15 June 1977, Solomon Mahlangu, Monty Motaung and two other cadres of Umkhonto we Sizwe were involved in an unplanned skirmish with the South African Police. The unit realised that they were being followed by the police and a gun battle ensued resulting in two civilians being killed in a warehouse in Goch Street.

I followed this incident assiduously because it made such a huge impact on me. These were young people who were fighting back, men of my age who were doing something about the unjust society that we were living in. We all talked about apartheid without really discussing what we could do about it. I was not aware of any legal forms of struggle or resistance to get involved in. This experience brought home the reality of a form of struggle. Perhaps it was the only form of struggle? It awakened something in me because it forced me to think about what I was going to do. Inaction was no longer a choice.

I thought a lot about what had happened and came to the conclusion that there was no alternative to the course of action that Solomon Mahlangu and his unit had embarked upon. I could find no other way to express myself politically or become part of changing the world around me. I could not stand by on the sidelines. My political understanding at this point in time was most limited. The only political organisation I knew of that was challenging the apartheid state was the ANC and I felt obliged to get involved. I had to become a part of this struggle because I believed in it. They were correct to engage in the armed struggle because they had already exhausted all the alternatives. I was convinced of this.

I could just not get over how senseless the death of Solomon Mahlangu was. Could there not have been better planning? There were obvious weaknesses, yet, even in failure, they inspired me. At least, they were doing something. I wanted them to succeed more than I was critical of them.

In my own naïve way, I felt compelled to find ways of helping MK cadres. I did not think of myself as an MK combatant then, but could see myself playing a support role of some sort, like providing units with the necessary transport and support to successfully carry out their operations. Nevertheless, supporting the ANC would obviously mean that I would first need to join the ANC and MK. I felt compelled to do something and was not prepared to remain on the sidelines any longer.

It was a major turning point in my life. From this point onwards, it was not enough for me to have a political sense of the world around me. I was driven to do something about it. I could not afford to be neutral. I had to throw in my lot as well. I was also beginning to get a sense of what I should do with my life. Suddenly, I had focus and my life had meaning. I now needed to find the ANC. This however proved to be a challenge greater than I had anticipated.

Then, on 12 September 1977, on my way from lectures to the student canteen, I met with Fazila Saleh who was quite emotional. I enquired and she informed me that Steve Biko had died in detention. Steve who, I asked? Until then, I did not know who Biko was and did not understand why there was so much emotion around his death. My interest was perked and I asked many questions and read all that I could find to understand what had happened.

The death of Steve Biko was different. Never before had the world paid so much attention to the death of an anti-apartheid activist. The government felt obliged to deal with the inquest very quickly. Fortunately for me, the inquest was held in Pretoria's Old Synagogue courthouse and started on 14 November. I made a special effort to attend as many of the sessions as possible and was fascinated by the legal team led by the legendary Sydney Kentridge, which made for the most riveting and inspiring legal examination. The inquest concluded a few weeks later in early December 1977 on a most unsatisfactory note, which left me totally angry. Despite the overwhelming evidence, none of the security policemen who were responsible for Biko's detention and interrogation, nor the doctors who were supposed to take care of him, were held to account for his untimely death.

Given the incredible political drama taking place in the country, I was totally distracted to be a good student and things did not work out too well for me academically. Despite the fact that I failed again, my poor parents refused to give up on me. Yet again, they borrowed more money for me to register for the following year. By this time, I too had grown a little wiser. It was clear to me by now that not only did I not have the inclination, but neither was I prepared to work as hard as would otherwise be required to make it to medical school.

In 1978, I registered for a law degree and started to experience a bit more academic success than my previous endeavours. I enjoyed most of the subjects I took except for Latin, but unfortunately it was still a requirement for a law degree. Two subjects I enjoyed greatly were African government and sociology.

That very same year I took a decision to become politically active in the ANC underground without actually understanding fully what this meant. I found the non-racialism of the ANC most attractive and it seemed like a natural choice. I did not give it much thought. This belief seemed to be reinforced even more, especially after reading Joe Slovo's 'No middle road',[11] found in a book kept in the Wits Library. Because this was banned literature, you could only read it in the library and not take it out. So, I managed to smuggle the book out of the library, copy it, and then return it to the library so that others could also read it. I also successfully used copies of the paper for distribution and then later for the political education of younger activists. I knew now that I needed to find the ANC.

I started making discreet enquiries as to how to find the ANC, but drew a blank. I wondered then if it was not because the ANC was so deep underground that I could find no trace of it. As weird as it may sound today when I think about it, back then we were even scared of mentioning the name of the organisation without referring to it in hushed tones and quickly looking over one's shoulders just to make sure that no one heard you. There was a real fear about this. Such was the state of repression.

Despite my efforts, I could not find any evidence of the ANC's presence. There was no organised activity of any sort and neither were there any leaflets or literature floating around that may suggest an underground presence. I could hardly find any graffiti in public places. While there may have been ANC people around, none of these were visible. The ANC was hard to find, which was an experience shared by many activists I recruited in subsequent years.

Through students in the Black Students Society, I came to learn that Saad Cachalia had studied in Botswana and I was sure that he would have had some knowledge of the ANC in that country. I was right. He knew Marius Schoon, who was a teacher at the school in Gaborone which he attended. After some discussion, Saad agreed to give me a letter of introduction and told me where to find Marius. I was so determined to meet the ANC that it did not occur to me as odd that the only way to do that was to leave the country.

Armed with the right information, I became totally focused and determined to do it the soonest. I decided to do this on the first possible weekend. This also made sense because Marius was a school teacher. I was so excited at the prospect of meeting the ANC that I could hardly wait. All this excitement did not of course escape my father's attention who had keenly observed my agitated behaviour without saying a word.

IV

Entering the Fold

Finding the ANC

Early on a Saturday morning in March or April 1978, I set off for Botswana. I crossed the border from Zeerust and got to Gaborone, the capital city, a very small city of not more than 30 000 people. The instruction I received was to drive through Gaborone and make my way to Molepolole, a rural settlement some 60-odd kilometres further north, which was where Marius taught, at the Kgari Sechele Secondary School. The village was rather small, dusty and barren. Upon some initial enquiries, I was led to the house where Marius and Jeanette Schoon lived.

Both Marius and Jenny were teachers at this school and lived in a basic prefabricated and rustic house. The road to this house was one that I would come to frequent over the next couple of years. It did not matter to me that much of the road from Zeerust and the Tlokweng Border gate on the South African side and then between Gaborone and Molepolole on the Botswana side were gravel roads. One had to be extremely cautious because of the loose sand and the occasional cow straying across the road. The total distance from home was about 450km and it would take me about five hours to get there. My car also did not have an air-conditioner. I was not bothered by the distance, time or discomfort of the journey. Neither was I concerned about my security. All I wanted to do was get to my destination. Needless to say, I was extremely anxious because I did not know what to expect.

As if the irony of having to leave the country to find the ANC was not enough, when I did, I went to meet an Afrikaner man who helped me understand the strategy of the ANC. It was this man who then recruited and deployed me in the underground. This irony was totally lost on me as I tried to soak it all in. I was so excited that I struggled to contain myself; I had so many questions but at that moment several things became clear. I was physically, politically, intellectually and emotionally in totally unfamiliar territory and not prepared. I had never before engaged a white person, let alone an Afrikaner, in a serious political conversation where we talked openly and freely about the ANC without it being in hushed tones. This was also my first engagement with the ANC, and I was every bit overwhelmed.

Both Marius and Jenny were chain-smokers and looked like ageing hippies. They were also the first intellectuals who provided me with a clear and cogent analysis of the South African political conflict. Marius and Jenny's first child, Katryn, was just a baby then and I have very fond memories of trying to entertain Katryn who became a part of our otherwise very serious political discussions and debates. In a surreal kind of a way, it gave meaning to a lot of our conversations. We were after all talking about the future of our country and its children.

But first, as I was to learn about the ANC underground, I needed to write my biography – the first of many that I would complete while in exile. Then came a lengthy debrief and conversation analysing the situation in the country. This was the start of my political education. As far as I was concerned, I came with an agenda – I wanted to work with MK. This resulted in quite a debate; one that I lost. Marius was adamant that our priority should be to establish a presence of the ANC in my community because the political struggle was more important than the armed struggle. I did not think this was possible because I felt that my community was still too conservative. Marius emphasised the importance of taking our communities along with us and tried to explain how he thought we should go about this. It was his argument that we needed to establish the presence of the ANC through our underground political work.

This meant recruiting people into a cell and making our presence felt by way of distributing ANC 'propaganda'.[12] We discussed techniques of recruitment and how an underground cell worked. We also discussed who I thought would be potential recruits. This was the first time that I had given the idea of recruiting people around me any thought. Until then, I was only thinking of my personal involvement and did not think about including anyone around me. I was given rudimentary guidance about the rules of secrecy.

We also talked about communications systems and I was taught the book code system. This system depended on both parties having a copy of the same book. The coding system was based on the page, line and word number that would provide the first letter. The system was therefore extremely elaborate with a large string of numbers and it could get confusing. It took huge effort. The result was that any report or communication would become an extremely long and difficult affair. A coded report would usually be compiled on very thin paper and crammed in a small space. The paper could then be hidden in a number of different places depending on how it was to be transported. A common technique was to place the report in a book between pages that were glued together to form a sort of an envelope. Needless to say, this system was never really very popular.

Perhaps the most important thing that I took away from my first engagement with Marius was a copy of the ANC's Strategy and Tactics Policy document, which was adopted in 1969 at the Morogoro Conference. This document resonated with what I had learnt from reading Slovo's 'No middle road'. Marius made sure that I read it and the discussion that followed was to be my first structured discussion and lesson in politics. I never forgot it. Marius also gave me other ANC and South African Communist Party (SACP) literature to take home. At the end of the meeting we agreed that I would return in the next three months to report on the progress made.

This was a defining moment in my life. I finally found the ANC, knocked on its doors, demanded to be let in and got myself recruited. I was a man with a mission. My life had purpose and direction. More importantly, this is the first time that I was given clear tasks and responsibilities as a young adult. I was not deterred by the possible danger that lay in the path that I had adopted. Perhaps, I had not given it enough thought. This was all very exciting stuff! My focus was clear. The most important thing to me was the goal of establishing the presence of the ANC in my community. To do this, I had to start by establishing a cell and distributing our literature to educate the people about the ANC's strategy. I was motivated and determined.

I returned home from my first political mission late on Sunday night. I was totally exhausted – both physically and mentally. For this reason, and perhaps because I did not want to explain where I had been, I retired to my room as soon as I could. But, I was not going to be let off that easy. My disappearance over the weekend worried my father. He was sure that something was going on. In general, my father was a person who never found it easy to express his emotions, be it love or concern. He also rarely ever came to my room. That night, he did so for the first time ever. In his usual blunt style, he simply asked me what was happening and where I had been.

I was taken by surprise and did not know how to answer him; so, I told him the truth. I told him that I had been to Botswana where I met with the ANC – and that was the end of the conversation. It was a very matter-of-fact conversation and very surreal. He did not ask anything further or make any comment and let me be. He knew what this meant because he was sufficiently politically astute. Despite this, he never raised this with me again. He obviously trusted me even if I did not recognise this then. I have always respected this in him and it remains one of my lasting and dearest memories of him.

Understanding the ANC

I accepted Marius' arguments and the guidance he gave, the logic of it becoming clearer over the coming years. The tasks I was given were part of a broader ANC strategy for the liberation of South Africa. At its core was the need to establish an underground structure that would provide the foundations of the ANC's revival, presence and to spearhead the struggle in the country. While this may seem to be trite, it is necessary to understand the context within which I was given these instructions.

There were several generations of underground operatives since the banning of the ANC and before I was recruited. Each of these generations was short lived, lasted for about three years or so, and came with its own unique set of disciplines, tasks, successes and failures depending on the objectives set out.

The first generation of the ANC's underground structures was established once the organisation was banned in 1960 and open political work was not possible. Umkhonto we Sizwe (MK) was formed to 'hit back by all means within our power in defence of our people, our future and our freedom'.[13] In the 18 months after its formation, MK carried out 200 acts of sabotage. This generation was however short-lived and ended in 1963. Police raided the secret headquarters of MK at Liliesleaf and arrested its leadership. This led to the Rivonia Trial when leaders of MK were charged with attempting to cause a violent revolution. Those ANC leaders who avoided arrest left the country. Many other ANC members left to undergo military training.

The next generation of underground operatives was a product of the agitation of young ANC soldiers, in exile, who became restless and demanded to be deployed back in the country to fight. The ANC was faced with the question of how best to infiltrate the country when South Africa was surrounded by countries hostile to the ANC. Rhodesia, Angola and Mozambique were all controlled by colonial governments that supported the regime. MK would first have to make its way through those countries before it could reach home ground. In 1967, MK began a joint campaign with the Zimbabwe People's Revolutionary Army (ZIPRA), who were fighting for the liberation of Zimbabwe. The intention was to find a route into South Africa by first crossing the Zambezi River from Zambia and into Rhodesia, then marching across through the Wankie Reserve, and crossing the Limpopo River into South Africa.

While the Wankie campaign gave MK cadres valuable experience in combat, it was clear that it would have to find other ways of getting into the country before they could even establish themselves. The ANC realised that it needed a strategy for the conduct of the struggle that took into account the conditions of struggle that it found itself in. The pressure to develop this strategy was made all the more urgent when it was faced with the demands made in the memorandum issued by Chris Hani and his fellow veterans from the Wankie campaign. Recognising this challenge, the ANC called a consultative conference at Morogoro, Tanzania in 1969 to look for solutions to this problem.

The Morogoro Conference, in a key policy document entitled 'Strategy and Tactics', called for an all-round struggle. Both the armed struggle and mass political struggle had to be used to defeat the enemy. But the armed struggle and the revival of mass struggle depended on two further aspects, the building of the ANC underground structures within the country and the campaign for international support and assistance from the rest of the world. These four aspects came to be known as the four pillars of struggle and were taught to all political activists.

The opening up of the ANC membership to non-Africans further consolidated the non-racial character of the ANC. To implement this strategy, the Morogoro Conference also established the ANC's Revolutionary Council (RC), which was jointly led by Oliver Tambo and Dr Yusuf Dadoo. The RC was the first structure of the ANC that was established for purposes of directing the ANC's underground struggle as guided by the Strategy and Tactics Policy. Implementation of the strategy was the responsibility of the military command structure, which was established and reported to the Revolutionary Council. At this point in 1969, no provision was made for the political underground, which clearly was not yet recognised as a critical component of the struggle.

The next generation of the ANC's underground emerged in the early 1970s with some of leaders who were at Robben Island. The ANC leadership took advantage of the fact that they were incarcerated along with some who were serving shorter sentences. With this in mind, the soon-to-be released ANC leaders were directed to establish structures of the ANC underground. Some of the leaders who led this development were Joe Gqabi, John Nkadimeng, Robert Manci, Henry Makgothi, Reggie Vandayar, Indres Naidoo and Harry Gwala, with

Albertina Sisulu working with them to build the underground. Hence, these structures of the underground depended very little on the ANC in exile.

Quite separately from this initiative, the ANC in exile also made some effort to establish its underground presence in the country. Examples of these initiatives can be found in the cases of Ahmed Timol and James April. Ahmed Timol was a young teacher recruited to establish a propaganda unit. Ahmed Timol's mission ended with his arrest in October 1971 and assassination a few days later when he was pushed from the 10th floor of the notorious John Vorster Square.[14] James April was a veteran of the Wankie campaign. After the campaign, April was infiltrated into the country in 1973 using a forged passport. He located himself in Durban instead of going back home to the Cape to avoid detection. This was however not to be because he was indeed detected within two months of his arrival, arrested and imprisoned.

Other examples of the ANC's attempt at establishing a presence in the country can be found in the instances of MK cadres infiltrated into the country and who eventually landed on Robben Island. Those cadres sentenced in 1969 were Bifana Matthews Ngcobo, Linus Dlamini and Amos Lengisi. Lawrence Phokanoka was sentenced in 1969 and Theophilus Cholo, Justice Mpanza, Sandi Sejake and Aaron Mtembu were sentenced in 1972. There were other cadres who were also infiltrated but later arrested and ended up serving sentences in the early 1970s.

Various other units were also infiltrated from London by the SACP. Some of the cadres involved in this were Tim Jenkins, Stephen Lee, David and Sue Rabkin, Jeremy Cronin, Raymond Suttner and Tony Holiday. While in each instance the propaganda units were established successfully, the units never grew or lasted more than a couple of years. These examples illustrate two important points. Not only were the number of units infiltrated limited, but so was their operational existence.

There were several important characteristics of the underground during this period. The ANC did not have any dedicated operational structure responsible for the development of its underground activities. The establishment of its leadership structures in Botswana, Zimbabwe, Mozambique, Swaziland and Lesotho, which came to be known as 'Forward Areas', only happened by the mid-1970s. Also, the underground structures that the ANC established were managed from the trenches of struggle inside the country with little organised or focused support from the organisation in exile. This only changed in 1974/75 when the ANC was able to recruit, train and deploy cadres back in the country to support the nascent structures being formed, which was mainly in the Soweto area even if it was in a very limited manner. Here, the work by Tokyo Sexwale, Naledi Tsiki and Siphiwe Nyanda are noted.

However, this generation of underground activists too were extremely short-lived. Most of its leaders including Joe Gqabi, Henry Makgothi, John Nkadimeng, Roller Masinga, Billy Masethla, Pitso 'Zakes' Tolo, and Keith Mokoape had to leave the country by 1978 and 1979. Those leaders, including Harry Gwala, who did not go into exile were imprisoned. The result of this was that the underground was once again decimated. However, those that did go into exile then became the key leaders in the ANC's Forward Areas and made responsible for the building of the underground.

The June 1976 uprisings saw thousands of young people leave the country to escape the terror that the apartheid regime had unleashed and to receive training and fight for their freedom. The ANC was unable to capitalise on the new revolutionary spirit that was unfolding. A change was necessary. The liberation of Mozambique and Angola by forces friendly to the ANC was most beneficial especially because it allowed them to established military training facilities in Angola.

To adapt to the new conditions, the Revolutionary Council was reconfigured in 1976 to express itself through two key structures: a military command and the newly established Internal Political Reconstruction Department (IPRD). The political and military structures were however separate. The mandate of the IPRD was to re-establish the political underground and establish a presence inside the country by growing its structures and disseminating its propaganda. Nearly 15 years after the banning of the ANC, the IPRD represented the first real organised attempt to establish structures within the country that were more suited to conducting political struggle from the underground. It was indeed more than a political reconstruction. It was starting on virtually a clean slate.

The IPRD was a full-fledge department based in Lusaka under the leadership of John Motshabi as the chairperson and Mac Maharaj as its secretary. Botswana, Mozambique, Swaziland and Lesotho were designated Forward Areas, and mandated to drive the strategy in the country. Because of the traffic between South Africa and the United Kingdom, London was also designated as a Forward Area. Each of the Forward Areas had an Internal Political Committee (IPC). Between 1976 and 1980, the Botswana IPC was led by Henry Makgothi and Dan Tloome. Jenny and Marius Schoon also served on this structure and were part of a political unit that focused on work in the 'minority' areas as part of a deliberate strategy of the ANC to establish a presence in these communities. It was therefore the IPC structure in Botswana under the leadership of Henry Makgothi, and through Marius Schoon, that was responsible for my deployment in the country.

I was therefore part of the fourth or fifth generation of underground operatives that was organised with the specific intent of taking advantage of the new conditions of struggle and prevailing revolutionary spirit. Consistent with the new strategy, my task was to establish an ANC presence in our community. The Indian community of Pretoria produced a number of activists and families that played an important role in our country's history and in the ANC. However, while there may have been individual members and supporters of the ANC at the time that I was tasked to establish an underground unit, Laudium did not have any history of an organised ANC presence in the area. In fact, at that point in time, the ANC had very little of an underground presence anywhere in the country, according to Stephen Ellis.[15] This was still early days.

I returned from Botswana alive, enthused and excited at the prospect of getting to work. I was freed from that feeling of helplessness in not knowing how to make my contribution to the struggle for liberation. I felt truly empowered and motivated. There was hope and I had focus. I was now part of the solution. Nothing to me was more gratifying than that and I immediately got to work. I knew exactly what to do. My life had meaning.

The trouble with this is that once I have a set of goals, I need to go out and get the job done. This has not always worked in my favour because I get to be so driven and focused, that I sometimes forget other important things that call for my attention

Establishing the Laudium ANC unit

My objective was to establish an ANC underground unit and presence in Laudium. For this, I needed to recruit fellow operatives, ideally two people. There were several qualities I was looking for in my team. While the most important was a political commitment to fight apartheid and to be aligned to the ANC's strategic perspective, cadres had to understand the risks involved and be willing to make sacrifices. Clearly, both political and security discipline was critical. I also needed people who I could trust and depend on.

The unit was set up against the backdrop of a very divided society. In addition to the obvious segregation of the racial groups, there was also the polarisation within communities based on political affiliations. It was a society in which there was an 'us' and 'them'. The sad truth of growing up as young radicals in the 1970s was our view that if people were not with us, they could be against us. There was no provision made for the so-called 'fence-sitters'. Friendships and acquaintances were formed around this belief. We were always wary of those we thought could be sell-outs. It was hardly conceivable to have friends who were not political.

As a logical extension of this belief system, when making friends, not only did we consider the politics of those we associated with, but we naturally considered whether people were disciplined and could be trusted or not. We were therefore also naturally very secretive. Very often, we operated on a need to know basis. This came quite naturally. It was our sub-culture.

Within such an environment, it did not take much effort to identify the people I considered ready for recruitment. Fazila Saleh and Yogesh Narsing were people I trusted implicitly and I was confident of their political views. Fazila was a fellow student at Wits University studying social sciences and was part of my lift club. She was also the sister of my classmate at school, Shaheda. I got to know Fazila quite well and knew she was a progressive intellectual with a developed political sense. She was also an independent thinker. I was able to observe her carefully enough to know that she would be a good candidate. Besides, her interest in journalism as a career would be of great value when doing propaganda work.

As for Yogesh, he lived in the flat directly opposite ours. He spent a lot of his time in our flat and was more of a younger brother than a friend. He was a couple of years younger and I was confident of his political views because I helped shape these in our many conversations.

Recruitment was not an easy task. We were instinctively very cautious. It was not until the early 1980s that we saw the emergence of structures of civil society in which activists could get involved and be trained. These latter structures also provided a useful place in which to observe the conduct of potential recruits. At that time, the only structure that was active was the Black Students Society. Activism was limited. I was therefore careful in approaching the possibility of each of them working in an ANC structure before I separately proposed their recruitment. It was a gradual process spread over a number of conversations. Fortunately, my instincts were correct and the recruitment of both Fazila and Yogesh was successful.

As a unit, we immediately set about focusing on two aspects. The first was our political education, and the other, the distribution of propaganda materials. Our ideological training was natural, and we took this quite seriously. We met once a week at my house to discuss political literature. We quickly made good progress and felt confident of ourselves. To consolidate their membership of the ANC and our underground unit, I made sure that both Fazila and Yogesh accompanied me at different times to Botswana when reporting. On each occasion, I made sure that we returned with new stock of literature and propaganda materials.

Our core function was to operate as a propaganda unit. This is where we experienced some challenges. Ironically, it was easier to deal with materials produced outside and smuggled in than to produce our own. The materials we brought back from Botswana came in different innovative forms. The most popular were beautifully designed stickers that were easy to peel and stick. These were extremely attractive and visible from a distance. Other materials were ANC leaflets and books in different forms. Sometimes, we brought in copies of *Sechaba*, a monthly ANC journal. On other occasions, literature from the SACP was also provided.

A very popular political tool was the January 8th speeches by Oliver Tambo because they provided a clear perspective and analysis of the struggle, identification of the issues and challenges, and a line of action. These speeches always ended with powerful slogans that became very popular. The speeches were available both in writing as well as in cassette form, the latter becoming extremely popular. There was a downside to this type of propaganda though; it was not always possible to infiltrate large quantities into the country.

The most ideal form of propaganda was those locally produced and printed materials. But the technology, logistics and resources needed to produce these were not easy to come by and also increased the associated risks. It was only in the late 1980s that technology in the form of roneo machines became more easily accessible and could be procured without attracting too much of attention. One also had to be careful of using typewriters because the type print was identifiable and could be traced. Besides these factors, the costs of production of material inside the country were prohibitive. Despite this, we did on a couple of occasions manage to produce leaflets on a smaller scale, which we had photocopied.

In Laudium, we targeted specific people and areas for the distribution of our materials. We established a little kitty into which we each contributed cash, which we used for the production of the leaflets. There were two methods we used for this. We either did anonymous cold-drops at the houses or posted materials to particular people. On campus, we put leaflets up on poster boards, into post boxes or under doors. We even once did a pamphlet drop from the top floor of Senate House during a busy moment. This was truly dramatic and worked to great effect. We went up to the top floor overlooking the courtyard, chose a moment when it was busiest and, when it was safe dropped the leaflets and watched these disperse over the courtyard. A hasty retreat was not difficult given the several alternative stairways down.

We always treasured the wonderful little booklets, which were cleverly disguised as something totally non-political like a novel or wine-tasting manual. The best amongst these was the political biography of Moses Kotane. We made sure that these were passed on to the young activists we were grooming for later recruitment. Getting banned literature was always a thrill! In a matter of a few months we were beginning to establish an ANC presence both in Laudium and on the Wits campus. For the first time, there was a consistent distribution of different types of materials both on campus and in Laudium.

The Pretoria Indian community had never been exposed to ANC literature or materials. Looking back, one would have thought that it would have been easy for the security police to come to the conclusion that the propaganda unit active in Laudium was also operating at Wits University. The deduction would then be that it must be students from Laudium who were responsible for the distribution of the propaganda. Fortunately for us, the apartheid security intelligence capacity did not connect these dots.

Politically, aside from the very useful workshops, seminars and journals at Wits, there were no structures of civil society such as residents' associations, unions or community-based organisations through which we were able to raise political awareness. This was to come later. It was therefore a great opportunity in 1978 and 1979 when there was a call to mobilise the public to come out in support of the Fattis & Monis and Wilson Roundtree strikes by organising consumer boycotts of these products.

This was a wonderful way to draw in the broader community and make them part of the workers' struggle. We were also able to start mobilising young people around these campaigns as activists. We had already started observing young school students for possible recruitment. Among the students we drew on were Nava Pillay, Razia Saleh and Thava Pillay. This was the first experience of political activism in Laudium. Our task was to distribute leaflets educating the community about the strike and why it was important to support it. But, we went further. We also started speaking to the shop owners in the location to explain the reasons for the campaign and encouraged them to stop buying these products. This worked much better than we thought. The community was beginning to stir and political debate was taking place. Support for the strikes proved to be subtle and soft, and yet an incredible vehicle through which to build political awareness.

Shopkeepers and residents gave us a hearing and were sympathetic. Some even donated money and clothes for the striking workers. We were connecting people in our community with the struggles of African workers and the rest of South Africa. The presence of the ANC was beginning to be felt, not any longer an organisation outside the country or in prison. The ANC was amongst the people. This was new.

As for the unit, we were making good progress and our confidence as underground operatives was buoyed by the impact that we were beginning to make in the community and on campus. It was always gratifying to listen to students or even members of the community in Laudium talk in hushed tones about the ANC literature that we were disseminating. Being responsible for establishing a presence of the ANC was good for our morale. We were beginning to capture the imagination of young people. Success was breeding success and we were gaining in strength. New opportunities were beginning to emerge. This opened up good prospects for further recruitment to take place.

While campus was a natural recruiting ground, this was not part of my brief. However, I took advantage of the opportunities that presented themselves. During this period, a major conundrum facing white democrats was the prospect of national conscription. Many students were angry.[16] I ended up recruiting four of these students. Because they were not within my scope of operations, I did no more than recruit them and sent them to Botswana to meet Marius, who discussed their further deployment. During this period, I also frequented the Institute of Race Relations building in Jorrisen Street where there were regular meetings related to the Fattis & Monis and Wilson Roundtree strikes. It was while attending these meetings that I got to meet two comrades who became important to me – Barbara Hogan and Rocklyn Mark Williams.

Crash at a roadblock

Barbara Hogan was a key activist in both these strikes and I learnt a lot from the way in which she presented the issues. Over the decades that followed, our paths would cross many times. The first occasion came late in 1978 or early 1979 when I returned to Botswana for a consultation with Marius. I took along a student from Wits whom I had recently recruited. When I got to Marius and Jenny's place in Molepolole, I was surprised to find Barbara and two journalists, Peter Wellman and Peta Thornycroft, also present. I remembered Peta because she was then at an advanced stage of pregnancy.

At the end of our weekend and after we all had our separate consultations with Marius, he asked me if I could give Barbara, Peter and Peta a lift to Johannesburg. I agreed and thought nothing of it. Passing through Gaborone, Peta wanted to stop at a butcher to buy some of the famous Botswana prime steak which was very cheap. As for me, I also wanted to take advantage of the stopover at a bookstore as I thought it would be useful to buy some of the political literature that was banned back home. We found some way of concealing these in a most basic way and without putting too much effort into it. We now had both meat and literature that was contraband in a car of multi-racial activists on their return from briefings with the ANC. We were clearly asking for trouble. The fact that we actually did this was an indication of just how naïve we were about our security.

I had another good reason to be nervous as we waited to cross at the border gate. While the police took their time inspecting our vehicle, there were several trucks that had been processed through Customs and made their way towards Zeerust. What bothered me was the fact that the road between the Tlokweng border gate and Zeerust was largely corrugated and it would be most unpleasant driving in the dust behind a horse and trailer truck. This is exactly what happened. After making it through the border gate, we travelled for about 20 kilometres in a cloud of dust making it difficult to overtake. All I could do was to patiently drive at the speed that the cloud of dust allowed. Fortunately, I had the good sense to ask that Peta sit in front and use her seatbelt. Then, disaster struck!

Along the road was a military roadblock. This was standard practice on that stretch of the road. The truck ahead of us was flagged down to stop. This was done on the road instead of being pulling off to the side. As the cloud of dust began to lift, all I saw in front of me was the back of this huge truck that I had been following since the border gate. I slammed on the brakes, but the car effortlessly glided on the gravel right into the rear end of the truck. I saw the front end of my precious car crumple up right before my very eyes. It was most fortuitous that I was not driving too fast because we could have sustained serious, if not fatal, injuries. An immediate check confirmed that we were all okay. I was sure that my world was about to come to an end. I had crashed into a military roadblock whose objective it was to apprehend the likes of us and there was nothing I could do about it.

The soldiers immediately made their way towards our car. I am not sure what came over me, but I jumped out and burst into tears. I started yelling that my father was going to kill me when he discovered that I crashed my car. I acted as a hysterical mess to great effect. The young soldier who witnessed this spectacle was not sure what to make of it and was sufficiently distracted from carrying out a search. Finally, good sense prevailed, and we immediately set about trying to get all my passengers away from the car as quickly as possible, by organising lifts for everyone from the vehicles coming through the roadblock.

This is an incident that would remain etched in my memory forever because we did everything that we should not have done and came through it by sheer good luck. Later, I called Barbara to let her know that I got home safely and sorted the car out. Not long after this, she was arrested and sent to prison and I had to leave for exile. The next time we would meet was more than 12 years later, in 1991.

Entering the Fold

Infiltrating the South African Defence Force

One day as I was entering the Institute of Race Relations building, I passed a tall young white male with a boyish face casually wearing a military jacket. Since I knew that some of the white students were already doing national service, I was more curious than surprised. The next time I saw him, I made an effort to greet and chat. He was very friendly and eager to engage. His name was Rocklyn (Rocky) Mark Williams. I quickly learnt that he held radical political views, which he was certainly not shy to share. Extremely intelligent and well-read, Rocky was also every bit a maverick. He worked in the signals section as a communications officer in the Defence Force at Voortrekkerhoogte,[17] which was the headquarters of the Defence Force where their key personnel also lived. It is also located adjacent to Laudium, which Rocky knew well. Rocky also enjoyed Indian food and this suited me perfectly.

I invited him home and tried to learn more about him and his work in the Defence Force because I was not sure what the signals section did. Over time, I got to learn that the signals section dealt with the communications and information support systems for the command and control of the combined armed forces. I did not understand the importance of this until I gave him a lift back to his place of work to resume his night duty. His office was in a standalone, prefabricated building, curiously, with no meaningful security on the premises. With the entire Voortrekkerhoogte perimeter secured, perhaps it was assumed that there was no need for additional security around each individual facility. Since it was night time and there was no one else present, Rocky invited me in.

It never dawned on me until much later that just as we did not take security very seriously, neither did the apartheid government. I was able to walk into the signals room without going through any security check and neither was the place guarded.

The main work room had little more than a series of telex machines placed along walls. This was obviously before the advent of computers and electronic communications as we know it today. As messages came in to each of these machines, they would be printed out on a perforated roll of paper, which had two additional carbonated copies for good measure. I was fascinated by this technology. Being curious, I wanted to know what the information was all about.

This is when the penny dropped. I was totally shocked by what I saw. Amongst other forms of military communications, the most critical military intelligence reports were sent to the signals room at Voortrekkerhoogte, the military headquarters of the apartheid army. The reports were printed in triplicate. I was told that the first copy went to the office of Tienie Groenewald, the chief of military intelligence; the second copy was sent for filing and the third copy was destroyed if it was not needed. This was a huge unplanned, and totally unexpected, breakthrough for me.

I immediately set about recruiting Rocky and also arranged for him to meet Marius. Over the next year, I kept in close contact with Rocky who regularly visited me at home and always had loads of information for me. I travelled to Botswana for a briefing almost every quarter and on each occasion, I would take a load of intelligence documents from Rocky with me. Naturally this was the highest grade of intelligence information one could hope for because it even included intelligence reports on our operations as well as reports from apartheid agents and spies who were working in our ranks. I worked quite hard to ensure that Rocky felt well supported and he was provided with a regular supply of political literature to continue his political education. In all my naivety, when I drove Rocky back to work at night after a meal, which was quite often, I would be bold (or stupid) enough to play O.R. Tambo's annual speeches on the cassette player in my father's car. We were extremely lucky not to have been arrested.

Rocky's recruitment was a major development and presented an enormous opportunity. Even if I was not trained in intelligence work, it did not take much to know that one should exploit the opportunity as best possible without compromising his recruitment. I was therefore looking for other potential recruits within the Defence Force that may be of value to us. Without much prompting, Rocky was very keen to help me recruit Gary, his best friend, who was also conscripted and deployed to the military base in Pietersburg. I met Gary a couple of times and was pleased to proceed with his recruitment.

Then in August 1979, I received a call from Rocky who asked to meet. He told me that he was picked up by the Security Police and detained for a couple of days. He reported that he had been careless with some political poetry he had written, and this was found by the authorities. Neither Rocky nor I made anything much of this. Rocky claimed that he managed to talk his way out of things and convinced the police that nothing much should be made of his poetry. I was too naïve to make anything of it. Soon after this event, I went to Botswana for another consultation with Marius. The meeting went well because my unit was performing exceedingly well. After submitting my latest haul of intelligence materials from Rocky, I also briefed them about his detention.

Both Marius and Jenny were shocked to hear this. It took me a while to understand what all the fuss was about. The meeting was immediately adjourned to allow Marius to consult with Henry Makgothi and take his advice. Henry was the most senior leader available and a member of the ANC's National Executive Committee. The response to this and the directive issued was earth shattering and would change my life forever. I was told that I had little choice but to leave home for exile with immediate effect. This was not possible, I protested. What was I to tell my parents? I was about to complete my second year of law studies. It was also the first year of university studies that I had actually performed well. They told me that I had no choice in the matter. As a compromise, they were prepared to allow me to complete my end-of-year exams and leave the country by November, which was in two months' time.

In their estimation, if I remained any longer in the country, I would be placing the members of my unit at risk and jeopardising all the work we had done thus far. There was no explanation for Rocky's detention or his release after two days. The circumstances were not clear and needed to be investigated. In the meantime, it was better not to take any chances because the risks were too grave.

I had become a victim of my own success. I was totally devastated. I drove back home that Sunday totally crestfallen. The world as I knew it had just collapsed. I had no idea of the full implications of the decision I took to become politically active in the underground of the ANC. Nothing could have prepared me for this eventuality. Besides, I simply did not know what I was going to tell my parents.

As for Rocky and I, while we too would part ways, we were destined to meet again.

Coming of age

I was a happy young man who had an ordinary upbringing even if it was in a home that was struggling to make ends meet. I was only 19 when the June 1976 uprisings took place. Like so many other young people of my age, my life would be irreversibly changed by these struggles. I stopped being a young adult and assumed the responsibilities of a grown-up. Playfulness had no place in this new world. Life had suddenly become serious; difficult choices had to be made. Gone was the luxury of having time to philosophise about matters of the world because we had to change it rather than ponder about it. I had also just started enjoying the development of the spiritual side of my life. All of this was to change.

The time now was for action more than just talking or thinking about it. We were no longer spectators making comment. We become protagonists in this alien world. People were dying and we could not afford to be idle. A battle was being fought and we could not stand on the sidelines. We were either part of the solution or part of the problem. We needed to do something about the situation in the country. There was a struggle to be waged, a war to be fought. This was a very different world for a young man like me from a community of conservative traders such as Laudium was. When there was no space within which to become politically active, it never occurred to me that it may be necessary to create one. I thought our community was far too conservative. Little did I think that it was necessary to go about changing this. The realisation that dawned on me was that it was up to us to change the conditions in the community we were living in rather than expecting someone to do this for us.

Politically, instead of coming of age, I was thrust into it. Despite this, the full reality of what I was getting myself involved in never dawned on me. I did not think about my security. I never gave much thought to the possibility of either going to prison or having to leave home for exile at the tender age of 22. This reality was a seismic shift. It was a shift that I was not prepared for.

V

Going into Exile

Traumatic break

I arrived home in the early evening on that Sunday, just in time for a shower and a meal with the family. After supper, I followed my father into the lounge where he would usually watch TV. He could sense that there was something on my mind. By this time, I had rationalised things in my mind and concocted a story to tell my parents. I told my father that I had long wanted to study in a foreign country and I now had the opportunity as the ANC had promised to get me a scholarship. After asking a couple of questions, he left me in the lounge, excusing himself to perform his evening prayers. He had seen through my lies and was not going to let me see him getting emotional. He was totally devastated.

In my utter foolishness, I thought I got through round one and was now ready to sell the same story to my mother. When she joined me in the lounge it was clear that she knew, as only mothers can, that something was amiss. I mustered all the confidence I had and tried to sell my mother the same story – I was going off for studies in this mythical 'overseas'. After a short while my father returned from his prayers.

Instead of focusing on the reason for this dramatic development, my parents immediately started to ponder on the practical aspects of this news. I cannot begin to fathom just how difficult this must have been for both of them. Instead, they were more concerned about me and my welfare rather than their loss. They wanted to know when I would be leaving. I told them that I would go as soon as my exams were over in November. And, when would I be back? I said I did not know. All my mum said to me is that she would appreciate it if she were allowed to take me to her family so that I could greet them before I left.

Culturally, this is what people did before leaving home for a long time or a distant journey. I was assured that the logic behind this was that it was necessary to take the families' blessings. This worried me because I did not want it to be known that I was leaving. I also did not want to answer the many questions that they would invariably pose. I told Mum that it was not possible to let anyone know that I was leaving. This did not bother her. She agreed that we did not say anything about my leaving home, I would just have to greet them. This was all that she would ask of me. How could I refuse?

I think my parents knew exactly what was going down, but just did not know what to make of it or what it meant. They knew that I was lying and that I was in all likelihood going into exile, but they were too decent to challenge me and demand more information. They were intent on protecting me from further exposing myself and this was the last we talked about the matter. No one said a word. Not even my sister. Throughout this affair, she stood by in total numbness. She watched the family being torn up and did not know what to make of it. She too was too respectful to demand answers.

The hours and days that followed were without doubt the most painful I have ever had to endure. A once-happy and cheerful home had been transformed into a totally sombre abode. To this day, neither of my parents ever asked me to offer them an explanation. They knew that it would be difficult for me to explain myself and respected and loved me too much to put me through this. Our home became a totally dark space. We stopped talking to each other and only spoke when it was absolutely necessary. Gone was the usual banter and petty sibling rivalry that would go on between my sister and I. Ours had become a funeral home – my funeral; and no one was allowed to grieve for fear of letting anyone know that I was leaving. I cannot remember a darker time in my life.

Going into Exile

In the next couple of weeks, I set out with my mother to visit the homes of various family members. On this trip, my mother bought me a gold ring and chain with a locket as a family memento. By September the pressure had become overbearing. The darkness and pain at home was too heavy. It was suffocating all of us.

Tragically, we did not know how to grieve for our imminent separation with all the uncertainty that it entailed. Neither did our circumstances allow us to do so. I suspect that it was the fear of the unknown that was most frightening. The most painful part was suppressing our sadness and not allowing ourselves to grieve. The break-up of our tight-knit family proved to be much more than I could endure. It was thus in September 1979 that I confessed to my parents that I could take this no longer and would leave that weekend. This would be before I wrote my year-end exams.

By this time, even my studies were the least of our considerations. All my father said to me was that if I had to go, then they would be the ones to take me there. They wanted to see where I was going and to be sure that I would be safe. He was firm about this position and left no room for debate on the matter. This was the first time that we actually spoke about the physical act of separation and where I was going.

That Saturday morning, the family went to the shop in Marabastad as usual. As soon as we closed the shop at midday,[18] we set off for the Botswana border. Both Fazila and Yogesh were there to greet and see me off. Crossing the border into Botswana was a great relief and took place without event. Fortunately, I had a cousin, Solly, who worked in Botswana. He was a mechanic of modest means but was always happy to open his heart and home to anyone who needed help. Both Solly and his wife, Hajira, were generous beyond measure and without any expectation. This was the beginning of a relationship that I have always been extremely grateful for and appreciated.

It took me years to figure it out, but this is not where the trauma ended. I was so busy feeling sorry for myself that I did not fully appreciate the impact that my departure would have on both Fazila and Yogesh. Like my family, they too were severely affected. The dangers of our underground work had dawned on them as they had on me.

We certainly did not see this coming. If this is what happened to me, how much longer would it be before they too would be affected? While I consoled myself with the fact that my departure was intended for their protection, I left believing they would continue the underground political work we started together as if nothing had happened. How wrong could I be?

With my departure, and because of my uncertain future, I relinquished my role in and responsibility for the unit. Both Fazila and Yogesh were now to report directly to the political structures in Botswana through Marius.

Gaborone

Botswana is a large land-locked dry country. In 1979, it had a population of little more than a million. Land was in abundance and the two largest cities, Gaborone and Lobatse, were small, but growing fast. For a number of years, the city continuously expanded as urbanisation grew. Roads were being tarred and new housing developments were sprouting everywhere. Gaborone quickly gained the reputation as the fastest growing city in Africa. The country was doing exceptionally well largely because it had huge deposits of diamonds and a large cattle industry. The economy was booming. While there was no industry of note, Gaborone transformed into a vibrant centre of retail trade boasting two shopping malls.

The shops were mostly owned by Indian people of South African birth. The growing suburbs had a significant population of foreign expat workers including many donor organisations. Another facet of Gaborone was its many popular watering holes, which were frequented by South Africans and often had good live music over the weekends. On the whole, Gaborone, and until the attacks and assassinations by apartheid security forces started, was quite a relaxed place and the people pleasant and welcoming.

I set off with my family for Molepolole to meet the Schoons the day after I arrived in Botswana. This was yet another strange experience for us all. My parents and sister helped me escape the apartheid government to come to Botswana only to find that they were to hand me over to an Afrikaner man, who looked like an ageing hippy, and his family who were living in a rural African village. The only relief in this surrealism was that my family was now able to put a human face to my exile. They were handing me over to someone. I was not disappearing into the sunset. In their minds, my exile had a destination and a face. It was not an uncertainty.

My parting with the family was quiet, sombre but very dramatic. My mum thought she needed to hand me over to Jenny. She asked Jenny to look after me as if she was to be my new mother. She also asked me to be good to them and to treat them as if they were to be my new parents. This was the only way she could deal with our parting and perhaps it was the best that could happen for my parents.

That is how my life in exile started.

On Monday morning, I was taken to the ANC offices to meet Isaac Makopo, the ANC's chief representative, and be processed as a refugee. I was then taken to a transit camp in a village called Mogoditshane, located about 10 kilometres north of the city. The camp was a novel experience for me. It had a house, which accommodated about 20 new recruits coming from home at any point in time. New exiles who wished to join the ANC were processed from this camp depending on whether we were going on to study or for military training. Most of us were very young with ages varying from about 16 to 25. Being a transit camp, no one remained for any significant period of time. There was no political or military training taking place at the camp. The purpose of my stay there was dependent on a decision as to how I was to be deployed. I was hoping to proceed to Angola for military training.

In the house, we had a collection of political reading material to keep us busy. Outside, was a big vegetable garden from which produce was sold to the villagers. The camp had running water but no electricity. Each of us were given a responsibility on the roster to carry out various duties ranging from cooking, cleaning, farming and the selling of the produce. This was the start of my new life. While I managed most of my tasks, cooking proved to be a major challenge for me. I had to learn fast.

It did not take long before the reality of my situation set in. Suddenly, I felt all alone and unsure of myself. I was out of my comfort zone, had no control over my life and did not know what the future held. I did not know what was to become of me. It is here that I learnt that the most honest moment you have in your day is the time between the lights going out at night and when you fall off to sleep. It is in that time that one is able to think about matters without distraction and with honesty. It was also during one of these nights that I burst into tears because I felt so helpless. For the first time in my life, I felt all alone. Fortunately, this emotional outburst was short-lived, and I regained my composure. Three months later and some time in December 1979, I was dispatched to Lusaka without any explanation. Movement at last. I was hoping that this would lead to some certainty as to what was to become of me.

Mac Maharaj

My trip to Lusaka opened a new chapter in my life. But first, my worst anxieties would be challenged. I was put on a plane and told that I would be met at the airport. I waited for a number of hours at the airport for a person I did not know to take me to a destination that I was not informed about or for a reason I was not entirely sure about. I was definitely not in control over my life. When I was finally picked up, I was taken straight to a house where I was told I had to be accommodated.

I learnt later that the house was referred to as the RC (Revolutionary Council) house. The house was located on a large plot that boasted a mango tree in the midst of long wild grass in the back yard. I was informed that I was going to meet Mac Maharaj who I later learnt was the secretary of the Internal Political Reconstruction Department (IPRD). Mac was, however, tied up in Maputo and I had to wait for his return.

During this time, several people passed through the RC House for varying periods. It was here that I saw the famed AK-47 assault rifle for the first time. There were several in the house for our protection, the sight of which suddenly conjured up all sorts of images of what our lives could be. I could already see myself marching in uniform with my AK.

The first person I met was Shaheed Rajie, who was also known as Steve. Steve was part of the MK command structures in Botswana. A tall and lanky person from the Cape, Steve was always neat and organised. He introduced me to Pitso Tolo and Keith Mokoape, both of whom were also part of the command structures in Botswana but were recently expelled under pressure from the South African government.

Another person who I would never forget was Francis or 'Shorty' (alias for Tlhomedi Ephraim Mfalapitsa[19]) who was also part of the Botswana MK command responsible for ordinance. The reason why I remembered him is that very soon after our encounter, he returned to Botswana, defected and became one of the notorious askaris. I also had the opportunity of meeting two other comrades who were returning from training in the German Democratic Republic and going back to Botswana where they were to be part of the political machinery.

I was most excited at the prospect of meeting with Mac. I quickly gathered that Mac was widely regarded as a struggle hero and an icon by many who looked up to him as a role model, as did I. What I discovered in Lusaka while waiting for him is that Mac also had a reputation for his razor-sharp mind, analysis and a work ethic that was very difficult to keep up with. My eventual meeting with Mac confirmed all that I heard about him.

Mac was always a difficult person to work with. He worked extremely hard, read everything, knew what he was talking about, had clear opinions, never sat on the fence and came to meetings prepared. Mac also expected the same from those he worked with and never suffered fools lightly. He took no prisoners. It took me years to understand Mac better. Under the boisterous, brash and rough exterior was an extremely gentle and sensitive soul. He was a great, but extremely difficult, mentor. Mac was someone I grew to respect, love and trust.

The upshot of my engagement with Mac was that I was to be deployed in the Botswana political machinery. It was clear to me that Mac was familiar with my background and the work I did in the underground. When I insisted on going for military training, Mac asked that I exercise some patience as this would come in time. I was tasked to focus my energies on helping to build the underground. I did not realise until then just how important the underground was. This meeting provided me with a better sense of this task. This was a major relief. I now had a mission and knew what the objective was. Once again, I had focus and the uncertainty that dogged me was immediately put to rest.

For now, it was more important to return to Botswana and set about working on my new mission. I was now formally part of the political leadership responsible for the building of the ANC's underground presence in the country. The Botswana machinery was responsible for operations from Masina in the north-east, down to the Vaal area including the entire Pretoria, Witwatersrand, Vereeniging (PWV) triangle and up to Upington in the north-west. While I was given some focus and knew what was expected of me, I was beginning to understand some of the challenges that we had to face in the execution of our struggle.

Difficult times

I returned to Gaborone where my cousin, Solly, very kindly accommodated me. I was always conscious of the fact that he was doing so at great risk and was most grateful for it.

The structures of the ANC were clearly in a state of flux and this was reflected in the frequent changes made in the leadership structures in Botswana. Security was a big part of the challenge. Working in the Forward Area was very different to working at home and it took some time to orientate oneself. Not being on the ground in the field of operations was an extremely difficult adjustment.

Underground structures of the ANC at home were few and very weak. This meant that ability of the political leadership structures in the Forward Areas to impact on the situation inside the country was limited. This was despite the increasingly favourable conditions for recruitment on the ground. Mass mobilisation was beginning in all earnest. An example of this was the establishment of the Congress of

South African Students (COSAS) in May 1979.

COSAS marked a decisive break from the past. Ironically, it was an organisation of students that was established with the support and direct involvement of the ANC. The inclusion of the word 'Congress' in the name boldly declared this. Until then, many in the country talked about being politically 'non-aligned', particularly because of the differences between the ANC, PAC and the Black Consciousness Movement. When I was amongst activists at home, we were even too scared to mention the name ANC aloud. When we did, we alluded to it rather than named the organisation. Now, an organisation of students had declared itself to be an organisation with the name 'Congress' in it. A clear statement was being made and this became patently obvious from the campaigns COSAS waged. Despite the weakness of the structures of the ANC, the organisation was becoming overtly popular.

It was therefore fortuitous that we were able to celebrate this new wave of militancy with the launch of the ANC campaign remembering the Battle of Isandlwana, which took place one hundred years before, on 22 January 1879.[20] This was the first major encounter in the Anglo–Zulu War between the British Empire and the Zulu Kingdom. The battle was a decisive victory for the Zulus and caused the defeat of the first British invasion of Zululand. Another was the commemoration of the life of the ANC freedom fighter, Solomon Mahlangu. This was a clear manifestation that we had entered a new era where the young were more determined than ever before to associate themselves with the ANC.

Botswana became a busy place with the building of the internal underground. Billy Masetlha and Rola Masinga, former Southern African Students' Movement (SASM) leaders who were intimately involved in SASM and then the establishment of COSAS, started drawing many young students out of the country for consultations, briefings and recruitment. I was asked to provide support.

On my part, I tried to start my work in the underground from where I left off. I turned to Yogesh from my original unit. Fazila had by this time left Laudium and not long thereafter also left the country. Yogesh had continued on his own with some propaganda work. Each time he visited, he would return home with the latest materials. He would also provide me with a report on developments taking place both at Wits University and in the Indian communities. I was looking at potential recruits.

I tried to get Yogesh to assist me with the recruitment of key activists that we had jointly identified. I was particularly keen on the recruitment of Nava Pillay and Neeshan (Shan) Balton, whom Yogesh had gotten to know at Wits. Nothing came of this. On one visit, Yogesh reported that he offered to connect key leaders in the Transvaal Indian Congress (TIC) structures with the ANC's underground. These offers were rebuffed. His attempts to create an explicit, if not formal, link between the ANC underground and the legal TIC were unsuccessful. He was disappointed that senior comrades within the TIC would not use the channel we had established for comrades who were wanting to be part of the ANC underground. In fact, he was given an ultimatum and had to decide as to whether he wanted to continue to work with the TIC structures on the ground or the ANC in the underground.

It soon became evident that I was not going to simply continue where I had left off as an operative inside the country. The conditions in the country and personal circumstances of each of us in our original unit had changed and I was not able to use my original underground unit as a platform from which to build further structures of the underground. I needed to find another approach and was finding it extremely difficult to do so. The best I could do was to gather political intelligence on developments in our communities and to identify people for potential recruitment. Beyond that, I was not very successful.

There was no easy road to getting back into the underground. My confidence was deflated. Exile was not only different, but difficult. I was frustrated and felt very useless.

The Green Book

It was not until much later that I understood that my frustration was not unique. The ANC, in general, was not able to take advantage of the wave of militancy brought on by the June 1976 uprisings to build its structures of the underground. Several generations of our underground structures had since the banning of the ANC been decimated. The challenge that the ANC confronted was that it had until 1978 adopted an approach which was premised on the idea that the struggle would be waged by 'specialist armed fighters' rather than by the people as a whole. It was essentially a militarist approach rather than a political approach.[21] This obviously meant that sufficient-enough attention was not paid to the establishment of underground political structures. Essentially, the ANC had no strategy to develop its underground political structures. This would also explain why it also did not have any dedicated structure at a leadership level to attend to this. It was not a priority.

This is why the Revolutionary Council established the Internal Political Reconstruction Committee (IPRD). As the name suggested, the ANC was intent to 'reconstruct' its political structures inside South Africa, albeit at the underground level. To give the ANC a better understanding of this mission, Oliver Tambo led a delegation of senior ANC leaders to Vietnam. Tambo was keen to learn what methods and structures were required in the execution of the liberation struggle. The outcome of this visit was the ANC's report in March 1979, which came to be referred to as the 'Green Book'. This was also the report of the Politico-Military Strategy Commission, which was established to report to the ANC's National Executive Committee. There were several key findings. In the main, the political leadership of the struggle was emphasised. The report found that in the absence of the ANC as a legal structure, people would naturally establish popular organisations to give expression to their daily struggles.

As ANC underground operatives, it was therefore necessary to establish relationships with the leadership in these organisations, which were re-defining the anti-apartheid struggles. However, the key injunction was that our interactions with these organisations were to be conducted in a manner that did not compromise these structures. Unfortunately, little emphasis was made on this requirement, because we were not privy to the Report, thus leading to some unfortunate results and exposure of leaders in the MDM structures.

Further to this, the importance of armed propaganda in support of these political struggles was emphasised. Responsibility for the implementation of this report and the execution of the struggle fell on the Revolutionary Council. The sad irony though was that while some leaders sought to give effect to the findings made in this report, the report itself was never published or distributed. In the Forward Areas, we heard of this document, but never got to see it. There was no attempt to educate or induct us into the approach proposed. One can only assume that there was no real will to implement the findings of the report, which would explain our weaknesses in this important area or work.

The Revolutionary Council was represented in the Forward Areas by a new structure, which had a title that lacked both imagination and inspiration: the Senior Organ. Like the Revolutionary Council, the Senior Organ also had a clear delineation between the political and military structures.

Between 1980 and 1983, the Senior Organ in Botswana was led by Henry Makgothi and later by Lambert Moloi. The political structures of the Senior Organ were represented (at different times) by Billy Masetlha, Dan Tloome, Wally Serote, Thabang Makwetla, Marius and Jenny Schoon, Patrick Fitzgerald and me.

VI

Exile:
New Beginnings

Leaving the comfort of home and going into exile was the start of a new chapter in my life. From here on, life was a bit of a rollercoaster ride with many new beginnings and dramatic changes.

Time to settle down?

My parents visited me regularly out of concern for the kind of life I was leading. At every visit, my father would ask when the situation would change sufficiently enough for me to return home. This became such a routine question that it irked me to no end because I did not have an answer for him. He was no more than a concerned father and I was a young revolutionary who got irritated far too quickly rather than understanding him. Each time my parents came, they brought me money, clothes and food in the hope of making me feel comfortable. It pained my father to no end to know that he had just built a beautiful big house which was mine to inherit and which I could not use because I was in exile.

In their attempt to make life better for me, my parents thought I should get married. A 22 years of age, they thought the time was right. This, they presumed, would give me a sense of stability, which I clearly did not have. I did not respond well to this. Each time they came, they would tell me about possible suitors in the hope that my interest would be perked. I was too much of a young hot-head to even think of marrying someone who was not political. Also, I could not afford to let my parents know that the life we were leading was totally abnormal and very dangerous. At one point, they even brought a young girl along. While their attempts did not work, the seed was sown. I began to think that it may be an idea worth considering.

In early 1980 my parents went on holiday to Zimbabwe and invited me to join them. I thought it was a welcome break and was very keen to see the newly liberated country. What a pleasant experience it was. It was not too difficult at all to fall in love with this wonderful country that was so richly endowed. Due to the weak Zimbabwean dollar, we were able to have a grand holiday very cheaply. Not surprisingly, with so many whites leaving in a hurry, beautiful houses were being sold very cheaply, and the country became an attractive place for one to settle down.

As things turned out, I met a young lady whom I fell in love with while on that holiday in Zimbabwe in early 1980. I made several trips to Harare during the course of the year in the hope of building the relationship, and for the first time in my life actually thought of settling down. I spoke to my parents and they were very keen, but unfortunately her parents had serious reservations about me being a refugee. Instead of dealing with this challenge, I hastily and in anger ended the relationship, otherwise a very happy situation, and quickly returned to Botswana to continue my life there.

Dukwe

The year 1980 would be a difficult one for another reason. Until now, ANC cadres were generally allowed to live and move about in Botswana without restriction. This was to change. Due to pressure from the South African government, all cadres with refugee status, and who did not have a work permit or other legal reason, were to be relocated from Gaborone and other towns to the Dukwe Refugee Camp. Used previously as the location for all Angolan, Mozambican, Namibian and Zimbabwean refugees, Dukwe was situated in a remote area north of Francistown on the edge of the Kgalagadi desert. However, I will always remember Dukwe as that place which was 120 km away from the nearest telephone or any other contact with the outside world.

I worked feverishly to avoid going to Dukwe and made every attempt to get a work permit. I discovered that the only way was to have specific skills that were sought after and not locally available. As a second-year university student, I would certainly not qualify. At Solly's house, I had met Ismail Bhamjee and his brothers who had come from Lenasia to establish a car dealership. Ismail and I became good friends and he offered me a job in one of their garages, but it was insufficient for me to qualify for a work permit.

Given no other choice, in March 1981 the entire contingent of ANC cadres without permits were moved to Dukwe. Dukwe was effectively a prison, fenced and guarded by soldiers of the Botswana Defence Force, with strictly controlled access to and from the camp. The camp was also managed by a mean-spirited policeman. The camp essentially resembled a village with some basic thatch roof mud huts. None of the basic conveniences existed. There was no electricity and a few communal taps with running water serviced the entire camp. It was a place that I would quickly come to hate with a passion.

In total, we were about 150 South Africans from the different liberation movements. Each political formation naturally established itself in a separate area. Fortunately for us, the good organisational skills of the ANC clearly showed itself to have great benefits. Billy Masetlha was appointed the commander of our group and a proper structure was put in place. Communal social, sporting and political activities were quickly organised. As refugees, we were given an allowance of five Pula[22] (Botswana currency) per month along with some supplies of canned foods, and ever since my experience in Dukwe I cannot bear the smell of mackerel. To make life more bearable, we used to club together our allowances to buy a goat once a month so that we could eat some meat. Food was therefore a collective and not individual exercise. We also kept ourselves busy with various activities including the clearing up of an area so that we could have a soccer field.

My hut had a hole for a window and a door that swung loosely on its hinges and had no lock. The cows from the nearby village would regularly come through our area leaving in their trail a fresh supply of cow dung. I quickly learnt how to maintain the walls and the floor of my hut by regularly plastering fresh cow dung on it. This, I was informed, had the added benefit of not only ensuring that no cracks in the wall emerged, but also kept the flies away.

Apart from the regular soccer matches, political debates and reading, there was little else to keep us productive and engaged over a long period of time. After a couple of weeks, I started getting restless because I could not make sense of a continued stay at the camp. One of the comrades that I befriended was Naledi Sehume. Naledi and I were able to chat about a number of things and it was not long before the two of us planned our escape from Dukwe.

We monitored traffic in and out of the camp and decided that our best way out was to stow away on the back of one of the trucks that used to collect supplies from Francistown. One Friday morning during May 1981 at about 5h30, we waited for the truck to pass along its usual route. With careful planning, we managed to get on to the back of the truck and hid underneath its tarpaulin without being noticed. We remained quiet for the journey of 120 km to Francistown. Once we arrived there, we waited for the vehicle to stop at a traffic sign so that we could jump off. We were free; but had no money or transport. We needed to find a way to get to Gaborone, which was some 450 km away. In town, I went to an Indian-owned shop and explained my plight. With little explanation, we were fortunate to be given money for train fare and a lunch. One of the most memorable meals I have ever had was the fish and chips Naledi and I bought and consumed on the pavements of Francistown.

Naledi and I were very proud of ourselves. This was no different to a jail break. That evening we bought a ticket on the train coming from Zimbabwe on its way to Gaborone. We got to Gaborone early on Saturday morning. Naledi and I parted ways at the station. This was the last I was to see him until about five years later when he returned to

Exile: New Beginnings

Gaborone as the regional MK commander.

The first thing I did on arrival in Gaborone was to make my way to Ismail's business place. He kindly allowed me to use his phone so that I could call my parents. It was a call that haunts me to this day. I knew that they would be really worried not to have heard from me over the past three months.

I called my parents at the shop in Marabastad and my mother answered it. Happy to hear her voice I greeted her with some excitement. To my horror, she responded to my voice with total silence. I knew something was wrong. She did not know how to answer me. After a while, my father came on the phone. The first thing he asked me was where exactly I was. I told him that I was back in Gaborone and would go to Solly's house. All he said was that I was to wait for them at the house. There was a real sense of urgency and concern in his voice. No sooner had he put the phone down that he made arrangements to close the shop early and immediately drove through to Botswana to see me.

What an emotional reunion it was! I knew my parents and sister loved me but cannot say that I understood it properly until that day. Unfortunately, it would be a long time before I would get to learn of the price they paid, the sacrifices they made and what they would have to endure for being my parents. For the most part though, it is me who thought that I was the one making the sacrifices and struggling. How wrong was I?

I learnt why my mother responded to hearing my voice with total silence. She was totally shocked and traumatised. Over the past months, with the evident knowledge of the absence of contact from me, the Security Branch called my home several times. On one such occasion, my mother had the misfortune of answering and they taunted her with the threat that they were going to assassinate me. She was totally mortified at the thought that my silence may well have meant that they succeeded.

Yet, on another occasion, the Security Branch sent a message to my parents to let them know that they were aware that I wanted to return home. They were asked to confirm this as they would be happy to get the authorisation from no less than the Minister of Justice, Jimmy Kruger, to allow me to return home with the undertaking that no charges would be brought against me if I collaborated. All my parents needed to do was to get this message to me and the Special Branch would facilitate all the arrangements if I agreed.

I often wondered about what could have allowed the Special Branch to come that conclusion. It could have been pure fabrication or a pure fishing exercise. On the other hand, I did, while in Dukwe, casually voice the concern that we were wasting our time there because it seemed so senseless. I often wondered whether an apartheid agent would have communicated this back home, but then cautioned myself not to be paranoid.

What I did not realise until then though was that every time my family crossed the borders to see me, they were being monitored and sometimes also harassed. In fact, almost every time my family came to see me, they would be paid a visit on their return by the Special Branch to find out about me. This naturally stressed the family out to no end. Sometimes, they were even harassed at the border gates. Still, they never shirked from coming to see me and neither did they complain.

Indeed I came to depend on these visits to sustain me emotionally, financially and, of course, with a fresh supply of home food. It is only later when I reflected on this experience that I got to realise how selfish I had been. I thought of my exile from my point of view and not the impact it had on my family. They were never spared during this ordeal and I wish I knew better then.

Apartheid strikes back

Historically, there has always been a very close relationship between the Batswana and South African people and cultural exchanges have persisted over the ages. One of the outcomes of this interaction was a vibrant South African community in Botswana, especially in Gaborone. With the influx of refugees, the South African community had grown in size and became very distinct. They made a huge impact on the local culture. The music of Jonas Gwanga, Hugh Masekela and Steve Dyer was extremely popular. The MEDU Art Ensemble equally made a huge impact. Because of the peaceful and welcoming nature of the Batswana, South African exiles, and the expatriate community in general, felt welcomed and were very relaxed in this environment. People moved about freely.

At first, South Africans threw great parties and had an active social life. There was a real community spirit. In fact, we were always happy to receive visiting South Africans and often accommodated them in our homes. This was a real break from the tension that many young people saw in the post-1976 period when South Africa was literally in flames. People felt safe. Botswana was peaceful and even free of crime. We felt so comfortable that little attention was given to our security as we should have done. We took it for granted.

The apartheid security forces did not sit by idly. Since 1975 when a noticeable presence of South African exiles in Botswana started, the apartheid security apparatus took various initiatives to neutralise the potential threat they believed the presence of the South Africans would pose. In general, they had hoped to keep their borders safe from infiltration by developing a 'cordon sanitaire'.[23] This policy was based on the 1977 Defence Force White Paper which laid the basis for P.W. Botha's concept of a 'total strategy' to protect its borders after Mozambique, Zimbabwe and Angola gained their independence and came to be known as the Frontline States.

There were essentially three different approaches used by the apartheid state to deal with their perception of the security threat. The first was on the diplomatic front. They issued warnings to neighbouring governments making up the Frontline States to take action against particular individuals, failing which they threatened direct intervention. Examples of this were the expulsion of Keith Mokoape, 'Zakes' Tolo and Snuki Zikalala, and later the forced removal of most of the refugees to Dukwe. Sometimes, too, governments such as Botswana would use the excuse of pressure from the apartheid government to manage the growing number of ANC personnel in their countries because they too started getting concerned.

The second approach was to infiltrate the ranks of the ANC. Here, the cases of Joe Mamasela[24] and Tlhomedi Ephraim Mfalapitsa come to mind. Another variation of this approach was sending out agents to infiltrate the organisation. Some of these agents even succeeded in inflicting serious harm in our military camps where they provoked and instigated dissent and discord. Some even went on to carry out various treacherous activities including assassinations. In the one instance, they even succeeded to poison an entire camp and report on the location of our training camps which were then aerial bombed.

The third approach was the use of hit squads and assassinations. This was the case in the instances of the infamous Matola Raid,[25] Maseru Massacre[26] and the June 1985 raid in Gaborone.[27]

I knew that it would be foolhardy to believe that we could carry out our work without drawing the attention of the South African security and intelligence community. However, I was naïve enough not to anticipate the brutality and ferocity with which they would execute their attacks. This is despite the first hint of their brutal action in using a parcel bomb to assassinate Abraham Ongopotse Tiro in the late 1970s. I suspect that while we all knew of the possibility of these attacks, we did not want to believe that this could happen to us. Needless to say, we did not always take the necessary security precautions.

The case of Mamasela stands out for special mention because of the approach used. Mamasela's recruitment into the ANC left us open to significant disruptions in several different respects, both in Botswana and South Africa. In Botswana, he got to know where many of our cadres lived and thus made them targets in later attacks. Back home, his work with Eugene De Kock's unit created specific damage because it took advantage of the recruitment of COSAS members into the ANC. Mamasela went on to provide members of COSAS with booby-trapped hand grenades, which detonated prematurely and were responsible for the deaths of several young people. The experience with Mamasela left many ANC people both inside and outside the country paranoid and uncertain as to how to trust people.

During the early '80s there were several trials of ANC who were arrested after coming from Botswana and in which a 'Mr X' would give evidence. Many activists in the country felt that the ANC in Botswana were either infiltrated or conducted themselves in a manner that did not adequately consider the security of its people in the country. This hampered our ability to build underground structures and made things more difficult for me to do my work. While activists in the country wanted to get involved, many were scared.

The reality of our vulnerability started affecting us. The case of Craig Williamson brought things home for me in a most painful way. Williamson infiltrated the white left through the student movement at Wits University and was later recruited by the ANC in London. Through his work in the international student movement, he funded a news organisation based in Gaborone in which both Patrick Fitzgerald and Heinz Klug worked. He also knew Jenny from Johannesburg and used to visit their house in Molepolole.

Williamson became bitter when he was eventually exposed and his cover was blown in 1980.[28] By 1981, he started exacting revenge. However, it quickly became known that there was a potential threat to the security of the Schoon family, Patrick and Heinz. Each of these comrades would leave Botswana in quick succession. Marius, Jenny and the children were eventually relocated to Angola where they taught at a university. Craig Williamson tracked down the Schoons, and a few years later, sent them a parcel bomb resulting in the brutal killings of both Jenny and Katryn. Nothing could have prepared me for this. These were people I knew and loved. They were also responsible for my recruitment into the ANC.

The challenges we faced were enormous. There was a lot of paranoia. I got to feel this first hand in a case that still haunts me to this day. I was approached by a comrade whom I trusted implicitly. He had recently received a contact from home. In the process of going through the debriefings and carrying out the usual security checks, it became clear the contact was in fact an enemy agent. The challenge the comrades faced was what to do with the person. Unfortunately, the agent was already exposed to several people and knew where they lived. If the agent was allowed to return home, this would immediately place many lives in jeopardy. At the same time, there were no facilities to properly interrogate or 'arrest' such a person. The only option left was to eliminate him. Should we proceed with this or not; and if so, what should we do?

This is a question that continues to haunt me. It haunts me now because of the weight of the burden that was placed on our shoulders. As a young man in his early 20s, I knew that I was definitely not mature enough to take such a decision; yet one was necessary. In the end, the problem was avoided because we found a way in which to convince the agent to travel to Lusaka where the ANC headquarters were better able to attend to the matter.

The year 1981 brought with it new developments that would yet again change the course of my life. This was the year that I went for military training in Angola and started my law degree afresh.

My military training

The permission to go for military training was one of my happiest moments. A dream had come true. Early in 1981 I was called to Lusaka for briefings and onward travel to Luanda, along with several other cadres who were also on their way for training. In Luanda, we were processed through immigration and were taken to a holding facility in the outskirts.

The first thing about Luanda that stood out was the familiar grandeur of Portuguese architecture, which I had seen before in our many visits to Maputo. The other reality that was evident was the ravages of war in an urban area. To me it stood out not only as a glorious symbol of the victory over colonialism but the brutality and the cost of that victory.

The journey I made to the training camp in the jungles of Angola was itself very educational. I got to learn a lot about war and its effect. While it may have been a romantic ambition to become a freedom fighter, I got to learn what happens when soldiers, like I was hoping to become, go to war. Wars result in destruction. The truth is that war is cruel and comes at a tremendous cost to the country and with a great deal of destruction of infrastructure and nature. Unfortunately, I would experience this same devastation much later in life, this time in Somalia.

There was also another lesson of war and revolutions that I learnt on my journey to our camp. It was clear to me that Angola had no easy victory. With revolution comes the inevitable counter-revolution. In Angola, the declaration of independence did not mean that the war was over because the counter-revolution came in the form of the continued banditry which the country had to endure. This was perpetrated by UNITA (National Union for the Total Independence of Angola) and remnants of the FNLA (National Front for the Liberation of Angola). The road we travelled was therefore dangerous. For this reason, we had to travel in an armed convoy of several vehicles.

We rode at the back of a truck and made our way into the jungle with extremely thick tropical vegetation. While the distance was approximately 65 km, the road was treacherous and took nearly two hours to reach our camp, Caxito.[29] Despite the reality that we found ourselves in, I was on my way to becoming a guerrilla, a freedom fighter and a soldier of the revolutionary people's army, Umkhonto we Sizwe. What exciting times these were! My spirits were extremely high.

Our camp was located on the banks of the Dande River and had a small complex of fixed buildings which were used by the camp administration, command personnel and fellow female trainees. The outer perimeter of the camp was defined by a trench that led to various dug-outs, some of which were used as living quarter and yet another for ordinance storage. There were also a few military tents in the inner area where we were to be accommodated. There was no electricity and only a couple of taps for running water. As for the men's toilet facilities, these were in an open space but blocked from view by surrounding bush. Logs were placed over a trench on which to squat.

There were several training areas surrounding the camp. These included a shooting range, a place to deal with explosives, and yet another to deal with exercises in military tactics. We also had a vegetable patch and kept few livestock that were intended for special occasions when it was appropriate to enjoy some meat. Occasionally, an animal was hunted and brought to the camp. There were no villages in the immediate vicinity of the camp.

After being processed by the camp administration as new MK

recruits, we were constituted into a new section of six cadres; each section usually consisted of up to ten cadres. We were also inducted into our platoon. With this done, we were shown our accommodation. I was allocated a space in a tent; the 'bedding' was an inflatable pool lounger.

The next morning, we were woken quite rudely by a big gong. This sound came from beating a hanging piece of rail line with an iron pole. This was the morning signal for our roll call and we were required to present ourselves in uniform and in our appointed formations. After hearing the roll call, the camp commander would then issue his commands and instructions as were necessary for the day.

The next part of the morning's ritual was most enjoyable with the camp commissar presenting us with the news of the day, which was continuously scanned and meticulously presented. This was an important mechanism designed to break the isolation of being in the jungles of Angola far away from home and put us in touch with developments in South Africa and the world at large. Apart from this, there were no newspapers, radio or television. Being young revolutionaries, our political lives and perspectives on world events were critical to us, and these reports would be the basis of the ensuing debates and discussions interpreting developments through the day. Naturally, we would carefully listen out for news on MK operations, political developments and what arrests were made. These news items would sometimes also include mention of operations carried out by fellow comrades who we trained or worked with. Politics was the lifeblood of the camp and it is what ensured cohesion and unity.

This item was followed by the daily run, which ranged in different distances depending on the instructor available. I did not enjoy this very much because I was not a very good runner and my boots were very big and uncomfortable. After the morning exercise, we would have our bath in the river, which early in the morning could be quite refreshing. Next would be our breakfast after which we would then proceed to our various classes. Our class consisted of our section of six cadres. Classes were located under some trees with makeshift seating and always on the outer perimeter of the camp. I remember sitting in class going about our lessons which would be punctuated by intermittent gunfire or explosions from units carrying out training in adjacent training areas. All of this often played out as if we were observing a battle unfolding. One got quite used to these sounds as it became part of our everyday life. Little did I know that later in life I would spend several years working in an environment where gunfire and explosions would also be a part of daily life.

We were issued with our uniforms and kit on the first day. These were of Soviet or Cuban issue depending on what was available. The Soviet issue was unfortunately totally unsuited for the climate we were operating in. But that's what we had, and we had to make do with it. I had the added misfortune of having a small body frame and feet, which meant that I had to find some needle and thread to alter my uniform to fit it to my size. Nothing could be done to alter the size of my boots. We were also issued with nylon tracksuits.

Being close to a river and in a very tropical area, the camp was infested with pesky mosquitoes and tsetse flies that were extraordinarily large and troublesome. Malaria was naturally commonplace because there was hardly a cadre who did not suffer at least one bout of it. The only thing we hoped for was to avoid getting cerebral malaria or the recurrent type. Despite the intense heat, I was forced to sleep in my nylon tracksuit in an attempt to cover as much of my body as possible to avoid being chewed up by the relentless mosquitoes. Invariably, I did not escape its affliction and succumbed to a serious bout of malaria as well. I have never been so sick or miserable in all my life.

Food at the camp was most unappetising. Our diet usually consisted of some form of canned meat that was not the most exciting and some fresh vegetables. For security reasons, only authorised staff were allowed in the kitchen. Fortunately, I had the good fortune of coming across some bird's eye chillies during a visit to some Russian instructors living in another area. I used the remains from cans of tomato paste to mix with the chillies to make some chutney to add some flavour and spice to my food. On national days, we were allowed to slaughter an animal. I missed having fresh milk and sugar the most.

The subjects we were instructed in included firearms, engineering, shooting, sabotage, military and combat work, and tactics. In the firearms class, we were exposed to all the different types of firearms and their uses, assembly and disassembly, storage and cleaning. I learnt very early on just how dangerous the equipment we worked with was.

One day, on returning from the shooting range, we went through the usual drill of cleaning our weapons. The standard practice was to start by removing the magazine and clearing the chamber of any rounds before proceeding with the disassembly. While this is taking place, we were all required to remain on the same side of the work table. On this occasion, we had all supposedly removed our magazines, cleared the chambers of any cartridges and then started the process of disassembly and cleaning. Most weapons were by now in different stages of disassembly. For a reason I cannot remember, I had to go over to the other side of the table. I checked that all was clear and proceeded to the other side. Just as I was returning to my place, the comrade who was next to me decided to release the trigger firing a 7.62 mm round from a PKM (which is a light machine gun) into the tree just behind me. Had it been a moment earlier, I would surely have been killed.

I enjoyed my shooting classes most and became quite proficient at using a pistol. My pistol of choice was a Makarov. I found it easy to handle, accurate and effective. In competitions, I fared rather well against more experienced comrades. My handling of both an AK and RPG proved to be excellent. However, of all the subjects being taught, I took a specific interest in military and combat work and engineering because these were areas that I believed I would need to train recruits in the underground. In this regard, I paid special attention in my training to the use of limpet mines.

At some point in our training, we were joined by several female comrades. Of this group, I would get to work more extensively with Sue Rabkin in the coming years because she was part of the Politico-Military Council Secretariat. There was a hilarious moment during our training in MCW involving Comrade Sue that I will never forget. Sue never took anything for granted and was always forthright. The instructor in this course was fondly referred to as T-Man (Ernest Lekota Pule). He was also someone whom I would come to work with in the following years.

T-Man tried to take the class through the basics of MCW and how to operate in the underground. Sue, who had already had a lot of experience in the underground from her work in the '70s was not having any of this. She took issue with T-Man for trying to give us information about tradecraft that we could pick up from reading Le Carre or any other spy novels. Sue demanded that we instead get the training that we could not get from casual reading. I don't think T-Man was ready for this. He was not used to being challenged by one of his students and was totally flummoxed. We all had a really good laugh about this later.

Another instructor that I met at the camp was Tommy (sometimes referred to as Chris). In the years to come, I got to work with very closely Tommy, along with T-Man. Yet another comrade that I got to know and would get to know in the field was, Mainstay Chibuku.[30] By the time I met him, he was already a trained and experienced fighter.

My training was full of memories that will remain with me. An interesting experience that I will never forget was an exercise in which we were required to plan and execute an ambush. We started with the theory and organisation of an ambush in the tactics course, with 'Makarov' as our instructor. Makarov was by then already a recognised war hero and a true legend who was also an exceptional athlete. We were all in awe of this great soldier. Makarov decided to take us on a practical exercise using live ammunition. The object of the exercise was to demonstrate what would take place in a live situation when you are in the middle of a battle with guns blazing and explosions going off around you all at the same time. We went into the field and prepped the site. Two large drums were used as the targets in our ambush. In this instance, the objects of our ambush were obviously stationary. We were asked to organise our formation and prepare to launch the attack. The exercise proved to be really exciting and a real adrenalin rush. We did the best we could and truly enjoyed letting rip on our AKs and carried out our attack. At the end of the exercise, we were asked to put our weapons down and inspect the site.

We learnt a few things. Firstly, on automatic fire we would empty our magazines before we knew it, unlike in the movies where they fired their weapons continuously for sustained periods without running out of ammunition. In truth, an AK47 rifle is capable of firing off about 600 rounds per minute on automatic fire with an effective range of 300 metres. Unfortunately, the magazine only had 30 cartridges, which could be fired off in little time if the rifle was in automatic mode. The more striking lesson that we learnt was that very few of our shots actually found the target, which was static. The point for me was that in battle one needed calm nerves and calculated action. Not only were we required to conserve our ammunition, but we also had to be very deliberate when firing. I would come to remember this lesson well in the years to come.

It was common, we were told, that new intakes would be initiated on the night of their arrival by a surprise mock attack. With us, the 'attack' on our camp would take place much later because the team that would execute the 'attack' was out on a survival march. On such days, care was taken to make sure that only senior people were armed to avoid any unnecessary injuries or deaths. These 'attacks' would usually be carried out only by well-trained comrades in the deep of the night. When it happened, it was one of the most dramatic events I have ever encountered. It was everything and more that the comrades promised it would be. I have never experienced the sustained explosions intermingled with gunfire for such a prolonged period. It was truly terrifying. The sky was all lit up and we had tracer bullets flying overhead in all directions. The intention was to sow confusion and it succeeded every bit in this.

The drill was that the moment an 'attack' took place, we would crawl through the trenches to an assembly area. Once the situation was 'stabilised', we were then commanded to get into formation at a designated assembly area to undertake an evacuation, which involved a long march carrying our supplies with us. This proved to be quite a gruelling exercise and meant to toughen us up.

While I did reasonably well with my training in general, my ability to march in formation was pathetic. I could not coordinate the movement of my arms and legs no matter how hard I tried. Besides being tone deaf, I have no rhythm whatsoever. In general, the camp was remarkably well organised. Cadres were kept well motivated with cultural and sporting events. However, after several months, the isolation of camp life did take its toll. The camp we were in was intended to deal with no more than refresher courses for those that had completed their training and were about to be deployed back home. Our training was therefore completed in about three months; but even then, it was not easy. I often spared a thought for those comrades who spent several years in the camps without being deployed. They would have completed their training programme lasting about six months; and if possible would have benefitted from further specialist courses of several more months.

Towards the end of our training, we learnt to wait for the M'China (or the Green Mamba) with great expectations. M'China was a green 4X4 vehicle that was used to collect cadres who completed their training and were on their way to undertake a mission. Everyone waited for their turn to be deployed. We sang songs about it. This was a great event. Unfortunately, we were receiving more cadres for training than we were deploying. This obviously frustrated many of our young people.

My first house

My training was a real motivator and gave me a great deal of confidence to pursue my tasks in Botswana. It gave the term 'Forward Area' new meaning because I was now looking at the struggle from not just a political perspective, but also as a soldier. Botswana was a 'Front'.

When I returned to Gaborone, I had the good fortune to take over a house from one of our comrades who had to leave unexpectedly. The house was extremely small and not unlike our RDP houses of today, but it was cosy and became my home for two years. With the help of my parents I bought some furniture and made the house very comfortable. I was very proud of this house and have many fond memories of my time there. I learnt to cook and enjoyed my house-keeping responsibilities. Saturday was the day to perform all my domestic chores. After cleaning the house, I would wash my clothes, cook a fresh pot of food, and have friends over for a meal. This was the first time in my life that I learnt to do this. Looking after this house was important because it made me feel like a normal person. My responsibilities made me feel like an adult. I had to think about buying groceries, cleaning the house and paying the bills.

I was determined to avoid arrest because I had no legal authority to be in Gaborone. Since I did not qualify for a work permit, I decided that the best legal reason to remain in Gaborone was to study. I therefore registered to study law. The University of Botswana (UB) had fortuitously just established their own law faculty with the help of the University of Edinburgh with whom they had a joint agreement. Until then, the faculty was managed across campuses in Botswana, Lesotho and Swaziland so that they were able to share resources. Fortunately for me, I also managed to obtain a scholarship sponsored by the United Nations. In terms of the new arrangements at UB, their BA.LLB degree was offered over five years. We would therefore spend our first two years in Botswana with lecturers from both Edinburgh and Botswana. Our second two years would be spent in Edinburgh and our final year of studies back in Botswana.

The following two years were hectic. I now had my own house. My father even bought me a new car. I surprised myself because I started enjoying my studies and doing well at it. Most of all, I was now politically engaged. Unfortunately, we detected increased activity by apartheid agents and it was evident that our security was in question. Thus, once settled in my house, I was issued with some weapons for my self-protection. My arsenal included a Makarov pistol, an AKM (with folding butt) and four grenades (two offensive and two defensive).

Despite my little arsenal, the weapon I was most fond of was something totally different. My father had always sensed that we were living dangerous lives but was not aware that I was now trained and armed. On one of his visits, he brought a toolbox full of a different tools that would be useful in maintaining the house. Tucked in between the tools, he fished out a tool that was a cross between a chopper and hammer – almost like a tomahawk – which he very proudly handed to me. He said to me that he did not think it was much, but at least it was something with which to defend myself should I need it. I thought this was most sensitive of him.

Living in my first house also taught me a lesson of just how tenuous an existence we had and the weaknesses in our security. In late 1982, I was asked by a comrade to host a young man at my house for a couple of days. This was not unusual, and I found nothing untoward in this. Unfortunately, the young man was arrested on his return home. He was intercepted in Bophuthatswana soon after he crossed the border and charged with membership of the ANC amongst other things. As a result of his arrest, his unit members were also arrested and charged.

As it turned out, a confession was beaten out of him. I followed this story as it unfolded in the media quite closely. Reference was made in one of the articles about an ANC operative in Botswana vaguely matching my description. The person was, however, described as a person of Arab origin. While no names or details were given, it demonstrated the dangers of hosting underground contacts who were going to go back into the country. The story made me quite nervous.

This period was also important for my political development. I had the opportunity to regularly meet with some of our key political and military leaders. Mac visited us quite often to strengthen the emerging political leadership in our Forward Area and brief us on developments. With the escalation in the number of military operations conducted by MK, both Joe Modise and Cassius Maake regularly travelled to Gaborone. Fortunately for me, both these leaders enjoyed staying over with me when they were in Gaborone. This provided me with much time with them and I learnt a great deal about their approach to strategy and our military operations. As a young cadre, this exposure was important.

What I learnt was that the focus of our military operations had shifted to the urban areas, most of which were acts of sabotage and armed propaganda. From the increasing sophistication in the operations, especially those from our Special Operations Unit, it was evident that MK was gaining in confidence, capacity and dare. These operations were also more widespread demographically. On the political front, there was also a surge in the number of community-based organisations that were beginning to emerge to take up people's issues in different communities.

The attack on Voortrekkerhoogte

Sometime in 1981, I was asked by our Military Command to see if I could assist in establishing contact with Rocky. This came as a surprise to me because I assumed that our military and or intelligence structures were already working with him. Evidently, Rocky's contact with Marius broke when the family left Botswana.

I was also anxious for a different reason. Rocky's detention had led to my exile, and no one knew what information was disclosed during his detention and whether I was compromised at all. This naturally raised many concerns. These anxieties were only perked when I re-established contact and he so eagerly responded by coming out so quickly. I was very nervous. For this reason, I made sure that he was accommodated at the Oasis Hotel, which consisted of a number of chalets which made it easy to monitor and observe.

As a general rule, I never travelled around Gaborone armed unless I had to. This meeting was an exception and I was sure to bring along my trusty Makarov. Rocky was most excited about our reunion. I was keen to extract as much information as I could. It was immediately evident that Rocky was just his usual effervescent self, showing no anxiety or concern and was extremely well composed. His calm demeanour put an end to my concerns.

The first thing Rocky reported was the unfortunate demise of Gary who was also his closest friend and first recruit. I had helped with this recruitment not long before my departure from home. While the official explanation given was that Gary committed suicide, Rocky believed that Gary was murdered while at his base in the Northern Transvaal by members of the South African Defence Force and was quite bitter about it. Rocky was also quite excited to see me because he wanted to hand over two sets of documents that yet again reconfirmed the value of his recruitment. The first was a set of manuals and operational plans for the South African Defence Force deployment in Namibia (South West Africa). The second was a detailed map of the layout of Voortrekkerhoogte Military Base, which he had painstakingly recorded in quite a bit of detail.

This map was hand-drawn, almost to scale, on individual A4 pages, which when assembled measured several metres in length and width. Rocky was very excited about this map and spent some time laying it out on my lounge floor. The map recorded details like the layout of the most critical SADF sites at the base. This was an exceptionally valuable piece of intelligence about the headquarters of the apartheid military force, parts of which I could verify from my knowledge of the area because I visited it on several occasions.[31]

This intelligence, I was later informed, was critical to one of MK's most daring military operations carried out on 9 August 1981. On this evening, the White Blocks[32] Residents Association of Laudium was holding a candle-lit march protesting against the appalling conditions that the community was forced to endure. At roughly the same time, and quite coincidentally, a couple of hundred metres away, an elite unit from the ANC's Special Operations Unit under the command of the legendary Barney Molokoane successfully managed to fire five 122mm high-explosive fragmentation rocket missiles using a Grad-P Light portable rocket system on the SADF Military Headquarters.[33] The launch of the attack from Laudium was most convenient as it was located so close by.

The attack was both audacious and historic. The timing could not have been more perfect. It was the first time ever that a sophisticated missile of this nature was launched as part of MK's offensive. Equally noteworthy was the fact that it was launched against the military headquarters of the apartheid army. The attack had such a devastating effect on the morale of the apartheid rulers that they felt compelled to retaliate and attack the ANC's London office on 14 March 1982.[34]

After 1990, when I met Rocky again, he told me that the South African government had understated the impact of the damage caused. He had seen it as a major success and was proud to have had a part in it. Rocky later joined the new defence force and played an extremely important role in developing its policy and strategies. Rocky also wrote extensively for the South African National Defence Force in their military journal. With this in mind, it brought a chuckle to me to read what he wrote about the attack:-

The year 1981 saw MK operations interfacing with the nationwide anti-Republic Day demonstrations and focussing on the sabotage of specific strategic installations. Targets sabotaged included major Eskom power plants in the Transvaal, attacks on military bases in the rural areas, the sabotage of certain government buildings, and further attacks on the police. On the 9 August 1981, MK Special Operations personnel launched a dramatic attack on the Voortrekkerhoogte military complex outside Pretoria. Five projectiles were fired from a 122 mm rocket launcher (the first time artillery was used within South Africa by MK units) and a number of targets within the complex were struck, including a near-miss on the fuel depot within the complex. What made the attack particularly audacious was the fact that it was launched from military property on the western perimeters of the base.[35]

Sadly, Rocky passed on after a brief illness in 2005.

Family milestones

In September 1981, I had started class at the University of Botswana for my law degree. This was a very different experience and a more pleasant one than my stint at Wits. There was less pressure, good lecturers and the classes were small enough to enjoy great debate.

Our class was the first batch of the new law faculty at the University of Botswana. It was also an important class that produced, in later years, several cabinet ministers, judges and leaders in Botswana's politics. My best academic performance took place in the next two years. The five-year course incorporated a moot court programme which was designed to provide practical court experience, and so did not require any internship or articles. To encourage students along, the chief justice sponsored a medal for the top student who won at the moot court competition.

In 1982, I was awarded the first medal by the chief justice of Botswana in advocacy. Between 1983 and 1985, I continued part of my degree programme at the University of Edinburgh. In 1985, I obtained a second award for advocacy in Botswana and represented the country in Zimbabwe in the African Moot Court competition. My grades were also excellent. I remember thinking that perhaps I did have a future at law after all.

The year 1983 also proved to be a momentous year in our family. My only sister, Hajira, got married. I had the good fortune of meeting with her husband-to-be, Razaak, a few months before the wedding. This was a bitter-sweet gathering of the family. While I was really excited about the wedding, the reality of exile was that my only sister would be getting married without me being present to take a part in the ceremony and to help give her hand in marriage.

Razaak and Hajira were married in August 1983 at the same time as the launch of the UDF and just a month before I left for Edinburgh. Unknown to me, just shortly before the marriage, my father suffered a massive heart attack. The family decided not only to keep this a secret from me, but to also continue with the wedding despite my father's grave medical condition. Unfortunately, my father's ill health continued into a rather protracted history that he would eventually lose.

In September 1983, after having successfully completed my two years at the University of Botswana, I was to start the second two years of my study, this time at the University of Edinburgh. I had very mixed feelings about this. On the one hand, I was very excited to have the opportunity to leave the shores of Africa for the first time in my life to the UK and to continue with my studies. On the other hand, tremendous political changes were taking place and I did not want to be away. After consulting the comrades in our structures, it was felt that it was necessary that I leave. This would be yet another new beginning in my life.

Edinburgh

The University of Edinburgh was founded in 1582 and is the sixth oldest university in the English-speaking world. The university is deeply embedded in the fabric of the city of Edinburgh. I will always remember Edinburgh as being grey and drab. I arrived in the city quite reluctantly and had the misfortune of doing so at a time of the year when it was really cold and miserable. While this image remained, there were many redeeming features.

Old College is also one of the most prestigious law colleges in the world, and my two years there were a great learning experience and opportunity. Old College is also opposite the medical school where Yusuf Dadoo studied. The student residence, Pollock Halls, was located in a most beautiful place at the foot of Arthur's Hill and within walking distance from campus.

My trip to Edinburgh was my first visit outside the African continent. I arrived one Friday in late September 1983 just at the beginning of winter. It was bitterly cold and stranger still were the short days with the sun rising late and setting early. My registration was processed on the morning of my arrival and with little fuss. After this, I was sent off to my student accommodation to get settled. I was surprised how smoothly it all went.

Edinburgh was very different. It was a cold, modern and organised place full of concrete and very few black people. Most of the black people I knew were my classmates from Botswana. One of the things I got to learn very early on was that even if people were polite, they were not entirely free of racism. Fortunately, most of the British students I got to know were welcoming and friendly and I discovered that the racists were just a minority.

Once I settled in, I began to realise that there was much to learn, gain and be happy about. For one, I became immediately conscious of the fact that I was free of the tension of threats to our security. This was a great relief and it was reflected in my academic performance. We were blessed with the incredible quality of lecturers. The standards were really high and we were encouraged to perform well and rewarded for it.

As a member of the ANC, I was required to report my presence in the UK to the ANC office in London. I did this as soon as I had the opportunity, which came during the vacations of December 1983. I took an overnight bus, which cost all of £12, and reported my presence to Aziz Pahad. After this, I returned to London whenever I could because I enjoyed my trips there so much. It still is one of my favourite cities.

London had a huge ANC community and a vibrant anti-apartheid movement. I was fortunate enough to experience the support of British people for our struggle. It was truly an incredible feeling to see so many people who were not South African work so extremely hard and be truly committed to the freedom of our people. Ironically, my first experience of mass-based anti-apartheid struggle took place in the UK and not South Africa. In general, London also offered a great political life and learning opportunities. I was offered part-time work at the International Defence Aid Fund (IDAF) offices in London during the holidays, and the pay was great for a student. One of the perks of having a UN scholarship was the generous stipend. The extra money coming in from working meant that I could buy all the books I wanted. Needless to say, my experience in London was memorable.

At university, jurisprudence very quickly became my favourite subject. The study of legal philosophy allowed one to explore a number of concepts, which I found most challenging. We had the good fortune to be lectured by Professor MacCormick, who was a staunch Scottish nationalist and wrote prolifically on the subject.[36] I did a critique of one of his books for an assignment and took issue with the arguments he made on Scottish independence using a Marxist-Leninist analysis. I was pleasantly surprised by the calm manner and grace with which he evaluated my paper. Without being patronising, he engaged with me and we had a most useful conversation. I did not quite expect it, but he was impressed by my audacity to challenge his ideas. At the end of our chat, he offered me a scholarship to study further at Edinburgh, which did much to boost my self-confidence. However, I was determined to return to the front in Botswana and had to decline the offer.

I enjoyed student life and my spirits were not dampened too much by the cold weather. Working with progressive students, we established a very successful structure supporting the Anti-Apartheid Movement on campus and used the nomination of Mandela for the position of University Chancellor to mobilise students. We ran a great campaign and managed to recruit a large number of supporters. It was a real blessing to know that so many people, despite being so far removed from South Africa, really cared for us and were prepared to do something about it. This was not only comforting but a great motivator too. It made me work that much harder.

It was during my anti-apartheid campaign work that I met Barbara, an arts student who also lived in Pollock Halls. Barbara was bright, knowledgeable and well read. Along with a number of other student activists, we spent a lot of time at the local student watering hole planning our anti-apartheid campaigns and fundraisers. These were memorable times. Barbara and I spent a lot of time together. We had the same political views on the situation both in the UK and South Africa. We shared a common commitment to justice and the struggle for freedom. We were drawn to each other and I enjoyed her company and quickly fell in love with her.

By the end of my two-year stint in Edinburgh our relationship had developed to a level where I felt ready to make a commitment and proposed to her. Each of us had still one more year at university before we qualified for our degrees – she at Edinburgh and me back in Botswana. I guess we figured that if our love could survive the additional year apart, she would then join me in Botswana and we would settle down. I was 28 years old and felt that I was old enough to settle down.

The two years I spent in Edinburgh leading a normal life made me think about many things differently. What became very clear was the fact that apartheid affected us well beyond the borders of South Africa. We were forced into leading abnormal lives. Our lives in the Forward Areas was abnormal. Having to continuously watch over our shoulders was not the way to live. It became clear that with struggle came great sacrifices. I found the imposition on us by our circumstances cruel and unbecoming.

The decision to get married was therefore an important statement to make. I was declaring myself to be a normal person. It was a refusal to succumb to the abnormality that apartheid imposed on us. Getting married would be a form of protest and making a statement. It was part of my struggle. This, however, was easier said than done. It was also selfish. What I obviously did not fully understand, and could not comprehend, was the impact that such a decision would have on Barbara and the children that we would later have. I had no idea of what was to come.[37]

Changing landscape

On 14 June 1985, a mere ten days before I returned to Botswana, the South African Defence Force troops, under the order of General Constand Viljoen, launched an attack in Gaborone called Operation Plecksy.[38] The raid, the fifth attack by apartheid South Africa on a neighbouring country since 1981, killed 12 people including women and children. Only five of the victims were members of the African National Congress. This attack made me more eager to return to Gaborone and served to strengthen my resolve to continue my political work there with greater vigour.

I returned to a totally different Botswana. The tension was palpable. Everything had changed, even our command structures. I immediately set about orientating myself and catching up with developments. The expatriate community I used to know was no more. Paranoia had set in. The mood was sombre and attitude serious. Even our underground command structures were being reorganised.

Little did I know that this was the setting in which my life was about to change so dramatically. The shift would be seismic. Life was never going to be the same. Suddenly, and without knowing it, I boarded a rollercoaster ride that was to continue for the next 20 years. It was going to be a life that was to become extremely intense, fast, dangerous and continuously changing. For the moment, however, I needed to get my head around what happened during my absence and make sense of the new challenges we were facing.

My family came to visit as soon as I returned. What a pillar of strength they were. Aside from helping me once again furnish my new accommodation, they bought me the latest computer – a IBM with a stunning 200 MB hard drive, floppy disk reader and dot-matrix printer. I also came back with a new attitude to my studies. I enjoyed the past four years of academic life and managed to do well at it. I was now into my last year of studies, eager to excel and quite excited by this. I was, however, more excited by the prospect of getting back to my political work in building the underground. I contacted Wally Serote, who was now responsible for the political structures, and got a briefing on developments.

VII

Changing Conditions of Struggle

A great deal had changed between October 1983 and June 1985. Several developments had changed the course of our history and struggle. Amongst the most important developments was the emergence of the mass democratic movement resulting in new conditions of struggle. The people began to revolt against apartheid, giving birth to the concept of 'organs of people's popular power'. The apartheid government responded with more repression and aggression reducing many residential areas to war zones. The new developments required a change to both our structures and approach.

Even if I did not see it then, it is clear to me now that by 1985 the ANC was confronted with a crisis – a crisis of relevance. This was a tipping point. The ANC had become a victim of the success of the people's struggle. While the ANC had become immensely popular and was recognised as the movement that was leading the liberation struggle, this popularity was not matched by its capabilities, structures or boots on the ground. While there were large numbers of eager young people ready to join the underground ANC, even prepared to give up their lives for the struggle, the ANC did not have the structures to take advantage of the fact that many young people regarded themselves as part of the ANC even if they were not recruited.

The failure of our structures in the Forward Areas was at the heart of this weakness. We did not have the capability or capacity to harness the new energy being unleashed and organise them into structures capable to escalating the struggle against apartheid in any meaningful manner. The ANC was really good at giving leadership from the top and providing strategic thought from the outside. However, on the ground and in the country, it was a different story. Throughout the country, new leaders started emerging from the struggles led by a host of new organisations that were being established. We in the Forward Areas, on the other hand, were struggling to catch up instead of leading.

The mood in the country and popular struggles compelled the apartheid government in the early 1980s to introduce some changes, which came in the form of the Tricameral Parliament Constitution of 1983 and the Koornhof Bills. The response of the people to these was incredible with a united front of opposition to both. More than 475 grassroots organisations committed themselves as part of the United Democratic Front (UDF) at its establishment on 20 August 1983. Politically, this major development would shape the struggles leading to 1990. Whilst most of the organisations and leaders were politically aligned to the ANC, the UDF was not an ANC structure.

The politics of localised protest initiated by the UDF quickly evolved by 1985 to give expression to popular grassroots struggles at the national level. This was made possible by a dynamic structure in the form of regional executive committees (RECs) and regional general councils (RGCs) that allowed for locally based affiliates. The local structures such as civic associations and local branches of sectoral organisations (such as the Congress of South African Students or the South African Youth Congress) were able to give expression to various local struggles and yet be integral to nationally organised campaigns.

UDF area committees and zonal committees proved to be an instrumental structure because it was built on a solid foundation with roots amongst the people, many of which were even at a street level. It made the mass democratic movement very dynamic because while there were national campaigns that could be run, it was based on the strength of grassroots struggles and organisation.

From our Forward Area in Botswana, we provided a great deal of support to comrades that were active in the UDF in several ways. Many cadres came out to consult with us on what they were doing, and we were therefore able to guide them politically and ideologically. Sometimes, financial support was also provided. At times, we even assisted with the drafting of some of their speeches and were therefore able to impact on the messaging. It is therefore hardly surprising that the UDF process generated a large core of activists that regarded themselves as ANC people.

I do not believe the assertion that the UDF was an ANC front to be correct. It certainly does not accord with my experience. We always dealt with activists and leaders of the UDF, who were also members of underground structures of the ANC, with respect. We recognised the UDF as a mass democratic movement structure and did not undermine it by treating them as an appendage of the ANC. The UDF was a front and not a political party.

The momentum of the mass democratic movement grew to such levels of intensity that many in the ANC started talking about the prospects of people's popular power. This development highlighted several important factors. The first related to the famous four pillars of struggle strategy of the ANC in which the mass democratic movement was one and the underground another. Our strategy was to build both these pillars. However, from the underground, we really did not do enough to take advantage of the opportunities created by the development of the mass democratic movement. Part of the problem was that we were so weak that we did not have the capacity in the underground to take advantage of the space created. Most of the new recruits that I was responsible for questioned me as to why it took so long for the ANC to recruit them. Years after the unbanning of the ANC, several activists who I knew continued to enquire why they were not recruited.

With structures of the mass democratic movement in place, the politics of protest soon graduated into the politics of actual resistance against the state. Apartheid had never before experienced a more effective challenge. The game changer was that the resistance was now people-driven. As local struggles spread and coalesced, the UDF was able to play a critical role in articulating common national demands for the dismantling of the apartheid state.

Communities were drawn into a movement motivated by the notion that the transfer of political power to the representatives of the majority was a precondition for the realisation of basic economic demands.[39] This was evident from the struggles involving the civic organisations and unions. Two further developments catapulted the importance of the UDF by 1985 in driving national politics. The first was the alignment of the majority of its affiliates to the Freedom Charter, and secondly, the establishment of the Congress of South African Trade Unions (COSATU).

The state responded to this militancy and resistance in the only way it knew – coercion and repression. After the army occupied townships in late 1984, communities became even more militant. The declaration of the state of emergency in July 1985 was therefore an admission that the state had lost control of many townships. The directive issued by Oliver Tambo in July 1985 was therefore most timely. He called on the people to make apartheid unworkable and the townships ungovernable. The people responded to this call with unprecedented fervour.

Suddenly, UDF area committees assumed an even greater importance. Self-defence units began to emerge as a response to the ongoing running battles between township youth and the security forces. For the first time since the formation of MK in 1960, we began to witness widespread incidents of armed clashes between untrained young people and the security forces. It was therefore logical that the call for ungovernability would soon give way to the call for a people's war. For the first time in our history, people began to speculate as to whether it was possible that an insurrection would soon materialise.

Still, neither the ANC underground nor the military structures were able to fully take advantage of these new conditions of struggle. We were just not ready or prepared for it. The tragic irony was that we already had several thousand fully trained and motivated combatants in our camps who were agitating to go into battle and we were not able to deploy them. This was the failure of the ANC's underground and political machinery. More importantly, the ANC was not able to give political leadership to the response and expression by people to the call for ungovernability.

Cadres in our military camps in Angola were also starting to show increasing frustration, leading to discontent and eventually a mutiny. There were disturbances in several camps that led to some unnecessary deaths.[40] The weak link in the chain between our soldiers in the camps and the people's resistance in the townships lay with us in the Forward Areas. We were unable to put the required underground structures in the country in place fast enough to absorb these trained cadres and support their deployment. The reality was that MK units could not be deployed in isolation and separate from the underground political machinery. Attempts to do so proved to be most unsuccessful.

The ANC's underground

The ANC responded to these dramatic developments in the country in the manner in which it normally did. Early in 1983, the ANC leadership instituted another set of far-reaching changes to operational structures. These changes followed the decision in December 1982 to establish a fully-fledged military headquarters. The Revolutionary Council (RC) was disbanded as the ANC's main operational organ and was replaced by a Politico-Military Council (PMC). The PMC, like the old RC, was to be chaired by ANC president Oliver Tambo, deputised by secretary general Alfred Nzo. Like the RC, it had two main operational arms – the political and military.

On the political side, the PMC hierarchy included a political committee chaired by Joe Jele, with Mac Maharaj as secretary. The newly created military headquarters was commanded by Joe Modise, deputised by Chris Hani, who was also MK political commissar and Joe Slovo, the chief of staff. The 'senior organs' that were introduced in 1980 to promote political-military coordination in the Forward Areas were disbanded.

In Botswana, the regional PMC went through a number of rapid changes between 1983 and 1985 because of a number of cross-border attacks and severe infiltration by the enemy. A coordinating committee was established in 1984 consisting of representatives from both military and political structures. This was chaired by Thabang Makwetla and later Thenjiwe Mthintso. The political representative was Wally Serote and the military representative, Lambert Moloi.

Unfortunately, the various changes made to these structures did not achieve its objectives. The leadership that we were able to give from the Forward Areas was limited. There was no real growth in the underground and the leadership once again were forced to make yet another change to our structures in 1985.

Security situation

Politically, Botswana had come under tremendous pressure from the South African government not to provide the ANC with a 'safe haven'. The raid in June 1985 shook everybody up. It was a turning point from a security perspective. The manner in which we operated had to change. Greater security measures had to be introduced. We stopped visiting each other's houses to protect the places we lived in. Everyone was more vigilant, if not paranoid.

There was however a more important development which forced another leadership change in our structures in the Forward Areas. The few underground structures that existed in Botswana and the country were severely compromised because of infiltration and could not be trusted. Structures were cauterised and those whose integrity was in doubt were cut off. We were left with very few cadres in the field. The truth of the matter was that the apartheid security forces had successfully managed to disrupt and stunt the development of the underground structures in Botswana. I found this quite demoralising. Paranoia had set in.

The Kabwe Conference

Despite the tension generated by the infiltration, there was a great deal of excitement within ANC ranks during the first part of 1985. Much of this was due to the developments taking place in the country.

There was definite evidence of the ingredients of an insurrection. In many places, people had begun to respond to the vacuum left by the absence of an administration by replacing structures of local government. Beyond this, the workers had begun to find greater strength in their increasingly organised numbers and militant organisation in the formation of COSATU. We were therefore seriously studying the possibility of forming organs of people's popular power.

At the same time, because of the serious problems in our military camps, there was a need to call a national conference. The Kabwe Conference was therefore called to address these challenges and to consider ways in which we could take advantage of the opportunities presented by the struggles of the people on the ground. It was therefore hardly surprising that the profoundness of Lenin's writing in *'Left-Wing' Communism: An Infantile Disorder* resonated well during our debates of that time. In particular, we looked at the following famous passage which would be useful to recount here:

> The fundamental law of revolution, which has been confirmed by all revolutions and especially by all three Russian revolutions in the twentieth century, is as follows: for a revolution to take place it is not enough for the exploited and oppressed masses to realise the impossibility of living in the old way, and demand changes; for a revolution to take place it is essential that the exploiters should not be able to live and rule in the old way. *It is only when the 'lower classes' do not want* to live in the old way and the 'upper classes' *cannot carry on in the old way* that the revolution can triumph [emphasis mine]. This truth can be expressed in other words: revolution is impossible without a nation-wide crisis (affecting both the exploited and the exploiters). It follows that, for a revolution to take place, it is essential, first, that a majority of the workers (or at least a majority of the class-conscious, thinking, and politically active workers) should fully realise that revolution is necessary, and that they should be prepared to die for it; second, that the ruling classes should be going through a

governmental crisis, which draws even the most backward masses into politics (symptomatic of any genuine revolution is a rapid, tenfold and even hundredfold increase in the size of the working and oppressed masses—hitherto apathetic—who are capable of waging the political struggle), weakens the government, and makes it possible for the revolutionaries to rapidly overthrow it.[41]

The Kabwe Conference produced a number of critical resolutions. It decided that instead of having separate political and military structures, area-based underground command structures or Area Political Military Committees (APMCs) should be established. Furthermore, it was agreed that the ANC should establish a presence in the mass democratic movement. Operatives responsible for the PMCs should be deployed regularly into the country to get first-hand information on the situation. We also had to ensure that we established a presence in the enemy forces such as the South African Defence Force and the police force. The directive coming from the Conference was that:[42]

- We should move beyond armed propaganda and directly strike at enemy personnel.
- We should shift the struggle, and our military operations, from the black ghettoes into the white areas.
- The stress should be on training inside the country.
- We should increase the presence of white, coloured and Indian comrades in the ranks of MK.
- We should strive to get our weapons from inside the country.
- We should work among enemy forces, including the Bantustans.

Special Operations

Special Operations was, as the name suggests, a unit of highly trained cadres whose task it was to carry out attacks on key targets of special strategic value. Established in 1979, it reported directly to OR Tambo through Joe Slovo. I had met Rashid (Ismail Aboobaker), one of the Unit's commanders, several times in Gaborone and over time with the rest of Special Ops team – Chris, T-Man and Victor (Johannes Molefe). Chris and T-Man had been my instructors in Caxito and I formed an extremely close relationship with them in Botswana, working together on a number of projects. I developed a deep respect and love for these remarkable human beings with an incredible zest for life. They were also great soldiers with lots of experience. With all of that, they were also very humble people.

Chris took over as the commander of Special Ops in 1987 when Rashid took over the responsibility for Ordinance after Cassius Maake was assassinated. As for Victor, while he was as affable as the others, I had a particular bond and respect for him because he was from Mamelodi and was involved in several operations, particularly the rocket attack on Voortrekkerhoogte. He also had the pleasure of working with Barney Molokoane on this and other operations.

Sometime in March or April 1986, I was approached by Rashid to help Chris receive Robert MacBride and his unit coming out for consultations and to collect a consignment of weapons. I was to receive them on the side of the main road from Gaborone to Francistown close to the new airport. We were to meet in the open and could be observed from far, parking their car off the side and opening the hood as if they had some car trouble. The meeting took place without any glitches. While I was not part of the briefings that Robert received, I worked most of that night with Chris packing a significant amount of weapons and explosives, particularly limpet mines into their vehicle. The bakkie they used had an extremely clever space in the undercarriage into which the cache was stored. I was amazed as to the amount that we could load in such a confined space.

Through the unit, I learnt about the spectacular work that Gordon Webster, who was the commander of the unit, carried out with Robert. It was therefore natural to take an interest in the progress of the unit and it was with great concern that we came to learn that Gordon was arrested and held in a hospital because of the injuries he suffered during his capture. This made big news, especially because of the number of weapons and explosives that were found in the boot of his car.

In May 1986, while at home studying for my final exams, Chris came to see me – most unusual for him because he took security precautions very seriously. He was clearly very agitated. Chris was usually an extremely calm character. However, when he was excited, he would start talking faster than usual and with as bit of a stutter. I learnt from him that Robert had broken Gordon out of the hospital in rather spectacular style with the help of his father. Gordon was obviously in a serious condition having just undergone surgery and was very weak. Robert bundled him into a caravan, placed him in a concealed enclosure underneath a bench, and drove him across the border.

Chris had nowhere else to take Gordon and came to me for help. There was simply no alternative and I could not refuse them. The challenge for me was that I was in the middle of the final law exams but Gordon clearly deserved priority attention. He also needed a great deal of care because of his condition and remained with me for nearly two weeks. Fortunately, we managed to get Gordon into a stable condition and had him safely evacuated to Lusaka.

Becoming a lawyer

The period between 1985 and 1990 was momentous at both the political and personal level. While there was much taking place politically, there were several personal developments of significance too. I successfully managed to complete my studies in June 1986, obtain my law degree and started working as an attorney for Rahim Khan, a South African lawyer who had been practising in Botswana for a number of years. With articles not necessary because of practical experience through the moot programme, I was able to immediately register as an attorney and start practising. I was, for the first time, able to obtain a proper residence and work permit.

As a new attorney, I was thrown in at the deep end right from the beginning. In the first week of my employment, I was assigned a case that was going to trial in the High Court in Lobatse. I had to attend to the matter without any hand-holding. This was my first formal work experience and I was grateful for it. My employment was critical to my cover as an operative of the ANC.

Shortly after this, Barbara, who by then had completed her degree, travelled to Botswana to start her life with me. An enormous change for me, but a bigger one for her, as she was coming to a country she did not know and was leaving the United Kingdom for the first time. Coming to Africa and being prepared to settle down with me was a bold move. This was not an easy task, especially since she was coming into a heavily charged security situation. It was indeed an extremely difficult experience for someone whose political involvement was limited to that of an activist in the Anti-Apartheid Movement in the UK. She was coming to Botswana because of our relationship and was intent on making a home with me.

Our first challenge came a few months later when I got a nasty surprise. For reasons I never got to know, I was issued with an order declaring me a prohibited immigrant. Not sure if this came about because of some pressure from the South African authorities or because of some arbitrary decision of an over-zealous government official, this obviously put everything in jeopardy and threatened all my plans. It made me realise just how fragile our status was because a prohibited immigrant order required you to pack up and leave the country within a short space of time. This really terrified me. I was already a refugee with no home and Barbara had just come to join me. Where would we go? What were we to do? I knew that the ANC would naturally deploy me to another location, but this still was not a pleasant experience and most unsettling. More importantly, what was to happen to Barbara?

Fortunately, after much pleading at the Office of the President in Gaborone and some hand-wringing, we managed to assure them that I was not a security threat and the order was reversed. Rahim Khan helped a great deal and I was very grateful for his efforts.

Then, Barbara's visa expired. We had two options: Barbara could find employment and be entitled to a residence and work permit or we had to get married. We chose to get married. It was a huge step in both our lives. Ordinarily, my upbringing would have required it to be a big event with much to fuss about. At the very least, the event would have to be solemnised in the presence of our families. Our circumstances however dictated otherwise.

Our marriage was a simple affair, conducted in the chambers of a magistrate and witnessed by two Batswana friends. The reception consisted of a visit to the Gaborone Sun Hotel where we ordered coffee and toasted sandwiches in the lobby and after which I dropped Barbara off at home and went back to work. We did not even take any photographs to record the event.

VIII

The Kabwe Generation

The mandate given to the underground by the Kabwe Conference was clear. The challenge was that I was now to start afresh; yet another new beginning. With no existing network or contacts to work with, new contacts had to be established. As for the Botswana structures, little was left of what had been built before because of infiltration. All that I was presented with was a unit of two young cadres, which was facilitated by Wally. I needed to help build underground structures that would be capable of taking advantage of the new conditions of struggle at home, capable of absorbing restless MK cadres in the rear and a difficult environment within which to work in Botswana.

With this in mind, I set to work on carrying out my mandate and started to build the foundation for the machinery we were to develop. I wasted no time in establishing contact with the unit I was given responsibility for. This did not take much time because they were as eager to meet with me as I with them.

Building a foundation

Taking my cue from the resolutions of the Kabwe Conference, I set about establishing an underground machinery that had both political and military capabilities. This was a whole new chapter in my life, one which I had little experience in. It made me very nervous and I was uncertain of myself. It involved people's lives. By this time, the number of friends or people I knew who were killed in action or assassinated was growing. We were involved in a dangerous business and I was painfully aware of this. At 28 years old, I had spent most of my adult life outside the country and my circle of acquaintances consisted of more people in exile than in the country.

Fortunately, I was quite driven and focused. I had a clear mission and was determined to deliver. I was conscious of the fact that my experience in exile over the past five years was not very successful and I had to do better. It was obvious that our struggle for freedom was not going to be an easy one, but I remained undeterred. This experience taught me a lot about my anxieties and myself. The only way in which to deal with my anxieties was to have a lot of structure. I cannot leave matters to chance and need to organise my thoughts and actions accordingly.

As a coping mechanism, I instinctively did a number of things. For a start, I made sure that my communication lines were effective, clear and always open. While I kept units informed as a matter of course, I also made sure that I knew what was happening. In general, nothing gets me more unsettled than not knowing. Everyone that worked in my machinery was given training in Military Combat Work[43] (MCW). I made sure that they all knew how to conduct themselves in the underground and take precautionary measures. Fortunately, the people recruited were extremely mature and level-headed. Looking back, the task everyone seems to remember and loathe is the copious reports that I would insist on when comrades came in for consultations.[44] This would prove most valuable because it made sure that I had excellent and dynamic intelligence information and was therefore able to make my own assessments and take the right decisions.

Like COSAS, Azanian Students Organisation (AZASO)[45] was an important organisation from whose ranks we would see a number of leading cadres coming into the ANC underground. MK too benefited immeasurably from the cadres produced in the struggles and campaigns waged by these organisations. The formation of the Kabwe Machinery would also draw heavily from these structures. In fact, throughout the existence of the Kabwe Machinery, its operatives continued to play leading roles in these and other organisations. Two of the foremost of these were young medical students, Confidence Ezras Moloko ('Confi' as we all called him) and Paul Sefularo.

Both Confi and Paul played a critical role in the formation of AZASO and were core to the early political debates and internal struggles that took place in the mass democratic movement in general and in the student movement in particular. Paul was a founder member of AZASO in 1979 and was subsequently elected its secretary in 1981. That same year he also became president of the Student Representative Council at Medunsa, a post he held up to 1984. During this period, he became active in the structures of the United Democratic Front (UDF) until its banning. Confi came from a religious background and was the son of a school principal and trader. He first got involved in student politics at Turfloop in 1978.

By 1983, both Confi and Paul were seasoned and mature activists who were married with families. They were level-headed young men and took their responsibilities quite seriously. By this time, they had also come to the conclusion that they needed to join the ANC if they were to make a greater contribution in the struggle. Just as I had experienced in 1977 and 1978, they too found it difficult to find the ANC inside the country. Like me, they too decided that if the ANC was not going to recruit them, they were going to go and search for it even if it meant going out of the country. This journey led them to Swaziland, Lesotho and Botswana without much success.

After much effort, their path led them to Greta Ncapayi in Soweto. Greta was an ANC veteran who worked very closely with Albertina Sisulu, June Mhlangeni and Sister Bernard Ncube. Collectively, they did much during this period to recruit young female activists who went on to organise women in the ANC underground. Greta also pointed Confi and Paul in the direction of the ANC leadership in Botswana where they met with Henry Makgothi and Dan Tloome. Dan linked them up with Thami Mnyele in 1984. Fortunately, Paul and Confi already knew Thami from home.

The Thami Mnyele Unit

Thamsanqa (Thami) Mnyele was a South African artist who moved to Gaborone in 1979 where he joined the Medu Art Ensemble along with poet Wally Serote. While in Botswana, he joined the ANC and was later trained in Caxito, Angola. By June 1985, most comrades knew that an attack was imminent and were asked to take the necessary precautionary measures. However, Thami was unfortunately not able to vacate his house quickly enough to avoid the attack by the apartheid security forces. He was killed on the morning of 14 June 1985.

With Thami's assassination, Wally, who was our political representative in the RPMC, charged me with the responsibility of attending to Confi and Paul. Together, they formed the first unit that I worked with in the Kabwe Machinery. The unit was therefore named in memory of Thami. I first met with the Thami Mnyeli Unit shortly after my return from Edinburgh. This was an auspicious start leading to one of the most fruitful collaborations I had the honour to be a part of; and, as will be seen from the ensuing account, much of what we managed to establish can be attributed to this collaboration. The performance of this unit was a very fitting tribute to the great freedom fighter that Thami was.

My biggest priority was to make a start, and the unit was my point of departure. I needed to make my contribution to the building of the underground structures in pursuance of the Kabwe directives. The unit was ideally suited for this task because of their profile, political maturity and history of activism. The first step however was to complete the unit with its third member, Sydney, who was recruited shortly after this. The unit was deeply affected by Thami's assassination and needed little motivation to be spurred into action. They were so driven that I often wondered whether they did so as part of a desire to avenge Thami's assassination. They operated with a deep and abiding respect for and memory of Thami.

Confi and Paul were two sides of the same coin and complemented each other with their differing skills and qualities. While Paul was the more profiled activist who worked in the front and held key positions in the student organisation, Confi was the guy who worked quietly in the background. Sydney was the more reserved one. The members of this unit all came from a middle-class background and were intellectuals with great organisational skills. Both Confi and Sydney came from political homes. Demographically, they had nothing in common. Confi was from Limpopo, Paul from the North West and Sydney from the Transkei. The unit gelled well, and this was well-reflected in their performance. The lesson I learnt with them is that the underground, like any other organisational structure, depends on the personal chemistry and interaction of the team players.

These were young medical students who were active in student politics and were respected by their peers. Their location politically was most strategic and the timing of their recruitment perfect. As leaders of AZASO, not only were they able to give guidance to the student movement but they were also exposed to most of the key role players and developments in the evolving and emerging mass democratic movement. They were at the centre of all the key political debates, knew the people and organisations, and, very importantly, had credibility.

The unit became the perfect cornerstone on which the Kabwe Machinery came to be established. Their field of operation was therefore not fixed to any demographic area, community or formation. The unit was deployed to assist with quietly providing structures of the mass democratic movement with the guidance and direction of the ANC as well as to sow the seeds for the establishment of a range of other units. As it turned out, they were perfectly fit for this purpose. They performed their tasks quite naturally without much adaptation. Critically, the unit assisted me with key recruitments that led to the establishment of underground structures in several areas. Fortunately, the unit was mobile and able to travel from the north in Limpopo to the Free State in the south and Mafikeng in the west. Despite the fact that both Paul and Confi headed families and were heavily committed to their medical studies, they performed brilliantly and were able to help me recruit prolifically.

Notwithstanding the risk of detection, they made countless trips to Botswana to provide me with regular reports and obtain further briefings. I remember well that on each consultation they would desperately also try to give some bit of their free time between intense discussions to do whatever studying they could squeeze in. There was never a visit when they were not exceptionally tired from lack of sleep. Yet, they persisted, never once complained and were ever ready to take on the additional tasks that I gave them. They performed brilliantly.

Confi and Paul came at a time when we were all very prickly about how we went about building our underground structures because of the high levels of infiltration and the damage we suffered. We were therefore obliged to apply stringent security measures. For this reason, we stopped taking contacts home and exposing our families to them. While this may appear logical with hindsight, this is what we did when we first joined the underground. This meant that we separated our personal lives from our political lives. A newly recruited comrade became a 'contact' who we worked with and it became difficult to form friendships from these relationships as we stopped sharing our personal lives with them.

One of the rules we introduced prohibited us from driving a 'contact' around without good reason, no matter how short a distance; and whenever we did, we made sure that they were not allowed to see the route we were taking and would not be able to identify any reference points. At first, I was quite apprehensive about applying these security precautions so stringently. However, both Confi and Paul had obviously discussed this, and they responded almost in unison that this is what they had expected of the movement and would not have it any other way. They were aware of and also very concerned about the levels of infiltration.

Needless to say, we spent a lot of time dealing with MCW. They soaked it all in and proved to be some of the most disciplined cadres in our machinery. Whether it be in their political argument or their conduct, they were quite dogmatic. They always applied 'the line'.[46] They continued to maintain this discipline even after the unbanning of the ANC.

There were several different categories of tasks that were given to the unit. Their leadership in AZASO and unique exposure to COSAS and a host of other UDF-affiliated organisations provided us with crucial political intelligence about developments as they were unfolding.

TOP LEFT: My grandfather (Dada), Hassen Ebrahim, Marabastad, 1945

TOP RIGHT: Dada's family – My father is the young man in the bottom right of the picture, Marabastad, 1945

BELOW: Issu Chiba, Nelson Mandela and myself during a fundraising evening, Lenasia, 1992

OPPOSITE TOP: Moulvi Cachalia, Aziz Pahad, Thabo Mbeki and Maniben Sita, with Hassen Ebrahim (standing), Laudium elections campaign, April 1994

OPPOSITE MIDDLE: Constitutional Assembly team at Bosberaad with Nelson Mandela, Arniston, 1995

OPPOSITE BELOW: Constitutional Assembly team, Cape Town, 1995

TOP: Constitutional Assembly – Consultations with the Judiciary led by Arthur Chaskalson and Ismail Mohammed, Parliament, Cape Town, April 1995

BELOW: Leon Wessels taking a break during negotiations in the closing days before the adoption of the final constitution. The clock shows 3h35 as the time, Parliament, Cape Town, October 1996

OPPOSITE TOP: Cyril Ramaphosa, Leon Wessels and myself during a briefing in the early hours of one morning towards the end of the negotiations, Parliament, Cape Town, October 1996

OPPOSITE MIDDLE: Cyril Ramaphosa chairing the plenary of the Constitutional Assembly meeting that adopted the constitution, Parliament, Cape Town, October 1996

OPPOSITE BELOW: Nelson Mandela signing my copy of the constitution, Parliament, Cape Town, October 1996

TOP: Hassen Ebrahim, my father Ismail Hassen Ebrahim, Mac Maharaj and June Walker celebrating the adoption of the constitution, Fernwood in Cape Town, October 1996

BELOW: Protection detail in Mogadishu, Somalia, September 2012

OPPOSITE TOP: Protection detail in Yemen on our way to Taiz, March 2014

OPPOSITE MIDDLE: Protection detail in the jungles of Cotabato, Philippines during a meeting with the leadership of the Moro Islamic Liberation Front, December 2014

OPPOSITE BELOW: Handover of archives to the Nelson Mandela Foundation, 28 September 2015

TOP: Meeting of the Kabwe Machinery, Nelson Mandela Foundation, Johannesburg, January 2017

BELOW: Myself, Fazela Malherbe and Yogesh Narsing – my first underground unit, Nelson Mandela Foundation, Johannesburg, January 2017

TOP: My daughter Ruby, myself, my granddaughter Lily Grant and Yusuf Ebrahim, York, England, 30 March 2017

BELOW: 60th birthday and 10th wedding anniversary with my family. In the front row is me with Mohammed, my mother, Zubeda Ebrahim, my wife Soraya with Imaan. In the back row are Amina with Yusuf, Aadil, Zaahid, Afsana with Zaeem, Aadila with Zahraa and Luqmaan, Pretoria, 11 November 2017

Because we often had multiple sources of information, we became well acquainted with the debates, discussions and personalities. This meant that we were able to test the veracity of the information gathered. It also provided us with the ability to ensure that we were able to influence the direction and policies adopted by these organisations. This is where our political briefings were of immense importance. We were able to provide political guidance and thought leadership – often interpreted to be 'the line'. That said, we had no doubt that while we sought to influence the direction of these organisations, we did not regard these as ANC structures. The integrity of these structures was at all times respected even where organisations were supposedly 'Congress-aligned'.

Because of the quality of the political intelligence provided, we were also able to carefully identify the key people needed to be recruited. This yielded impressive results. The first person I identified for early recruitment was Mandla Nkomfe. Mandla was a young and respected activist with influence in the greater Johannesburg area, particularly Soweto, who was critical to the work of the UDF and its key affiliates. Confi was tasked to approach Mandla and did so very promptly.

With a toe-hold on Johannesburg, we moved further north to Pretoria and Limpopo. While Limpopo was home ground for Confi, his wife was from Attridgeville, and so got to know the Pretoria area very well. This was most convenient because I was eager to make an impact in the areas of Attridgeville, Mamelodi and Garankua. From Medunsa, we identified Gwen Ramakgopa. In Attridgeville, it was Matthews Sathekge and Freddy Nephawe in Masina. Confi was also tasked with these approaches over the course of the next couple of years. While Confi focused his energies on the establishment of contacts from Johannesburg to Masina, Paul focused on the North West and Free State from where he dispatched several cadres to be recruited and deployed.

Soweto

The recruitment of Mandla Nkomfe provided me with a timely entry point into Soweto and also further helped lay the foundation for the building of the Kabwe generation and the machinery that was to emerge. Mandla was an activist I had started observing the moment I became operational again in mid-1985 because his name cropped up in many contact reports.

Born in 1961, Mandla hailed from Emdeni where he was based. In senior secondary school during the June 1976 uprisings, his experience of it initiated his political life. By nature, he was always calm and amiable, a good listener and very bright. He never dominated a conversation, but when he spoke people listened. This explains why he rose so quickly as a leader in the structures that he operated in. Generally considered to be wise and level-headed, Mandla became critical to the development of mass democratic movement structures in Soweto, particularly the civic movement and the Youth Congress. He was a senior founding leader of the Youth Congress and displayed all the characteristics of a good leader. He demonstrated a good political sense, was dedicated and had a steely resolve.

Mandla was however not the ideal operative one would want in the underground because of his public profile. Despite this, I thought it necessary that he be recruited into our structures fully conscious of the security constraints. Mandla was well placed to help me establish the presence we needed in Soweto. This turned out to be a strategic move.

Confi arranged with Mandla to come out for a consultation in early 1986. Mandla responded immediately and, when he arrived, asked me a pertinent question which many of the recruits who followed also asked – why did it take the ANC so long to recruit them because they had hoped for this to take place a long time ago? Where was the ANC?

Mandla's deployment was unique. He was to operate as an individual rather than in a classic underground unit. While it was not by design, it soon became apparent that Mandla was politically located in a manner that would be able to provide the vital relationship and complementarity between the underground and mass democratic movement pillars of our struggle.

With Mandla's location as a leader in the Soweto Youth Congress (SOYCO) and credibility, he was able to identify key activists who were ready for recruitment, thus resulting in the establishment of several units that were important to the political life of Soweto. Some of the key recruits from this space were Ephraim Nkwe,[47] Brian Hlongwa, Pule Buthelezi and Huni (Sylvia) Phala. The units established were of strategic importance and made a huge impact. Each of the recruits was a leader and played a critical role in the different formations of the mass democratic movement. They were pioneers that helped establish new forms of organisational structures taking the mass democratic movement further than ever before and giving it new form and shape.

There were also other cadres that Mandla helped me recruit from outside of Soweto. The cadres sent out by Mandla came in a steady stream. In recruiting them, I was most impressed by their political maturity and the quality of leadership being produced by our youth structures. This gave me a great deal of confidence about the future of our struggle.

Soweto was a vibrant place. For a long time, these cadres participated in seminal intellectual debates that shaped and developed new organisational structures and forms of struggle. The structures established allowed the people to give expression to their struggles in diverse ways involving all levels including students, youth, residents, women and the community in general. Most promising amongst these structures were the sophisticated street committees. These experiences naturally led to vigorous debates in our ranks trying to make sense of the direction the struggle was taking. By the mid-1980s, we were beginning to speculate about the possibility of establishing what we thought could be 'organs of people's popular power', people's war and the conditions that could lead to a possible insurrection.

While on the one hand, we were learning from the experiences of the people of Soweto and the developments taking place, having underground units that were key to these developments offered us an opportunity to give strategic direction and make an input from the Botswana front of the ANC leadership. This interaction between the Forward Areas and the comrades in the trenches of struggles provided, on the one hand, for a powerful interplay between the subjective and objective aspects of struggle, and on the other, the strategic and tactical implications in guiding it.

The timing of the recruitment of the comrades from Soweto also offered us an opportunity to infuse political and ideological direction into the development of the organisational structures on the ground. Some of the ideas the units discussed with us were the argument that workers and residents should be seen in the same way when it came to organising people. Everyone in the community had to be organised into some form of structure. This approach found expression in the call by COSAS who argued that you are first a member of the community before you are a student or a worker.

Each of the cadres recruited would go on to individually and collectively make an incredible contribution to the struggle. As was usual with new units of this nature, they were put through their paces with propaganda work. They excelled and proved to be most creative. In part, they were spurred on to do better than the comrades in the Black Consciousness Movement who set brilliant standards. Different types of posters, leaflets, flags and the use of different mediums were experimented on.

Building on the struggles of the 1976 uprisings

The value of the political and organisational experience that the Soweto structures provided us with can best be understood when we consider the background and context of the developments that unfolded.

In the wake of the 1976 student uprisings, the Soweto Committee of Ten was formed hoping to lend support to the ongoing struggles taking place. However, with the passage of time, the increasingly militant youth argued that they were elitist in their orientation. In response, the Committee of Ten was transformed in 1979 into the Soweto Civic Association (SCA) which sought to be more deeply rooted within the communities of Soweto.

The young activists pushed ahead, and their militancy found expression in the formation of the Congress of South African Students in May 1979. This was to signal an important development in the struggle against apartheid. It came with a new brand of political mobilisation and political perspective, that of the banned ANC. Until 1979, no legal organisation ever dared to show an alignment to the ANC, let alone have the name 'Congress' in its title. It was a level of defiance not seen before.

During this period, a post-Rivonia generation of the ANC leaders who had either come out of prison or survived in a few underground structures in Soweto emerged. Among these were Joe Gqabi, Castro Mayethula, John Nkadimeng, Winnie Mandela, Samson Ndou, Elliot Shabangu, Curtis Nkondo, and Lawrence and Rita Ndzanga. This group was complemented by a younger grouping of cadres who were recently released from Robben Island and immersed themselves in building trade unions, civic organisations, student and youth structures. Among these were Amos Masondo, Kehla Shubane, Murphy Morobe, Dan Monstisi, Eric Molobi, Brian Mazibuko, Pule Thate and Ephraim Butshingi. Internally, there were people like Popo Molefe, Sydney Mufamadi, Nat Ramokgopa, Vincent Mogane and Jabu Ngwenya who were also active.

Despite the efforts of these leaders, which were monumental, the ANC still did not have a strong enough presence either on the ground or in the community. This was the respite the apartheid security forces needed to gain some ground. They recruited without challenge and infiltrated a number of institutions. This took place in three specific ways. Firstly, places of education such as the Soweto College of Education were infiltrated by apartheid agents who occupied key positions in the student structures. Secondly, members of the apartheid security police operated openly, were full of confidence and even brutal. Security officers enjoyed their public notoriety and were quite boisterous and boastful. Thirdly, agents of apartheid were appointed as key figures in the black local authorities and enjoyed the power they held over the people. They were corrupt, arrogant and aggressive. It is hardly surprising that the challenges experienced in Soweto were also reflected in the infiltration that we were experiencing in the Forward Areas.

With this background, progress was clearly not going to be made unless these challenges we confronted head on, and sometimes with force. The ANC's political leadership of Soweto could not be assumed. It had to be earned and fought for. To do so, it was first necessary to fight back and wrest control over the area and community from the agents of apartheid. In each instance, apartheid agents were isolated, exposed and harassed making them largely ineffective. This was the public role played by the emerging structures of the mass democratic movement. These public struggles were supported and reinforced by the efforts of the newly established underground political and military structures. This support became possible only because leaders of the underground structures occupied key roles in the student, youth and civic organisations and were able to provide for a dynamic relationship between the two fronts of struggle.

There was however a further tension that was also at play. This was the tension between the Congress perspective and that of the Black Consciousness Movement (BCM). A useful snapshot of this dynamic comes from the manner in which cultural forms of struggle were harnessed. Until then, most of the media skills in the township capable of producing posters and banners using silk-screening methods were amongst the BCM comrades. BCM produced the best poets, writers, and artists to great effect.

It was now time that the ANC-aligned structures also played their part. This they did with great effect. It was a common thing to test the courage and commitment of young activists by tasking them to carry out some propaganda work using graffiti and putting up posters, banners and hoisting the flag of the ANC. The propaganda work done immediately changed the complexion of political work in Soweto. The ANC was visibly seen to have a presence and a critical change was to take place. The units were also in a sense marking their territory which they saw as important in the ideological battle with the BCM. We were moving from protest to mass mobilisation and organisation to political direction and leadership. Things began to move at an incredible pace and it did not take a long time before the ANC had begun to out-organise the BCM. With the structures in place, the streets belonged to the people and discipline was tight.

From the student to the Youth congresses

By 1982 the young leaders of COSAS had grown into a generation of young women and men who were no longer in school and needed an organisational home. They could not remain in COSAS. It was therefore a logical development to establish the Soweto Youth Congress (SOYCO). This fortuitous development was also very timely and necessary because the youth throughout the country needed a structure through which to express themselves. It was therefore hardly surprising that the establishment of SOYCO took root throughout Soweto so quickly.

From an organisational point of view, a new space or front opened for a generation of young leaders to emerge in a manner that would change the way in which the mass democratic movement functioned. Whereas COSAS and AZASO were structures that were located in educational institutions and a formal environment, SOYCO took its structures into the communities right down to the street level. The decision taken by its leadership was that it would be more practical to establish separate structures for each of the townships and regions. Working in close cooperation with COSAS and AZASO, 20 new youth organisations were launched by 1983. By the end of 1986 there were some 600 youth congresses across the country.[48]

The notion that emerged was to develop SOYCO into a mass-based organisation. This concept also took root in the Soweto Civic Association (SCA). In 1983 when Kehla Shubane was released from Robben Island and got involved in the SCA, he insisted on also adopting this form of organisation. The close relationship between the SCA and SOYCO went further. To build the SCA, Kehla recruited young activists, amongst whom were Mandla, Ephe, Brian and Huni from the Soweto Youth Congress (SOYCO), as full-time organisers in 1983. This was a useful development from many points of view.

These young activists, had dedicated their lives to the course of their communities and needed employment. Their employment in the SCA was therefore extremely helpful. However, this also meant the infusion of organisational structures and methods of mobilisation from SOYCO to the SCA. This came at a time when the SCA began to also assume the form of a mass organisational structure. The difference though was that it was membership-based. For practical purposes, each township was organised into zones, each with its own street committee. A new organisational form was taking root. It was a radical change that resulted in a very resilient mass-based organisation. The value of this development is that while it provided for an organisational form that allowed the community to participate in the resistance to apartheid, it also became a vehicle for more militant struggles to take root. The nature of the struggle was to change in a fundamental manner.

The establishment of the SCA in the form that it adopted helped bring the period of protests and 'deputations' to an end. The organisational form and approach allowed for door-to-door work to be carried out. This was an important development because with this, the demands of the community started becoming more radical. Because the SCA now consisted of people from the street levels, they were now dealing with more basic 'bread and butter' issues and started taking ownership of the townships. They even entered into direct contracts with Eskom.

This changed the complexion of politics not only in Soweto, but the country as a whole. It was the first time in history since the banning of the ANC that the country witnessed mass organisations developing at this level. By 1985, SOYCO had through its experience in building the SCA also established its own formidable organisational structures that were able to withstand apartheid repression. The banning of COSAS was followed by the formation of the Soweto Student Congress (SOSCO). This added impetus into the ongoing organisational work by Congress-inclined formations in Soweto. It was using this as a foundation that the Soweto UDF area committee achieved the great successes it did in coordinating the different struggles that were taking place. These militant youth structures debated with the structures of the UDF the value of organs of people's popular power.

Counter-attack

Unknown to us, the MK command decided to launch Operation Zikomo, the infiltration of several hundred MK combatants, which began in mid-1985.[49] Whatever the efficacy of this operation was, it resulted in the return of fully trained MK combatants to several townships in Soweto who were provided with basic arms and instructed to become part of the street committees and the defence committees that were beginning to emerge.

Fortunately, because of the effectiveness of the underground structures led by Pule, Ephe and Brian, they were able to detect the presence of these newly infiltrated cadres. There were several benefits in all of this. Firstly, units of our underground machinery were now exposed to trained and motivated cadres on the ground. We therefore had the opportunity of providing these cadres with training on the ground, and sometimes operationally as well. The units were now able to engage in both political and military forms of struggle. In turn, our underground units were then able to give direction to these combatants and deploy them with great effect. Secondly, with the added infiltration of weapons, the newly and locally trained operatives could be made functional. Thirdly, we now had armed support that made a huge impact on the battles being waged in the townships. This armed support helped wrest the physical control over several of the townships.

This counter-attack led by our units helped ensure that many local authority leaders, security police officers and police agents were driven out of the townships and had to be relocated to a secure area referred to as 'Power Park'. This was done by harassing them and sometimes attacking these individuals. While this deserves more detailed discussion elsewhere, the important point to be made is that our underground units began to give leadership in the community and managed to effectively roll back the authority of apartheid local government structures and security forces. By physically driving these apartheid forces out of the townships, even their intelligence started drying up. The action of the units effectively created new space within which to operate. This also gave us in the Forward Areas the opportunity to intensify our efforts and provide more direct and bolder political leadership.

People's War

With the escalation of the struggle, the apartheid security forces resorted to greater repression by deploying troops in the townships, particularly Soweto. The people resisted, and this often erupted in running battles in the streets. The quality of the ANC leadership we had in the youth movement proved its mettle. Fortunately for us, street committees were well established and proved to be a remarkable force that were able to ensure that the apartheid troops did not control our streets. Barricades were set up, convoys were attacked, and petrol bombed, and an elaborate system of signals developed to indicate the presence of troops in the area. Incredibly, unarmed young people – through shear grit, determination and very capable leadership – were able to ensure that the sophisticated apartheid security forces were not able to control the streets of Soweto. The youth of the country were responding to the call by Tambo in July 1985 for ungovernability with great vigour.

Some of the most exciting political discussions I had while working from Botswana took place with these units between 1986 and 1988 when we explored the concepts of organs of people's popular power, people's war and insurrection. Needless to say, the lead given by the Kabwe Conference regarding the integration of political and military struggles were critical in guiding us. The phrase that became common in our discussions was: 'all men and material to the front'. Our units were able to quickly understand the political direction given and translate this into positive action on the ground. The unmistakeable leadership of the underground in the leadership of these youth structures helped guide communities and structures on the ground through a most difficult time.

The strength, dynamism and resilience of SOYCO was seriously tested in 1986 during the state of emergency. Despite the detention of most of the senior leadership, the organisation on the ground remained largely unaffected because new leaders quickly emerged to assume the mantle of those detained. This gave space for the growth of a second level of leadership and also gave some respite for those in detention to learn, organise and plan, and to regain their strength, networking and political education.

This dramatic growth in the youth movement and their phenomenal role was remarkable because youth congresses were being established throughout the country. In spite of the state of emergency and the devastating effect it had on the mass imprisonment of key leaders, the South African Youth Congress (SAYCO) was successfully launched on 28 March 1987. The underground units clearly demonstrated their maturity in pulling off such a feat despite the repression. The rules of secrecy were successfully applied. Representatives from nine regional structures were elected to the national executive. It adopted the Freedom Charter, pledged itself to work closely with COSATU and the NECC, and was affiliated to the UDF.

It was with this confidence that we took the bold initiative in 1987 to take the entire SAYCO leadership out of the country for consultations with the ANC's leadership. Ephe assisted us in making the arrangements for them to illegally cross the border into Botswana and then be successfully infiltrated back thereafter. The effect of this was phenomenal! The fact that we were able to execute an operation of this magnitude gave the youth leadership a great deal of confidence.

It was not long after this that the underground machinery in Soweto was called upon to pull its weight in the reception of the ANC leadership (Walter Sisulu, Andrew Mhlangeni, Wilton Mkwayi and Elias Motsoaledi) that had just been released. The same applied when Nelson Mandela was later released from prison. The ANC/MK command relied on this group to provide security while the other MK commanders were still in transit into South Africa. Of note was the role played by Brian Hlongwa and the units that he was associated with.

In addition to the work that Mandla did in Soweto, I was very keen for him to help me establish structures outside. With his help, I recruited

Neeshan (Shan) Balton, who was responsible for the establishment of the very successful APMC in Lenasia, and Azhar Bham, who established our units in Central Johannesburg. This presented a major breakthrough for me. I was finally making some progress. Each of these activists in turn went on to recruit their own units collectively producing some spectacular results. Unfortunately, Mandla was detained in 1988 and this put him out of action for a significant period.

Lenasia

Lenasia is the largest Indian township outside of KwaZulu-Natal in the country. With a large working-class population, like many other black communities, it had long been a site of political activism. Lenasia first experienced a groundswell of student political activity between 1977 and 1979, drawing inspiration from their contemporaries in neighbouring Soweto. This milieu also saw the emergence of several progressive civil society organisation other than the Transvaal Indian Congress (TIC), which was also very active. This was the environment in which Shan Balton, Jitendra (Jeets) Hargovan and Shamim Hargovan became activists.

The vibrancy of the youth found expression in the Lenasia Youth League (LYL) which was established in 1982 and was the second such structure to be established in the country after the banning of the ANC Youth League. The LYL became an influential structure. This period also saw the re-emergence of the TIC which became the primary political organisation representing the interests of the Indian community. It was during the TIC's Anti-South African Indian Council Campaign in 1983 when Alan Boesak made that famous call for the formation of the UDF.

The conditions were perfect for the emergence of a generation of young activists that would remain committed and continue to serve the public. Shan, Shamim and Jeets were some of the best of this generation. Shan and Jeets were active in the Lenasia Youth League and served on the LYL executive. Shan was also a teacher and a founding member of the Progressive Teachers Union (PTU). Shamim started her political activism at school in 1979 through COSAS. During this time, she used to travel to Soweto with other student activists to interact with the COSAS leadership. Later, Shamim was employed as a national administrator first for the Construction and Allied Workers Union (CAWU) and later the South African Railways and Harbour Workers Union (SARHWU).

Lenasia was politically alive. The experience in the development of its community organisations as well as the underground was different to Soweto. Progressive political thought and activism was gaining ground. Naturally, repression was also rife. Detention and arrests were common. There was even a strong view amongst some leaders in the TIC that they represented the interests of the ANC in the community. This meant that there was therefore no need for any other contact with the ANC. Some even resisted the idea of establishing underground structures of the ANC and discouraged activists from establishing ANC structures.[50] This view was however not shared by all.

The Ahmed Kathrada Unit

Shan came from a working-class family with no history of political involvement. It was only when he got to Wits university in 1980 where he was studying to be a teacher that he first took an interest in politics. Typical of Shan, once he took up an interest, he would pursue it with passion and vigour. The spark that ignited his interest in politics was the school boycotts in 1980 which affected his younger sisters. This interest was pursued by his involvement in the LYL, and later prompted him to become a founder member of the PTU where he played a leading role in 1985 when he started teaching. After this he got involved in the Lenasia Students Congress (LESCO) and the Federation of Residents Association in 1986. Shan had already by this time started working with Jeets, whom he trusted implicitly and would later help recruit.

Shan was detained in 1986 during the emergency for two weeks. Instead of being discouraged or intimidated, he learnt to covertly continue his political work. It was also during this period that he got to work with Prakash Napier. I took an interest in Shan in 1980 when he was identified by Yogesh as a possible recruit, by following his political development with some interest over the next few years.

It was therefore a great relief when I managed to finally establish contact with Shan, some six years later. During this period Shan had matured politically through his involvement in various struggles of the mass democratic movement and was already well schooled in the ANC's theory of the four pillars of struggle. Over time, Shan managed to master these concepts sufficiently enough to give classes to other younger activists on these ideas.[51]

It did not take long before Shan had come to the conclusion that working in mass political struggles on its own was insufficient and he needed to get involved in the armed struggle and political structures of the underground as well. It was therefore fortuitous that I asked Mandla to call Shan for consultations when we did. The timing was perfect! Shan was eager to join the ANC and Mandla was the right person to approach him and make the arrangements for him to see me in Gaborone.

I found him at the agreed spot in front of the mosque, a convenient place to meet a new contact because it was in a public spot which I could easily monitor from a distance. When I met Shan, he was visibly anxious. On enquiry, I discovered that this was because he had already come to see me the previous week but was not met because of some miscommunication.

The rule that we used when making an appointment to meet was that one should wait at the agreed spot for no more than 10 minutes and then leave so as not to attract any unwarranted action. This would be repeated an hour later and possibly one further time on the hour after which the meeting was to be regarded as being cancelled. The result is that Shan would have had to abandon the meeting and return home only to come back the next week.

It was therefore not surprising that he was already quite uncomfortable when I finally got to meet him. It is only later that I discovered that he was so anxious about this meeting that he felt obliged to inform Jeets that he was coming to meet with the ANC. He chose Jeets to confide in because of the trust between them. This was just in case something happened to him on his visit. Apparently, Jeets let him know that he too would want to be part of the ANC should he succeed. In this way, Shan had really started establishing his unit even before his recruitment. Such was the state of readiness and willingness to serve.

What immediately struck me about Shan was his forthright and direct manner. The first thing that Shan wanted to know was why it had taken so long to recruit him? He demanded to know what the reason was. I simply had no answer and had to apologise for this. This embarrassed me immensely. With Shan there was no small talk. We went to work immediately. After setting him up in a hotel room, he was tasked with writing up his biography. This became a ritual with all new contacts. It was necessary for security purposes and important to get to know who we were dealing with. I usually spent a lot of time with new contacts talking about their biographies so as to get to know them better. I needed to understand their character, background, strengths and weaknesses. By understanding the environment from which a contact came I was then able to understand the contribution they could make and how best to deploy them.

Shan was always ready to accept responsibility for tasks given to him. He took most things quite seriously. He was politically matured, had an ability to think out of the box and was not scared to take on new challenges. He came across as brave and determined and self-confident. From my assessment, he was just the well-rounded and seasoned person that we would want to have in our underground structures. I found him to be a natural leader and an organiser who would lead from the front. It was obvious that his experience as an activist and the leadership role he played in a number of community-based structures would be of enormous value.

Our first consultation was extremely productive. We agreed on his mission and tasks. Shan identified a number of possible comrades for recruitment. Among them were the husband and wife team of Shamim and Jeets. Once this was settled, Jeets came out for consultations and his recruitment confirmed. It was not long after that Shamim also came out and was recruited. This was the only time I had to consider the recruitment of both the husband and wife. This had obvious benefits but also huge risks. It was unusual. I was uncomfortable with this but after considering the case at hand, agreed to go ahead. Fortunately, they were still young and had not started a family. I never regretted this decision. They were great partners and drew their strength from each other.

Like Shan, Jeets first got involved in the struggle in 1980 at the height of the school student boycotts. He was a member of the SRC and was soon detained in the same year. In 1981 he became involved in the Anti-SAIC Campaign and in 1982 in the steering committee of the LYL and was elected onto the LYL executive. From this, he got involved in the organising committee of the TIC. Much of these activities were undertaken while on the run from the security police. These activities soon found him scouring for information on the ANC. It was only in 1985 when he travelled to Zimbabwe that he came to find some copies of *Sechaba* and the *African Communist*. He devoured all the information he could get hold of.

Shamim Akhalwaya also became involved in student politics at high school from 1980. She was a member of the Congress of South African Students (COSAS), which led to her working with students from surrounding areas such as Ennerdale and Soweto. She later become active in the LYL and the Lenasia Women's Congress. Her activism continued through to university where she was elected onto the AZASO executive at the University of Durban-Westville (UDW). It is here that she met Manoj Pema, a fellow student activist and SRC member. Manoj's political activism started with the 1980 national student boycotts. While at UDW he worked as an activist in Durban communities and in the political struggles brought into focus by the UDF. Later, Jeets recruited Manoj as the fourth member of the APMC. Manoj was initially part of the propaganda unit but later in 1989 also tasked with the establishment of a further MK unit which he was on the verge of initiating.

The commitment displayed and sacrifices made by both Jeets and Shamim were not only incredible but commanded my respect. Both Shamim and Jeets got to know each other through their involvement in the struggle. After a few years of courting, they got married in 1986 during the emergency, and it was during the first quarter of 1987 that they were recruited into the ANC. Whereas many activists were lost to potential underground work once they got married, with Shamim and Jeets, their marriage really started shortly before their induction into the underground. Because of their commitment and involvement in the struggle, they even sacrificed the joys of a honeymoon.

The unit composition was perfect. Shan was a teacher, Jeets an accountant with good skills and a passion for technology, and Shamim steeped in the work of trade unions. They were integral to the political struggles of Lenasia and each, a leader in their own right. The team was a good match and proved to work together well, perhaps because of the maturity of each of the characters involved. The speed with which they moved and produced results was indeed stunning. They had mutual respect and were clear about their common objectives. This unit taught me about the importance of human relations in building underground structures.

Very early on in the development of the Unit, it was evident that its members had all the qualities that I would look for in the establishment of an APMC in line with the Kabwe Conference decisions. When I broached the matter with Shan, he was willing to explore the idea. While the concept of an APMC had been around for a few years, it was only until the Kabwe Conference that we were directed to build these structures. The intention was to establish a third layer of ANC leadership and command structures. The PMC was the first layer of leaders and responsible for all ANC work under the leadership of the National Executive Committee. The second layer of leadership came from us as the regional political military committees in the Forward Areas; and, the third layer of leadership – the APMC – would be inside the country in each of the designated areas.

The function of the APMC would effectively be to represent the ANC at the area level in their community. This was a fundamental and historic break from the past because until now, the ANC leadership operated from outside the borders of the country. This meant that we now had leadership back home through the APMCs. The strategy worked and by 1988, the APMC made sufficient enough progress to start preparing the ground for the reception of a senior member of the ANC to be infiltrated into the country to work with them.

As the leadership of the ANC, the unit was required to establish both a political and military presence. Politically, they were to represent the interests of the ANC in their interaction with structures of the mass democratic movement and through their propaganda work. In time, a military unit would also be established. The unit performed beyond expectations. As soon as they were settled, they said they wanted to be referred to as the Ahmed Kathrada Unit. The Ahmed Kathrada APMC was, to the best of my knowledge, one of very few APMCs ever to be established in the country.

One only had to scan the reports produced by this team to see the depth and quality of their leadership. Their reports were always clear and precise. They provided me with a very thorough understanding of the developments in the community, what each organisation was doing, and what each member of the APMC were doing. The reports presented were not about what they heard and saw, but what they were doing to influence the political developments in the community. And, on each occasion, they would look at what further could be done to take the struggle forward. These were leaders indeed.

The establishment of a propaganda capability was carried out very quickly. This was the responsibility of Jeets. He started by recruiting Kim Morgan and Roshnie Naidu. A roneo printing machine and typewriter was purchased. A back room was rented and effectively became the unit's print room and place to store their materials.[52] Activation of this capability immediately provided a public presence of the ANC in the community which boosted morale and gave confidence to activists. This was a major development. Where appropriate, the leadership of mass democratic movement structures were each anonymously sent ANC propaganda materials to reinforce the political training and to provide them with an ANC perspective and analysis.

With time, they became confident enough to extend their work into two further areas. They started producing propaganda material for other areas such as Laudium, Benoni and Johannesburg. These materials were either 'cold-dropped' at the houses of activists or at bus stops. Besides reproducing ANC materials I sent them, they also produced their own leaflets with analyses on current strikes, boycotts and in support of the struggles of the day. Later, Jeets recruited Manoj Pema. Manoj was initially part of the propaganda unit but later in 1989 also tasked with the establishment of a further MK unit which he was on the verge of initiating.

While it was standard to provide all units with the required MCW training, I was pleased to also provide Jeets and Shamim with an introduction to the use of firearms. Late one night while they were in Gaborone for consultations, I took them to a safe house and gave them a thorough briefing on the weapons we used including an AK47, Makarov, grenades and a limpet mine. We went through a basic run including the assembly, disassembly and how to use these weapons. Shamim was the first woman I gave training to and I was always very proud of this. I suspect that she was one of the first Indian women in the Gauteng area to be exposed to the weapons we used. Shan also had the benefit of this training. To follow on this training, both Jeets and Shamim registered with a shooting range to gain expericnce. On various occasions, when Jeets and Shamim came out for consultations, they would return with weapons secreted away in false compartments that we created in their rented vehicles, with specific instructions to be cold-dropped for other units to pick up later.

The Ahmed Kathrada Unit managed to survive undetected for nearly five years – which in itself was unusual. With this unit, we were constantly exploring new ways of executing our tasks. We paid a lot of attention to our communications. While it may appear to be a simple matter today, our methods of communication were rather limited because it was dependent on either personal interaction, over a fixed line or by post using the traditional book code method. For obvious security reasons we looked to reducing the number of visits by members of the unit outside the country.

We explored the use of modems which then was cutting-edge technology. We depended on Jeets's knowledge in this area. He made a special trip to meet me and we then tested out the modem on a 16kb line in the middle of the night. Success was limited, but it did provide the equivalent of instant messaging. Not satisfied with this, we also explored the use of a fax machine, which at that point time was also new technology.

The Ahmed Timol Unit

The establishment of the APMC's military unit was the responsibility of Shan. The establishment of the unit presented us with a major breakthrough which was greater than that which I could have hoped for.

Prakash Napier was recruited by Shan in October 1986. He came from a working-class family, went to school in Laudium and moved to Lenasia as a young man. In his early youth, Prakash was apolitical and held a very cynical view of the struggle. Because he was a friend of several activists, Prakash witnessed police brutality during various clashes with activists. Never one to stand on the side lines, Prakash was thrust to the fore in defence of his friends. Very soon after these experiences, he was drawn into the LYL and took part in various campaigns. It was when Prakash became a worker, doing his bit to feed the family, that he became aware of the exploitation and oppression of the working class. Needless to say, he immediately threw in his lot with the workers and joined the unions, and in 1986 was elected a shop steward for the General and Allied Workers Union. His activism in the union and interaction with comrades in the townships only served to increase his political consciousness. This was the experience that made Prakash determined to commit himself to the struggle.

Jameel Chand, like so many of his fellow student activists, was also affected by the struggles of the day between 1980 and 1984. However, his interest in politics started much earlier in his Standard Six history class when he discovered that the first people to arrive in the Cape were not the Dutch in 1652, as was commonly taught. He wanted to learn more about this history and so his journey of discovery began, and it was not long before school became his first terrain of struggle. He became active in the LYL and LESCO and cut his teeth as an activist in the campaigns waged during this period.

Also coming from a working-class family, Jameel developed a deep political consciousness. This was further shaped when he went to Westville university where his political thinking developed, and he came to the conclusion that he wanted to join the ANC and become a member of MK. During this period, he read prolifically about the lives and struggles of Fidel Castro, Che Guevara, Mao Tse Tung and others. He too was by 1986 ready and willing to be recruited into the ranks of the ANC and MK.

Prakash, with the approval of Shan, recruited Jameel in December 1986. In April 1987 Prakash and Jameel came out to Gaborone for a consultation and formal recruitment into MK. During this visit, the unit was given basic training and were introduced to the handling of firearms and limpet mines. Prakash was appointed as commander of the unit and Jameel the political commissar. Towards the middle of 1987, Yusuf Akhalwaya was recruited into the unit too.

Careful consideration was put into the recruitment of Yusuf Akhalwaya. He was Shamim's younger brother. Yusuf moved to Nirvana Secondary School in 1980 at the height of the school boycotts and matriculated in 1984. The violent response of the security forces to the struggles against the tricameral parliament elections profoundly influenced Yusuf as he began looking at more effective ways in which to resist apartheid. When Yusuf joined Wits in 1985, he very soon got drawn into the activities of the Black Students Society and Muslim Students Association. He later became the *amir* of the latter organisation. However, Yusuf's political training and influences came from working in the community, particularly the LYL and the Federation of the Resident's Association. By 1987, Yusuf was a disciplined activist with developed political views and ready for recruitment into the ANC.

Each of the members of this unit could not have been more different but gelled together incredibly well. Prakash was always self-confident, jovial if not mischievous at times and extremely pleasant to engage with. Despite his playful demeanour he was quite serious about his business and knew exactly what he wanted. He gained a reputation in the community for his bravado.

During the student uprisings a few years earlier, the riot police had decided to take aggressive action against the protesting students. They used teargas and decided to mount a charge against the students. The students started to flee the moment they had thrown the stones they had in their hands. Through the haze of the teargas, while you had the police charging and the students fleeing, there was this image of the lonely scrawny figure of Prakash who decided that enough was enough. Prakash decided to run in the opposite direction to the students and started charging towards the police. He was armed with nothing other than a knife in hand and was quickly making his way towards the police. Fortunately, a confrontation was avoided by Shan who intercepted Prakash and discouraged him from proceeding with his counter-attack. This image left a lasting impression in the minds of many students of that time. The incident also convinced Shan of Prakash's bravery and militancy.

Both Yusuf and Jameel were university students and also had the opportunity of looking at the struggle from an intellectual point of view. However, while Jameel was always keen on communications and therefore outward looking, Yusuf was a very private person and also deeply religious. Shortly after the establishment of the unit, I was informed that they had decided to name and operate it as the Ahmed Timol Unit.

With the establishment of the Ahmed Timol Unit, we now had the opportunity of engaging in both the political and military aspects of struggle. Conditions were perfect. The question was: How were we to transform this group into an MK unit that would be effective and successfully achieve its objectives? The objective as I saw it was to establish an MK unit that did not have to engage in direct combat with the enemy forces, or at least not immediately. The primary function of the unit was to undertake armed propaganda. The main purpose would be to carry out military operations that would directly support political struggles. There was no intention of engaging in purely military operations. The express instruction I gave was to avoid any direct engagement of the enemy.

With this in mind, we needed to consider how best to train the unit.

There were three possible approaches to dealing with this challenge. The traditional approach was to extract some or all members of the unit for a short crash course in Angola. I decided against this approach for security reasons. I wanted to limit the unit's exposure outside and to reduce their time away from home to avoid any suspicion. The second approach would have been to infiltrate a fully trained MK cadre into the country to work with the unit and provide them with training on the ground. This was a possibility and it worked with the Soweto units; but, the circumstances were different. While in Soweto, we were forced to improvise; in Lenasia, we were able to plan. I therefore decided on a different and novel approach. I decided to train the unit in the field and operationally. In this way, we would find a way of graduating this young unit into a powerful fighting force that had operational experience and understood the challenges.

The approach adopted was to start the unit off with a basic training course. Training of the unit took place over a couple of visits and over several days. The first part of the training dealt with the political imperatives and context of our armed action. They were taught the importance of carrying out armed propaganda and why it was important to ensure that our military actions were guided by our politics. We had to be sure that we did not carry out military actions for its own sake. Ours was a political struggle and they needed to be sure of this. The next part of their training was in MCW. Because of the risks entailed and the sensitive nature of their operations, we needed to be extra sure that they observed all the rules of underground work.

The unit was given a thorough course on the use of the different weapons including firearms and explosives. The focus, however, was on the use of limpet mines. This was to be their weapon of choice and we wanted them to know it well. To give this training, I was fortunate enough to be able to call on Chris and T-Man, who were commanders of the MK's elite Special Operations Unit. These guys were the best in their field and had trained many units and saw some of our greatest operational successes. Once the unit knew their weapons well, understood their mission, and had a clear political orientation, they were ready to become operational.

The intention was that, over time, the unit would be afforded further and more specialised training. In December 1987 Prakash and Jameel were sent to Angola for further training. While in Luanda they were trained in urban guerrilla tactics, surveillance, small arms and military engineering. The unit returned home after three months to continue with their operations. Prakash was sent for a further commander's course in June 1989 to the Soviet Union.

The unit was provided with several consignments of weapons, mainly limpet mines, each time a member of the unit came across to Botswana. The standard method used was for them to rent specific types of vehicles because of the ease with which we were able to create concealed spaces to store the weapons. The most popular vehicle for this was the Nissan Skyline because of its deep boot. It also had integrated bumpers that could hold a large number of mines. In addition to this, Jeets and Shamim also took responsibility for some shipments of weapons.

Over time, our ordinance people had mastered the art of expertly building false bottoms and concealed spaces or compartments in different makes of vehicles. This was dealt with expertly using wrapping and packaging that would ensure that the weapons would not be detectable even with a careful search using sniffer dogs. None of the weapons thus transported were ever discovered.

The Ahmed Timol Unit was under the political and operational command of the Ahmed Kathrada APMC. This meant that we would provide no more than strategic guidance. The tactical command, however, was left to Prakash as commander of the Ahmed Timol Unit. I can remember only one occasion on which we issued a specific call to action. This was because there was a lull in MK's activities and, for political reasons, we thought it necessary for some action to take place.

It was against this background that the Ahmed Timol Unit became operational. In doing so, I issued some guidance and direction particularly as regards their first few actions. I wanted to build their confidence and give them practical experience on the effect and impact of the weapons that they were to use. This was particularly important because they did not have the benefit of their training actually taking place in a live environment.

I know from personal experience that going into a live operation is very different to the theory. It was also necessary that they understood just how dangerous the materials were that they were dealing with. I was also keen to ensure that they learnt how to apply their training in undertaking MCW. They needed to become aware of the method to be adopted in carrying out reconnaissance, the value of good intelligence information, and being vigilant and security consciousness. For example, they needed to learn to place one person on guard while the actual operation of placing the charge was dealt with by another. It had to become second nature to know what weapons they were to use in going on an operation, how to approach a target, how to place the charges and then to retreat. The idea of back-up plans in case things went wrong was also discussed.

The instruction given was that the first few operations carried out had to be those where there was minimal risk and the greatest certainty of success. I advised that they should choose a railway line or some such target in an in area which their presence would not raise any suspicion. They should do this after carrying out the best of reconnaissance before and make sure that it was easy to approach and lay the charges. It was critical that the operation would not involve any direct engagement with the enemy forces. I wanted them to lay the charge, retreat to safety and observe the type of damage caused.

More than the training, the unit was also street-savvy, mature and clear-headed enough to carry out their first operations according to plan. Despite Prakash's playfulness, he took his command responsibilities very seriously. Their first operations took place soon after their training in July 1987. The approach adopted and the training given proved to be effective. With the correct balance between the maturity of the cadres involved and the quality of the training given, I effectively proved that we could build MK units that could effectively and successfully carry out armed propaganda operations without having to go through the process of training people over extended periods in our camps. That said, I did commit myself to a plan to give the unit professional military training in our camps.

Once the unit was deployed, there was no stopping them. They gained confidence and expertise with each operation they carried out. They also became more daring. While at the beginning they attacked one target during an operation, over time they gained the confidence to attack several targets in one evening. This gave the impression of a campaign rather than a series of isolated attacks and proved to be of enormous political value and made a big morale booster. This approach clearly confounded the security forces both as to the number of units involved, and where the unit was located or operating from.

The targets attacked that we were able to verify are identified in the table below.[53] From this, it is easy to see the frequency of the various attacks, their geographical spread and propaganda value.

	Target	Date
1	The National Peoples Party office near Lenasia	1 October 1987
2	Substation at or near Pageview	21 December 1987
3	Magistrates' Court at or near Vereeniging	March 1988
4	Electricity pylon at or near Carltonville	3 March 1988
5	City Hall	14 March 1988
6	Railway line at or near Langlaagte	10 April 1988
7	OK Stores	28 April 1988
8	Score Furnishes	28 April 1988
9	SA Railway Service transport truck	28 April 1988
10	Home of Mr Abramjee, Member of Parliament	12 June 1988
11	Home of a member of the Laudium Management Committee Dr. Shamiss Laudium	12 June 1988
12	Home of I. Jugbhai	28 July 1988
13	Municipal offices, Actonville	3 September 1988
14	Home of a member of the Lenasia Management Committee R. Ebrahim	10 September 1988
15	Lenasia Bus Service	10 September 1988

	Target	Date
16	Offices of the House of Delegates	10 September 1988
17	Unknown police station	22 September 1988
18	Home of a member of the Laudium Management Committee S.D. Goolam	22 September 1988
19	Offices of the Lenasia Management Committee	31 October 1988
20	Receiver of Revenue offices at or near Boksburg	2 December 1988
21	Offices of the Department of Home Affairs at or near Brakpan	December 1988
22	Magistrates Court at or near Benoni	9 December 1988
23	Randfontein police station	15 December 1988
24	Regional Services Council offices	15 December 1988
25	Home of MP Salam Mayet Ryansoord	4 January 1989
26	Electricity substation at or near Mayfair	6 March 1989
27	Yeoville police station	6 April 1989
28	Cleveland police station	April 1989
29	Home of Management Committee Member Hassen Varachia Azaadville	18 July 1989
30	City Hall and damage to property;	14 March 1988
31	Home of councillor A. Lambert Palmridge	30 August 1989
32	Railway line near Kliptown/Klipspruit	21 August 1989
33	Hillbrow police station staff quarters	11 December 1989

Starting a family

For different reasons, including at a personal and emotional level, the Ahmed Timol Unit will be associated with the start of new and great things. It was certainly a new chapter in my life. The unit came out for their second training session in July 1987 which is also when my daughter Ruby was born. This is also when I first met Yusuf. I remember well having to shuttle between the hospital where Barbara was struggling through a rather prolonged and difficult labour, and the unit who were being trained in a room at the Oasis Hotel in Gaborone.

Ruby was born in Princess Marina Hospital in July 1987. The quality of the patient care at the hospital left much to be desired and resulted in many anxious moments. They were short-staffed and pretty much left us to our own devices. The nurses only checked in on us when they could. Nonetheless, Ruby was my first child, and nothing could possibly rob me of the excitement of her birth. It was every bit magical. I was pleased to witness the miracle of birth. Ruby's birth made feel human. I was more than just a soldier, political activist or a lawyer. I was now also a father.

With Ruby, I had to learn what being a father was all about. But first, I would need to learn how to deal with colic. Ruby suffered quite seriously with this and I often resorted to driving her about in the middle of the night just to get her to sleep. As new parents, we went through the usual anxieties and had to regularly visit our family doctor, usually at rather odd hours. It took many consultations and false diagnoses only to discover that Ruby's colic was brought on by lactose intolerance and needed to be fed soya-based milk.

This was the start of a realisation that I was going to learn a great deal about myself from my children. I soon recognised that I had suffered being lactose intolerant all my life. Unfortunately, I did not understand it and it was a normal part of my life.

Ruby brought us enormous joy and added real meaning to my life. She was a ball of energy. She also became the reason why I had to be a successful revolutionary. I was now a family man and needed to ensure that I also earned enough to support them.

Fortunately, my reputation as a lawyer was recognised in the legal fraternity and I was headhunted by one of the bigger law firms who offered me a post with a huge increase in salary. This was a great boost to my legal career, and I took up my new post early in 1988. It gave me an opportunity to start focusing on corporate civil litigation and insurance work which I enjoyed immensely.

Working as a lawyer

Great new beginnings also come with new challenges. Ruby's birth brought to the fore a major challenge that I would have to contend with throughout my life. I was not only a revolutionary fighting an armed struggle, but a lawyer by profession and now also a father. I needed to find a balance between these different commitments, which I found enormously difficult because I simply cannot multi-task.

One of the perks of working in a law firm is the exposure to people and opportunities. I soon chanced upon an opportunity to buy a house at an extremely good price, the first investment of any significance that I was to commit to. Within a short space of time, I started feeling like a normal person. I had a career in law, married with a family and now owned a house. It did a whole lot for my morale and self-confidence. But it was even more important because it helped me deal with the challenges of the life that came with being part of an underground machinery.

The changed living and family conditions provided me with a legitimate and a fantastic cover. But it came at a cost of leading a double life. I was a successful lawyer and family person by day and required to undertake my underground activities at night. I was in a perpetual state of exhaustion. The only way I coped with this was to introduce a rigid structure and routine to my day which was quite mechanical.

In general, I have a very tense relationship with time. I get extremely anxious about meeting my commitments on time. To cope with my new life, I would start my day in the office at about 4 am or shortly thereafter. The routine I adopted ensured that I complete the load of files that were diarised for attention by 7h30 every morning. This meant that I worked through my files and dictated my instructions onto mini-cassettes which would be given to my two legal secretaries, which kept them busy for the day. If I had no court duty scheduled, the remainder of the morning was left for the library to do my research. I used the afternoons to consult with clients. This routine was reinforced by Barbara's firm ideas as to how to manage Ruby's day and I had to align myself to this. It meant that I had to be home by 5 pm so that I had some time to play with Ruby, bath her by 6, then feed and read to her before she was off to bed by 7. Clockwork! It was quite a regimented affair.[54]

This is when my second shift would start as I attended to my commitments with the underground structures. These engagements would often last until up to 1 am more regularly than I care to remember. As a coping mechanism and because I lived so close to where I worked, I would come home at lunch, eat a quick meal and then have a short power nap which worked incredibly well. Without fail I would fall into a deep sleep the moment I put my head down. This would usually last for 15 to 20 minutes. Unfortunately, this work style would carry on for many years without any respite.

Given the fact that I was newly married and having started a family so quickly, my inability to give more time to my new family did me no favours. It started putting an enormous amount of strain on my marriage from early on. Barbara was quite isolated. My lifestyle and security considerations did not allow for an active social life and, as a new parent, she was not working. Fortunately, Barbara's mother, June, regularly visited us for a few months each time. This helped give Barbara some relief. Both Barbara and I took a lot of strain but miraculously soldiered on, more because Barbara persevered as I stubbornly insisted that I have no choice.

To celebrate Ruby's first birthday in July 1988 we decided to go to the UK and also participate in Barbara's mother's 50th birthday celebrations at the same time. This is when I also got to realise the seriousness of the difficulties we were facing. On a road trip to Edinburgh to see old university friends, Barbara asked whether I would consider relocating to the UK which would be better for raising Ruby and where the quality of life would be infinitely better. True to character, I refused without giving it much thought. Barbara asked me to choose between keeping the family and going back to Botswana. My response was that I had no choice. I suspect I took some comfort in believing this because it obviated the need to consider the options as I then felt compelled to merely go back and continue my political work. This was a serious challenge and I did not know how to cope with it.

I knew it was terribly unfair on both Barbara and Ruby, but I could not find it in myself to give up the work I was committed to, especially not at this stage because we were beginning to make some progress. As usual, I tried to ignore the problems we were facing for as long as I could. My response was to put even more focus on my work and hope that the problems would simply go away. Work was, and sometimes still is, an escape.

And so, the struggle continued.

Central Johannesburg

Mandla had arranged for Azhar Bham, a law student steeped in student politics, to visit Botswana for a consultation. From my experience in the Black Students Society at Wits, I got to know some of the other Bham family members who were from Limpopo. By this time, I had a fairly clear idea of what was going on in the student community and was keen to meet with Azhar.

Azhar was tasked to establish a unit in Central Johannesburg and set about doing this over several months in 1988. He recruited Maya Sooka and Dipak Madhav. This unit was an important development because it was operating in an area that once had a very proud history of struggle during the 1960s. Other than the brief interlude in the early 1970s because of the pioneering work that Ahmed Timol and his unit carried out in this area, the ANC lost its active presence. The establishment of this unit was therefore most welcomed.

Both Maya and Dipak were able to come out for consultations. They were well connected with a network of activists and because Johannesburg was such a hive of activity, their political intelligence was most valuable. Each member of the unit focused on specific structures of the mass democratic movement which they had been active in. Both Dipak and Maya were central to the work of the Johannesburg Youth Congress (JOYCO). Azhar focused on AZASO. The unit also did a significant amount of propaganda work, giving the ANC an active presence in this area. They even bought a Gestetner roneo machine to print their materials and managed to successfully reproduce copies of January 8th statements and other leaflets for distribution.

The unit was unfortunately not able realise its full potential. Before they were able to get into their stride and develop their capacity, they suffered the same fate as many other operatives during this period. Dipak was detained early in 1989 while distributing propaganda material and Azhar was also detained some months later for his work as the secretary general of AZASO.

Pretoria

Pretoria was my home and where I started my life in the underground. If I were to be active in the ANC's underground machinery, what good would I be if I was not able to establish a presence in my own community? I felt obliged to do this. Beyond this, I was also committed to ensuring that the ANC had a presence in the Indian communities of the Transvaal. I saw this as my task, which was one I was unable to deliver on for the first five years of my life in exile. The reality was different now.

My objective was to re-establish an ANC presence in Laudium. There were however two realities that were not lost on me. The first is that Laudium had marched on after my departure and it was not simply a matter of picking up from where I left off when I went into exile. Secondly, the road leading back to Laudium was facilitated by African comrades who had also assisted me in building structures of the underground, including in neighbouring Attridgeville.

It was in 1980 not long after I left that Laudium experienced its first school boycott. Nava Pillay, Razia Saleh and other activists started organising students around the quality of education. Amazingly, for the first time ever in Laudium, both a high school and the primary school came out in boycott. Spreading to other schools, these boycotts, as they did in other communities, produced many student activists that would grow on to becoming the engine of the resistance in the community later.

We were beginning to see the emergence of progressive community-based organisations despite the fact that Laudium was still a very conservative community. The first was the election of a parent and student representative council that was established during the school boycotts. As was typical of developments like these elsewhere, the apartheid state responded by detaining people they thought were leading the protests. For the first time, 12 people were detained from Laudium. When these boycotts continued, both Yogesh and Nava got arrested for distributing leaflets.

The year 1981 saw these struggles mature into something more meaningful. Activists made contact with leaders like Pravin Gordhan from Durban who helped provide some training in the building of community organisations. The exposure that the activists got was invaluable. Nava and others got to attend their first political school which took place in Phoenix in Natal, and later on at a place called Botha Hill. This is where people like Pravin and other leaders of the newly emerging mass democratic movement provided political education classes guiding people as to how to go about building a mass movement.[55]

This training helped. Soon, activists like Razia went on to establish structures such as LIPSA, (the Laudium Inter-Primary School Sports Association). Because of the ensuing repression, activists needed to find different and innovative ways of mobilising support and bringing people together around common issues. LIPSA was such a structure. It proved to be a fantastic base for the recruitment of people into political activity.

From these activities, Laudium established its first residents association for White Blocks, a complex of cheaply constructed prefabricated duplexes for the poor people of Laudium. After that, they went on to establish the Bangladesh Flats Association and the Claudius Residents Association which then led to the overall community structure called the Laudium Ratepayers and Residents Association. Another key structure established in 1981 was the Laudium Bursary Committee, and in 1982 we saw the establishment of various sports bodies calling for non-racial sports.

These naturally provided the base for the struggles to follow under the auspices of the revived Transvaal Indian Congress (TIC) and then the formation of the UDF in 1983. These developments meant that activists from Laudium were exposed to struggles elsewhere and started getting involved at a broader level. Razia started working for the TIC in Johannesburg, Yogesh for the Education Policy Unit in Johannesburg and Nava got involved in the civic associations structures of Pretoria and became the Secretary of the Pretoria UDF regional structure.

As we saw with the Soweto comrades, activists like Nava were able to find full-time employment as organisers. In Laudium, an advice centre was set up using funding from the Kagiso Trust. Using this as a base, Nava started working on regional civic and UDF structures of Pretoria. This is where he started working very closely with comrades like Matthew Sathekge who was servicing Attridgeville.

A valuable lesson that activists learnt in these struggles was the value of a support network within the community. This became one of the key drivers for their success. Ordinary people were able to participate in the struggle by providing food, money, support, a hiding place or even just transport necessary to make the community organisations come alive. The important part of this was that the community started taking ownership of the struggles that were being waged. They got involved in whatever way they could, and it did not have to be just as activists.

The development of the underground machinery in Pretoria presents a unique experience and case study. We managed to merge three of the four pillars of struggle (the political underground, military and the mass democratic pillars) by deploying people in each pillar in an integrated manner. In so doing, this resulted in both our underground structures and community organisations assuming a non-racial character at a regional level. This assisted us in deploying activists to work in all areas of the region rather than being restricted to their communities. It was therefore not unusual for comrades from Laudium to work in other areas of Pretoria, or for comrades coming from Attridgeville to be active in Laudium.

Because Pretoria was the capital, repression here was most brutal. The units responded to this reality in a most creative manner by mobilising both the above and underground forms of struggle in an intricate set of networks. This resulted in activists being able to support each other without it being known that they were part of the underground. This method of work allowed for greater political coherence and yet protected cadres from being known as such to each other. This method of building structures also helped us to reach out to areas outside of Pretoria as we saw being developed towards the end of the 1980s. We built a camaraderie between activists from various areas crossing boundaries that laid the basis for what the new South Africa should look like. Unfortunately, the unintended consequences of rebuilding ANC branches specific to apartheid-defined areas destroyed effectively undermined this development.

Reconnecting with Laudium

The trail leading me back to Laudium started with Confi, then to Mandla who led me to Azhar, and then Maya who finally led me to Razia Saleh. What happened is that sometime during the state of emergency, Maya was approached by senior activists to accommodate a young Indian woman who needed a quiet place to work from. This was Razia. Maya accommodated Razia in her parents' home in central Johannesburg. I got very excited when I heard this because it offered me an opportunity to meet with Razia. The possibility of meeting Razia was fantastic news. It opened the way for me to politically get back into Laudium. I wasted no time in pushing for Razia's first consultation and subsequent recruitment which took place in the latter part of 1987.

Razia was a well-grounded and mature activist by the time I met her. She grew politically in the period between 1979 and 1983. By 1983, with the revival of the TIC and later with the establishment of the UDF, there was also direct political work that she was called upon to undertake in the mass democratic movement.

Razia finished her studies at Wits in mid-February 1985 and immediately took up employment with the TIC as coordinator and organiser. When the emergency was declared in July, the TIC office was raided by the Security Branch, and a decision taken to close it.

Initially, they operated from the offices of various executive members and then found 'quiet' offices that were known to just a few comrades. This was when Razia took up accommodation at Maya's parents' home.

Because of the commitment of comrades like Razia and Nava, Laudium went through an incredible growth in the establishment of new civil society structures, including student organisations, bursary committees and residents' associations, which collectively played an invaluable role in Laudium's political life. With the absence of ANC structures and leadership in the community, activists successfully focused their energies on these.

The TIC presence in Laudium was managed by a TIC area committee. Community leaders such as Apmai Dawood, Omar Motani, Omie Ayob and Maniben Sita served on its leadership structures. Because Razia was working full-time for the TIC, she attended all its meetings as an ex-officio member. Both Yogesh and Nava also attended these meetings. The TIC became an effective vehicle for the mobilisation of the community during the campaigns against the tricameral and municipal elections in Laudium, providing a platform to distribute leaflets, put up posters and organise demonstrations.

This is the history that I had to familiarise myself with when I finally got to meet and recruit Razia in the latter part of 1987. Razia was tasked to establish the first ANC unit after the unit I established was disbanded in 1979. She agreed that Nava was a natural choice for recruitment. In the meantime, Razia started working full-time for the UDF Information Office in Johannesburg in 1988 – again operating from secret offices.

The Stanza Bopape Unit

In parallel to the help I got from Maya to reconnect with Laudium, I turned to Confi who knew Attridgeville well. He had family there and had a good working relationship with the activists in that community. One of the young COSAS leaders that Confi helped develop was Matthew Sathekge. Matthew was a regional organiser for

The Kabwe Generation

COSAS in the Transvaal. When he left school, he got involved in the youth and UDF regional structures. Matthew grew as an activist to assume significant responsibilities both in the civic structures as well as the UDF. Matthew was also involved in the struggles against the Bophuthatswana Bantustan structures.

Confi sent Matthew to Gaborone for consultations. I recruited him. He was an important recruit because of his background and influence in the mass democratic movement. He also offered me an opportunity to establish an ANC presence in both Attridgeville and Mamelodi. Before long, Matthew identified Benny Theko from Mamelodi for recruitment.

Benny started his political awakening in the Young Christian Workers in 1977. He later joined COSAS and then the Mamelodi Youth Organisation in 1983. By 1986 he was co-opted into the leadership structures of the civic organisations where he contributed significantly to the struggles of the community. This is the context within which Matthew worked with Benny. Benny was sent to Gaborone in 1987. Soon after his recruitment, I arranged for the same crash course that we gave to the Ahmed Timol Unit. Chris, the commander the Special Operations Unit, once again happily obliged.

Benny established the Stanza Bopape Unit after recruiting Bheki Nkosi and Ryder Mokgothadi. Strike Bila was recruited later and went on to become a critical player in this unit assisting greatly in our ambitions to establish a firm base in Pretoria. He had the added value of being previously trained in Angola as an MK cadre.[56]

Together with Strike, Benny recruited a number of other units in different areas doing both political work amongst structures of the mass democratic movement, propaganda work that focused mainly on graffiti, as well as the distribution of ANC literature. This was a wonderful partnership because it provided for a dynamic synergy between the political and military forms of struggle. A unit was established under the command of Matthew Malaza to carry out their military operations. A cold-drop of a consignment of weapons was successfully arranged to support the unit with its efforts.

The unit immediately set about establishing themselves. They carried out successful operations against notorious local members of the Security Branch, and local government councillors. With this, we were now able to maintain a consistent political and military presence of the ANC in the Pretoria region. It helped demonstrate that MK was able to come out in support of local political struggles and even able to deal with troublesome police and local councillors. It was also during this period that Mainstay Chibuku was infiltrated into the country and started becoming active in the Pretoria area with a series of military operations. I came across Mainstay when I went for my training in Caxito, by which time he was already a seasoned and experienced commander.

The stage was set. My late entry into Pretoria had the benefit of establishing structures consisting of operatives who had a great deal more experience and maturity. Our structures were evolving and in a short space of time were strategically positioned within the broader Pretoria area. The units established were responsible for the regional UDF, civic movement, COSAS and Youth Congress structures. Our strength was growing exponentially. It was now possible for us to develop a more senior level of organisational structure.

I set a plan in motion to do this sometime late in 1988. Benny was called to Gaborone where he was introduced to Razia. The other member of this structure was to be Matthews Sathekge. I wanted to establish a structure that would assume responsibility for all political and military activities in the greater Pretoria area. For this reason, the structure was to assume the role of a Regional Politico-Military Committee (RPMC).

Given the close proximity of Attridgeville, Laudium and Mamelodi and the fact that these areas were already politically connected at the MDM level, it made sense to establish them into one RPMC rather than establishing several APMCs. In this way, they were able to support each other. The other attractive possibility that the newly established RPMC offered was that of a non-racial structure that did not operate within the confines of the apartheid group areas. We were redefining our politics. For me, Pretoria was the natural place to do so. It was the citadel of apartheid and this is where I believed we should work the hardest to establish a non-racial approach.

When Strike was sent out to meet with me in Gaborone, he was asked to rent the preferred Nissan Skyline. After a refresher course in firearms and explosives, we provided him with a load of materials to replenish their stock. They also successfully established a Dead Letter Box (DLB) to store their materials in the Mamelodi area which they established as their base of operations. Most of their operations were designed to support community struggles. Very often, their targets were chosen to strengthen support for rent and consumer boycotts. Local government councillors were also frequently attacked. As a matter of policy, there was no loss of life. Over a period of two years, 12 operations were executed. At some point, Thava Pillay was drawn in from the Laudium unit to participate in some of the military operations of the unit. He was quickly put through his paces by Strike who trained him in small arms in the bushes surrounding Mamelodi.

Duma Nokwe Unit

The RPMC, consisting of Benny, Razia and Matthews, resolved of its own accord to adopt the title of Duma Nokwe Unit as the name of their structure. The agreement was that each member of the unit would assume responsibility for underground structures in their own areas which would then be coordinated at the regional level. The idea was that they would be able to draw strength and support from each other. To consolidate the unit, they had to be exposed to further training. It was my view that there was value in training the entire unit together as it would assist in the building of the team. The first part of this training took place sometime late in 1988.

Because of the tense security situation in Botswana, we decided to send them to Zimbabwe with the help of the MK regional command structures. The unit was first driven by car from Gaborone to Francistown. There, under cover of darkness, they crossed the border illegally at a point close to the Plumtree Border Gate. They were then picked up on the Zimbabwean side and taken to a safe house in Bulawayo. Later on, they made the journey to Harare where their training took place. The unit was trained in small arms, grenades and explosives, including the use of limpet mines.

While in Zimbabwe, the unit greatly benefited from their interaction with members of the NEC. They met with Thomas Nkobi, Steve Tshwete, Ronnie Kasrils and Lehlohonolo, the MK chief of operations. During this training, the unit was also introduced to Mike,[57] an MK commander who was later infiltrated into the country with his unit of two other MK comrades. Once inside the country, Mike then became a member of the Duma Nokwe Unit.

Unfortunately, the attachment of the MK unit to the RPMC did not work out well. The arrangement was short-lived and proved to be most disruptive to the RPMC's. The two MK combatants from Mike's unit who were infiltrated with him were arrested in circumstances that were never clear to us. What was clear however was that these arrests compromised Mike and this could have impacted on the RPMC itself. Accordingly, Mike was forced to retreat to Zimbabwe to avoid arrest.

The RPMC tried to recover from this by replacing Mike with Strike on the RPMC. This helped refocus the RPMC and under the leadership of the Duma Nokwe Unit, several other units were established, two of which were in Laudium. That said, the RPMC had limited success and not enough time to prove itself operationally.

The Thambi Naidoo Unit[58]

Soon after Razia's recruitment, she arranged for Nava to come out sometime in 1987 for a consultation. Nava was extraordinary and went to work immediately on his recruitment. He waited nearly seven years for this to happen and our meeting was something both of us hoped would take place sooner rather than later.

Nava came from a rich family history and tradition of struggle. He grew up in the shadow of his grandmother, Mrs Thayanagie Pillay, who fed the treason trialists when the trial was moved to Pretoria. Mrs Pillay's father, Thambi Naidoo, had been a close associate of Gandhi and steeped in the political struggles of the Indian Congress Movement. With this pedigree, Nava's commitment to the struggle was total and he proved this by the way in which he lived his life. He was a hard worker with a determination to succeed on the tasks given. He was also a natural organiser, and this stood him well in providing leadership to his generation of activists. Nava spent all his working life serving the community and developed an admirable expertise in local government matters which was respected well beyond Pretoria.

Nava's association with Razia was a natural fit. Both grew up in the struggle together and were critical to the political life of Laudium where they helped establish a range of civic structures. In fact, they were in the same class at school with Thava and organised the 1980 school boycott at Laudium High School in their matric year. The unit established with Razia and Nava was referred to as the Thambi Naidoo Unit. This unit reported through Razia to the Duma Nokwe RPMC.

The scope of work of the Thambi Naidoo Unit was to give political leadership to the community primarily working through the various structures of civil society. At the same time, the unit also operated as a propaganda unit. They secured a roneo machine and typewriter, and rented a back room to run their printing press and produce materials for distribution. The purpose of this was to ensure that we were able to establish an active physical presence of the ANC in the community. This was the first time that Laudium experienced this activity on such an organised and consistent basis. Politically, it was an important breakthrough.

Roy Naidoo Unit

While Razia served on the Duma Nokwe RPMC, in 1987 Nava established his own unit in Laudium called the Roy Naidoo Unit. He recruited Thava Pillay and Paresh Devchand, and once established, the entire unit came out for consultations to Botswana. I drew on the support of January Masilela (Che O'Gara) who assisted me in providing the political training and briefing for the unit. Over the next year, the unit came out as a team for one more consultation. This unit continued the political and propaganda work in Laudium started by Nava and Razia. Because of their efforts, they effectively managed to move the community through local struggles to hold more progressive positions. The unit also successfully managed to establish a unit that carried out political and security intelligence.

Mesina

Ndivhudzannyi Freddy Nephawe was one of the foremost activists of the north. He was instrumental in the formation of most of the key structures responsible for advancing the struggle against apartheid in the now Limpopo region. Humble and truly committed, he served in various organisations including the Sanco, Cosatu, the National Education Crisis Committee (NECC), the Azanian Students Organisation, United Democratic Front, and the SA Youth Congress. Freddy also helped to establish both the Congress of South African Students and the Congress of Traditional Leaders of South Africa.

The recruitment of Freddy in 1988 was a major step forward for us because of the leadership role that he played. Besides his political role, Freddy also provided critical support to our military efforts. At the time, the seemingly all-powerful Defence Force and its Bantustan appendage, the Venda Defence Force, believed they had the north of the country sealed. Freddy, however, managed to skilfully help organise the logistical support to bring in trained cadres, and take out recruits headed for training.

IX

Stepping Up – In Full Flight

I have always associated the period from the birth of Ruby in July 1987 to the end of 1989 as my most productive and successful years in the underground of the ANC. It was also a very challenging and exhausting time. It made me realise that progress would not come any other way. It was not until 1987 that I could honestly say that I felt as if I was beginning to make real progress in the underground and beginning to make a political contribution.

The operational environment in Gaborone was a different one to that which existed in the years after I arrived in 1979. The command structures were more stable and mature. The provision of ordinance and training was sophisticated and successful. We were now able to transport a full unit illegally across our borders with both Zimbabwe and South Africa for training or consultations without much fuss. We also changed our behaviour to be more security conscious, but without the paranoia. We were more vigilant now.

On 28 March 1988 we were again brutally reminded of the need to be vigilant. Naledi, the friend who I escaped with from Dukwe and a comrade who became the regional MK commander, was assassinated in an attack by SADF Special Forces. We were greatly angered by the callousness of their actions. Not satisfied with just killing him, they proceeded to burn his body and the house around him. A grim reminder that death was never far.

This is something that I had become more conscious of especially because I was no longer an individual. I was a family man with a young child in my house. I still shudder at the thought when I am reminded of just how terrifying it was for me to think of what I needed to do in the event of an attack. My options were rather limited. On the one hand I needed to make sure that we lived as normal a life as was possible. How else was I going to raise a family? On the other hand, this was a luxury and life I could ill-afford. I was a target and the increasing success we were beginning to experience made me increasingly so. This meant that my family too were targets and I knew that the apartheid security forces drew no distinction. They did not care. I am still not sure how we managed to cope with this constant threat.

By 1987 the Kabwe Machinery, which I was responsible for, had a firm foundation. It was a sound structure that I was able to build on. The machinery had started achieving a lot that I had hoped for. The machinery we established extended from Masina in the north-east of South Africa to Mafikeng in the North-West part of the country and stretching down to the Free State in the south where we were beginning to have a presence.

The greater Pretoria area shared a similar experience to that of Soweto. Pretoria also presented us with as major headache because of the high levels of infiltration. These challenges effectively remained with us until about 1983 when we were able to turn the tide and start making inroads. By 1987, we effectively managed to overcome this legacy and started building an effective political presence, particularly in the UDF structures and even impacting on most area committees. Once again, our underground cadres assumed full responsibility for all youth and student structures.

Of personal and emotional value to me was the impact that we began to make in Laudium after an absence of more than six years. Laudium now witnessed vibrant political activity as well as some military action. These were great victories. I was also pleased that we were beginning to see women involved in various units. Perhaps, the greatest excitement was the non-racial character of the Kabwe Machinery which now consisted of both an Area Politico-Military Committee and Regional

Politico-Military Committee.

By 1989, we had recorded significant progress in several other areas of operation. Paul Sefularo had been very active in the Mafikeng area stretching down to the Free State where he had recruited several comrades. We even had a presence in the coloured community of Riverlea in the Johannesburg area. However, it was in the greater Pretoria and Johannesburg areas, particularly Mamelodi, Attridgeville, Soshanguve, Laudium, Johannesburg Central, Lenasia and Soweto that the Kabwe Machinery was most effective. In these areas, we were able to provide leadership to most structures of the mass democratic movement, area committees, and youth and student structures. By now, the Ahmed Timol Unit had become a critical driver that was making a dramatic impact.

The Kabwe Machinery was by this time politically embedded in key centres of the mass democratic movement from Masina down south to the greater Pretoria and Johannesburg areas. Our operatives participated in key structures of the mass democratic movement. This meant that our political intelligence was accurate and timely. In fact, many of our cadres were also senior leaders in various organisations and therefore party to many of the decisions made.

Very uniquely, we were able to witness the interaction between three of the four pillars of struggle that marked the ANC's strategy. Our cadres were involved in the mass democratic movement, underground as well as the military structures in our area of operation. What emerged clearly in this period is that the messaging and language used became consistent across all democratic formations and resistance structures. A remarkable feature of this period of struggle is the ease with which our operatives who came from the student, youth and civic organisations were able to move from one sector or site of struggle to another with a great deal of ease because of the commonality of the messaging used.

There was unity in struggle and there were common demands across the different platforms. An interesting feature of this period was that many of the meetings of these different structures would often involve people from different underground units of the ANC talking to each other without knowing that they all belonged to the same machinery. Our presence in these structures made it easy to ensure that the political struggles were supported by armed propaganda where this was necessary. The Ahmed Timol Unit, for one, did this incredibly well.

Needless to say, the intelligence information we were receiving was the best it had ever been. It could not get much better. Not only were we able to know what was happening after the fact, but we were now also participating in what was to happen. We were often even assisting in drafting the speeches on public platforms. The importance of this is that our structures in the Forward Areas were now totally immersed in the work at home rather than the operational issues affecting us in Botswana or Lusaka. Even if we were located in Gaborone, we were making our presence felt at home in various communities.

We had also developed effective supply lines for both information and material. Our machinery was sufficiently well developed to allow me to engage in discussions with Rashid, who was now responsible for ordinance, and helped in various instances to move weapons inside the country. In one instance, there was a DLB of a significant size that was dropped off in the Northern Province which our ordinance structures were uncertain of. They wanted it to be cleared. Rashid asked if I had the capacity to take this over. I did and passed this over to the Ahmed Timol Unit. They were able to professionally lift this stash and used it to great effect in their operations. Other units too were now in a position to pick up material and to move it effectively without detection.

By the end of 1988 and 1989, the Machinery was quite mature, effective and had operational experience. There was definitely an operational confidence. If anything, I detected a measure of over-confidence among some. I have seen this in other units and cadres I interacted with. Cadres who thought nothing was a problem and they could attend to anything without much fuss. This is a measure of confidence, or even arrogance, which did concern me a bit. But, that says more of my own character than anything else. I have always been of the view that a bit of self-doubt is a healthy thing because it forces one to be more alert and careful. Never be too sure because one could easily become careless.

While there was a great deal to boast about, we were still not in a position to promote the infiltration of trained MK cadres into the country on a significant scale. Even though it was now easier to move information and material, this was not the case with moving people in the numbers sufficient enough to make a difference. I kept telling myself that it was only a matter of time before this could take place.

The pace at which the Kabwe Machinery was growing and its operational activity increasing, presented another emerging weakness. Despite the fantastic support I got from the other structures in the RPMC, Special Ops and even Lusaka, it was not going to be possible to sustain and support the Machinery by myself. At some point this was going to have to change. In particular, servicing the Machinery now required an increasing number of consultations and engagements with units that committed more of my time than I had. Naturally, this was not good for my family life. They suffered immensely because of my absence. I too, would suffer because these were formative years in our family life.

X

Finding a Political Solution

As young soldiers we had dreams of marching through the streets of Pretoria with our AKs slung over our shoulders as we seized power. We wished for this moment to be as dramatic as the entry of the Cuban revolutionaries in Havana when they liberated their country. But, these dreams needed to be tempered by some political and historical realities which I paid little attention to. I was too preoccupied by what I was busy with and did not properly see the big picture.

The visit by the ANC leadership to Vietnam in October 1978 highlighted a number of realities, one of which was that ours was a political struggle and not a military one. No matter how important our armed struggle was, it was not going to be won on the military battlefield. Since the Second World War, with few exceptions every liberation struggle fought ended around the negotiating table no matter how long the military struggle was fought. This was a reality that the ANC was going to have to understand. It was definitely the way in which African countries gained their freedom. We learnt this from Algeria and later other countries too. This lesson became even clearer after the liberation of Mozambique and Angola was negotiated in 1975 and Zimbabwe which gained its independence in 1980 after the Lancaster House Talks.

A year after the formation of the UDF in 1983, a meeting took place in August 1984 between H.W. van der Merwe from the Centre for Inter-Group Studies at the University of Cape Town and the ANC exploring the possibility of dialogue between the South African government and the ANC.[59] There was some seriousness in this initiative because it was followed up several times before the end of 1984. Over the next six years, nearly 150 meetings took place between the ANC and various formations, including opposition political parties in South Africa and other interests representing the apartheid government.

There was obviously a momentum being generated for a negotiated settlement. Tambo was wise to this and once again proved to be a master strategist. He responded in several ways with the objective of ensuring that the ANC was placed in the best possible position to deal with a new terrain of struggle.

At the level of our underground structures, Operation Vula was established for purposes of ensuring that leaders of the ANC had an effective presence inside the country.

On the legal and constitutional front, Zola Skweyiya was instructed in 1985 to set up the ANC legal and constitutional committee. Others in this committee were Kader Asmal, Frene Ginwala, Penuel Maduna, Matthews Phosa, Bridgette Mabandla and Albie Sachs. Should negotiations take place, the ANC would be in the strongest possible position to engage in this new terrain of struggle.

On yet another front, the approach adopted by the ANC would need the support of the Organisation of African Unity (OAU) and international community. Thus, began an intensive lobby of the frontline states. It was during this lobbying that Tambo's health took a turn for the worse and he suffered a stroke. Nevertheless, he persisted and managed to get the Harare Declaration passed by the OAU on 21 August 1989. This document was later pursued in the UN General Assembly which also adopted a version of this.

It is worth noting that the Harare Declaration expresses its support for negotiations in its statement of principles, which states as follows: -

- We believe that a conjuncture of circumstances exists which, if there is a demonstrable readiness on the part of the Pretoria regime to engage in negotiations genuinely and seriously, could create

the possibility to end apartheid through negotiations. Such an eventuality would be an expression of the long-standing preference of the people of South Africa to arrive at a political settlement.
- We would therefore encourage the people of South Africa, as part of their overall struggle, to get together to negotiate an end to the apartheid system and agree on all the measures that are necessary to transform their country into a non-racial democracy. We support the position held by the majority of the people of South Africa that these objectives and not the amendment or reform of the apartheid system, should be the aims of the negotiations.

The declaration then proceeds to define the key constitutional principles that the negotiations should relate to. It also demands that before any negotiations take place, that the *necessary climate for negotiations be created* and then defines the guidelines for the process of negotiations. The adoption of this declaration took place against the backdrop of the biggest battle (Cuito Cuanavale 1987–88) on African soil since the Second World War. The battle was one of the turning points in Southern African history.

Angolan government troops, the Armed Forces for the Liberation of Angola (FAPLA), in an attempt to defeat UNITA (the National Union for the Total Independence of Angola) fighters in 1987, advanced deep into the south-eastern parts of Angola from Cuito Cuanavale to attack them. The South African Defence Force (SADF), whose primary objective was to protect UNITA and prevent the South West African People's Organization (SWAPO) from using the region to launch attacks into Namibia, intervened on UNITA's behalf. The Cuban forces then intervened on the side of the Angolans. The South African troops suffered serious losses resulting in their confidence and morale being shaken. It also made them realise that even if they had a powerful army, it would not be sufficient to keep them in power for too long. The battle eventually led to the withdrawal of the South African, ANC and Cuban presence in Angola, and to the Independence of Namibia in November 1989.

With the independence of Namibia and the Harare Declaration, it was clear that negotiations were on the agenda and the ANC leadership wanted to deal with this very carefully. Had the ANC leadership raised the profile of this possibility in any measure, it would have only served to distract or demoralise those of us in the trenches.

XI

Closing of a Chapter

The closing years of the 1980s brought to an end one of the most vibrant chapters of our struggle. There were a number of critical developments that marked this closure. It was also evident that many of our cadres and structures were beginning to take huge strain. This is hardly surprising because by this time, most of these cadres had given the prime of their youth to the struggle.

During 1988 and 1989, Mandla, Azhar and Dipak were detained. Mandla and Azhar were detained for work related to their involvement in structures of the mass democratic movement. Dipak was arrested in January 1988 distributing propaganda materials, amongst which was the ANC January 8th statement. Ephraim Nkwe was also distracted by personal and health matters.

During this period, it was also noticeable that some of our units were being distracted. It only became evident much later that some cadres in these units were being called upon to perform tasks related to Operation Vula. These tasks included the movement of some of their weapons and support for their communications.

Then, in December 1989, disaster struck and both Prakash and Yusuf, who were involved in an operation, paid the ultimate sacrifice.

Ahmed Timol Unit

During 1988, the Ahmed Timol Unit recorded its greatest success with more than 30 successful operations. They had clearly found their confidence and were consistent. Their operations were spread over a wide demographic area, so it was clearly not possible for enemy intelligence to figure out where the unit operated from, or even if it was one or more units that were operating. Their operations were beginning to be noticed and respected by regional and national commanders in MK.

When things were slow on the MK front I heard comrades in the regional command ask if the Ahmed Timol Unit could not do something to keep the spirits up. The benefit of armed propaganda was becoming obvious. Avoiding direct combat and conflict with the enemy meant that we were defining the battlefield and dictating the rules. All the fire power, numbers and resources that the apartheid army had was of no value. We were scoring victories against them without incurring any losses. From an efficiency point of view, the Ahmed Timol Unit was one of the most efficient, effective, consistent units that we had.

We were now ready to move things a notch further. The Ahmed Timol Unit's deployment strategy was clearly working and effective. However, we could now afford to get bolder and undertake bigger projects. The unit too was beginning to insist on getting involved in more daring and ambitious projects. They started reconnoitring the Lenz Military Base and had considered different options. We had also started talking about the value of attacking troops being carried to and from the base, even considering the possibility of an ambush.

From the reconnaissance the unit carried out, they discovered that soldiers in an armed personnel carrier regularly followed a particular route and stopped at a bakery. We went through the sketch of the targets and possible operations and concluded that it was a project that we could undertake with minimal risk and maximum impact. There were two ways in which to approach the operation. The troops had a routine. We could either plant a limpet on the troop carrier when it stopped there or rig an explosive device along the road as the carrier was returning to the base. An operation of this nature in the greater Johannesburg area would have had enormous value. The unit was ready and had my full support for an operation of this nature.

Closing of a Chapter

It was standard operating procedure that the commander of the Ahmed Timol Unit met every Thursday with Shan as their commander in the Ahmed Kathrada APMC. This operation was discussed with Shan in detail. What I was not aware of was that the project was vetoed by Shan. The reason was that Shan was not yet ready to embark upon a project that would take human life, even if it were that of the enemy.

It was clear that we were now in a position to graduate the unit from armed propaganda to hitting the enemy directly. This was a bold and audacious prospect but was the unit ready for it? We had started considering this in 1988 and concluded that more comprehensive training was necessary for the unit. I therefore started consultations with comrades in the regional command as well as Chris and T-Man from Special Ops about how we could go about providing this training.

There was a combination of two possible options; they could do their training in either Angola or in one of the other countries such as the Soviet Union, German Democratic Republic or Cuba where we sent cadres for specialist training. The point about this was that the training would last for a couple of months at least. Once we had a sense of what our options were, these were discussed with Shan as commander of the Ahmed Kathrada APMC and Prakash in his capacity as commander of the Ahmed Timol Unit.

We decided to do this over the festive season as it would provide for a plausible legend explaining the absence of the comrades for a significant period of time. We had planned for this and even arranged for each of the members of the unit to prepare postcards which would be posted at different times from Cape Town to show that they were on holiday. When the unit finally arrived in Botswana, Yusuf was not with them. Apparently, he had domestic matters that were important and urgent enough for him to be excused. This meant that Prakash and Jameel had to continue with their training without him. We arranged for new travel documents bearing pseudonyms. In the absence of Prakash and Jameel, Yusuf proceeded to carry out some operations on his own. This was important as it would then give the impression to anyone observing that the unit was still operational.

Prakash and Jameel were trained in Moscow and Angola. They

did intensive MCW training as well as an advanced military course for commanders which lasted for three months. They returned rather excited about their experiences and were raring to go back into the field. They returned in January 1989 and continued from where they had left off.

During this last year of the Ahmed Timol Unit's illustrious history, there were several events and developments that were of significance. Yusuf married Farhana and they became parents soon after. I have no doubt that these milestones in his life would have given him, as it did me, a new perspective and meaning in life.

On 15 October 1989, Ahmed Kathrada was released together with Andrew Mlangeni, Walter Sisulu, Raymond Mhlaba and Elias Motsoaledi. Demonstrating the leadership responsibilities of the Ahmed Kathrada APMC, it was decided that since Ahmed Kathrada was released into their area, the APMC would naturally also assume direct responsibility for his security. Without hesitation, the Ahmed Timol Unit immediately went into action and provided Ahmed Kathrada with 24-hour armed protection in the most discreet of manners. This was not the easiest of tasks, especially given his profile and hectic schedule. Nevertheless, they carried out this function with distinction.

As a reflection of the maturity of the Machinery, the comrades in our Soweto unit under the leadership of Brian and Pule, took a similar decision to provide protection to the leaders based in Soweto.

In the last couple of months before the end of 1989, there were important debates and discussions that reflected the quality of the leadership that was emerging. Most prominent amongst these was a discussion in the Ahmed Kathrada APMC as to the number of attacks that were being planned in a single operation. In fact, when the planning of the Ahmed Timol Unit's last operation was discussed, a view was offered that it may not be wise to plan several attacks together. The APMC was taking its responsibilities seriously and considering the nature of their operations carefully. They were extremely level-headed and gave serious thought to what they were doing.

Prakash was the type of commander that took his leadership responsibilities extremely seriously. Even if he had a mischievous streak in him, there was a serious side which few knew. This was evident when dealing with matters of internal discipline. While Prakash had discussed these matters with Shan because he was being transparent, he was adamant that matters of this nature were his to take care of. I noticed this characteristic in him when he returned from training. Apparently, Prakash and Jameel had a most unfortunate experience with some of the cadres they were in training with. Both of them decided that they were not going to allow this experience to get them down. The important thing was that Prakash took charge and decided the matter should be resolved without escalating it or informing me about it. That was the nature of Prakash.

On the evening of 11 December 1989, less than two months short of the unbanning of the ANC and the release of Madiba, the Ahmed Timol Unit undertook their last operation. The intended target was the Hillbrow Police Barracks. It was a Monday night and after placing their limpet mine, they thought better of it because there was a risk of life being lost. The unit then decided to recover the limpet mine and proceeded to a secondary target which was at Park Station. Here, they hoped to place the charges on the rail carriages. This was in support of a strike by the South African Railways and Harbour Union.

While Jameel stood guard above the bridge at Park Station, Prakash and Yusuf proceeded to where the rail carriages were parked in the station. They did not make it. The limpet, which was already primed after it was placed at the police barracks and with the detonator which was evidently still in place, prematurely detonated resulting in the loss of both cadres.[60] As per his training, Jameel was forced to retreat and make his way back to base in Lenasia. This must have been the most difficult journey that he has ever had to make.

When none of the unit members reported back, the Ahmed Kathrada APMC had by early morning started searching for them. Instinct and good judgement led Jeets to immediately make a call to alert me of a possible problem. It was however only when they heard the early morning news broadcast on the radio about an explosion that they then realised what had happened. They reported this to me immediately upon hearing the news.

Each year, ever since, each of us who were responsible for the Ahmed Timol Unit will automatically replay these events in our minds and repeatedly suffer the same anguish and pain we felt on that day. This is an anniversary that will continue to haunt us for the rest of our lives. When we got involved in the struggle, we knew well that there were risks involved. We were aware that we may have to make the ultimate sacrifice. However, talking about it is easier than having to experience it. There is no training that could prepare us to deal with this terrible and devastating tragedy. The pain will always be there and the only thing that happens is that we try to find better ways in which to manage it. Nothing we say or do can rationalise this loss or make the pain any lighter. This is something that each of us have to live with.

Jameel was naturally severely traumatised by the tragedy and it was thought best to withdraw him. He was brought to Gaborone where I debriefed him and arranged for his onward transfer to Lusaka and the Soviet Union where it was thought best that he be sent for counselling. A few months later though Jameel returned and asked to go back home where he was received by Shamim and Jeets who took care of him. After a brief period, Jameel felt confident enough to resume his underground work. Jameel also established a further unit after recruiting Mohammed Adam and Brandon Morgan, on the recommendation of Shan.

The entire experience and history of the Ahmed Timol Unit was marked by and took place between the birth of my two children – Ruby who was born in July 1987 and my son, who was born in September 1990. It was therefore natural that he was named as a celebration of the life of Yusuf Akhalwaya and in his memory.

Ruby

As dangerous and abnormal as exile was in Gabarone, this is where my family home was located. Ruby brought us a great deal of joy, I had a flourishing legal career, and the years between 1986 and 1990 was also the time when I was most successful in my underground world. Like most new parents, Ruby was the centre of our lives and much of our family time revolved around her schedule.

The security situation imposed very restrictive conditions on us. Few ANC people came home and our circle of friends was limited. I also worked long hours. Despite this, Ruby brought a special kind of energy to our home. Bright, bubbly and eager to learn and read, my time with Ruby was therapeutic because it came at the end of a full day at the office and the beginning of my evening meetings in the underground. Ruby gave me focus and constantly reminded me of why we needed to succeed at our efforts to liberate our country.

Freedom at last

On 2 February 1990, the last apartheid President, F.W. de Klerk, summoned sufficient courage to deliver a speech at the opening session of the Parliament of South Africa announcing sweeping reforms that marked the beginning of the negotiated transition from apartheid to a constitutional democracy. De Klerk promised the unbanning of the ANC and other anti-apartheid organisations, the release of political prisoners including Nelson Mandela, the end of the state of emergency, and a moratorium on the death penalty.[61]

On 11 February 1990, I sat in our lounge in Gaborone, totally transfixed to the television as millions of people all over the world were, to observe the seemingly impossible – the release of Nelson Mandela. This was obviously the beginning of the end of a chapter in our lives. All that we knew had suddenly changed. This was the point of no return. Needless to say, the senselessness of the tragic deaths of Prakash and Yusuf, which came two months before the release of Nelson Mandela, was not lost on any of us.

I had so many questions about the way forward, but no one was available to answer these. The PMC did not offer any guidance. It was as if the ANC was taken completely by surprise and did not know how to respond. There was no leadership. With the unbanning of the ANC and the release of Madiba, my family wanted to know when I would be coming home. A dream my father thought impossible had just come true. To demonstrate his seriousness, my father came along with an application form for a new passport which he made me complete before returning home.

I had my doubts. Going home would be a drastic action. I was uncertain as to what the risks were. Until then I was a target for assassination. What changed? Would my return home place any of my units at risk? What permission would I need to make the journey home? Besides, I had a well-paying job, was a home owner and my family were settled. What was I was going to do back home? These questions, as daunting as they were, were overshadowed by the excitement of the prospect of going home.

The year 1990 was momentous for another reason. I was blessed with my second child, a son, at the beginning of September 1990. Yusuf was born in the UK and brought me a great deal of joy. Fortunately for me, I was able to assume greater responsibility for feeding and attending to his needs as a baby than with Ruby. This was a real blessing.

I could not believe it when the South African government issued my passport. With this in hand, there was no logical reason not to go home. What a bizarre moment it was for me. The single most important objective over the past 11 years was to get back home. I was stripped of my birthright and forced into exile. I could now return home but hesitated. A thousand different conflicting thoughts crossed my mind as I struggled to make sense of this new reality. The biggest challenge was uncertainty. I quickly put this aside and immediately started consulting some of the leaders of the Kabwe Machinery and informed them of my intention to return. The idea of returning home was more than overwhelming. I was however concerned that the comrades at home may fear that I would be compromising their security if I returned. Eleven years before, this was the reason that I left home. It was a relief to learn that I had their support.

The first step was to make arrangements to cross the border legally for the first time since leaving in September 1979. Because I was uncertain as to whether it would be safe, I decided not to let anyone know. The first trip was going to be a reconnaissance mission. I did not want to travel alone and made arrangements with Jeets to pick me up at the Ramatlabama border gate, which is 25 km north of Mafikeng.

I crossed with no fuss at all. No questions were asked. My first trip back home was incredible. After spending a couple of days with Jeets and Shamim in Lenasia, they dropped me off at my parents' home. I arrived without announcement. They were totally shocked to see me. There were tears of joy all round. A dream they had had materialised. The strange thing though was that shortly after returning home, it was such a natural thing that I almost forgot that I had been away for such a long time. After spending time with the family, I went on to meet with a number of comrades from different units.

I returned to Gaborone with a new resolve. There was no doubt in my mind that I had to get back home. From this point on that was all that was on my mind. I focused all my energies on it. A new beginning beckoned.

This meant that I would need to sell my house, which I loved, resign from the law firm and give up a successful and promising career in law, look for a new job and find a new home for the family. I still did not know what I was going to do with my life. What was my role going to be? Would the ANC deploy me? How would I earn a living? These and many other questions began to loom large. But I was not daunted, I was going home. Over the next few months, I would make several trips back home to plan my return and spend time with the family.

My father offered to have us stay with him. Barbara and I thought differently and felt that I had to establish our own home. My father relented and offered to help me buy a home. As with Zimbabwe, the political transition brought with it a great deal of uncertainty in the property market and houses could be bought reasonably cheaply. Besides, we were no longer restricted to live in terms of the Group Areas Act. While the law was not yet repealed, it was not enforced. This meant that I could buy a home anywhere I wanted to. We found the Midrand area to be most convenient because it was on the highway between Johannesburg and Pretoria and with easy access to the airport if need be. During these trips home I also took time to continue meeting my units on the ground.

The most memorable of these was my meeting with Freddy

in Masina. Freddy, a down-to-earth cadre with no ambitions, was a committed activist with significant respect in his area. Freddy undertook each of his tasks most diligently and you could always rely on him. This was unfortunately also the last time I met with Freddy because he soon succumbed to cancer leading to his untimely demise. We lost a great cadre in him.

On one of my trips back home, I got to meet Barbara Hogan. This was the first time that I got to see her since 1979 when she was a passenger in my car on our way back from a meeting with Marius Schoon. This was a fortuitous meeting because when she discovered that I was returning from exile immediately insisted that I join them in the ANC's interim Pretoria, Witwatersrand, Vereeniging (PWV) regional office that was required to rebuild the ANC in the country. How could I refuse? This answered the question as to what I was going to do when I returned home. This was indeed a new beginning.

XII

Kabwe Machinery's Closure

According to ANC hierarchy, I reported through the RPMC in Botswana through the IPRD[62] to the PMC, which was accountable to the NEC. When the ANC was unbanned, no attempt was made to call for reports from the leadership in the Forward Areas to account for the units, people, materials and work undertaken. Had this been done, there would be an official and accurate record of the organisation's strength on the ground in the country.

Instead, the ANC focused on matters regarded to be of greater importance, the most pressing imperative being the establishment of its branches, the first legal structures. No consultations were undertaken with the underground structures. It was as if they did not exist. The branches were to be new structures, rather than a continuation of the existing structures of the ANC.

The ANC started on a clean slate with the organisation almost reinventing itself. Underground operatives became ordinary members without any status. To their credit, they immediately refocused their energy to the political struggles of the day, with some even elected to government and executive functions.

MK cadres, however, were recognised through a legal process to integrate members of non-statutory forces. Underground operatives such as those of the Kabwe Machinery, which was one of the most successful ANC machineries in the country, were ignored. Throughout its existence, none of the Machinery's more than 50 operatives were arrested or detained for their ANC activities. Our structures were never compromised in any way. They provided political leadership in their areas and managed to successively execute more than 70 military operations with no civilian casualties. Armed operations were always in support of specific political struggles or campaigns. Even Operation Vula relied on the capabilities of units and operatives from this machinery.

XIII

My Homecoming

The return home

My entire focus in life had suddenly changed. It was indeed yet again a new beginning and I became consumed by the move back to South Africa. Once the house in Midrand was bought, I returned home on 1 April 1991 to prepare for the family's homecoming.

The ANC meanwhile focused its energies on the establishment of its legal branches. To guide this process, they established interim regional leadership structures to help establish the branches that would in turn elect its regional leadership. This would then allow for the election of the ANC's national leadership.

As soon as I set up home and even before I could get the family settled, I started work as one of the ANC's six PWV regional coordinators. Our function was to facilitate the establishment of the ANC's branches. This meant a daily trip from Midrand to the Johannesburg city centre where our offices were located, very different from the two-minute drive I had in Gaborone. It took some getting used to driving along a busy highway with traffic jams. Another difference that I was going to have to get used to was the drop in salary. As a senior attorney, I had been earning approximately R13,000 a month with decent gratuity. Working for the ANC, I earned R1750 per month.

Moving our family home was neither quick nor easy. Much of this burden fell onto Barbara's shoulders who also had to take care of four-year-old Ruby and Yusuf at barely a year. While this was a very exciting time for me, it was a daunting experience for Barbara who now had to cope with yet another major change in our lives.

This is also when we began to notice Yusuf's extreme hyperactivity. It quickly became evident that he was allergic to food colours and preservatives, and had to avoid sugars. I remember well those anxious moment as we consulted different doctors to make sense of the diagnosis of Yusuf's condition. It took a while before it was confirmed that it was Asperger's Syndrome, which is a high-functioning autistic condition. Unfortunately, the medical profession was still coming to grips with Asperger's as it was not yet properly understood. This also meant that the management of Asperger's by medical practitioners was found wanting.

I was determined to remain politically active in Laudium. Yogesh was the first ANC branch chairperson and Nava the secretary in Laudium. I was asked to become the chairperson, which forced me to very quickly familiarise myself with the day-to-day politics of the area. The branch was extremely vibrant with a mix of younger activists and stalwarts. Nava was an excellent organiser and well-grounded in the issues of the day. He was a fantastic coach to expertly guide me through nuances of the politics of the community. Laudium was a very conservative community and would need to be convinced to support the ANC. Being an activist at the local level and an organiser at the regional level meant that I had less time to focus on my personal and family life.

There was however a strange irony in the establishment of an ANC branch in an area like Laudium, which had never before had a legal ANC structure. While the establishment of the first ANC branch was a big step forward, it came at a time when this usually very conservative community was beginning to develop a political identity and profile that was part of a broader non-racial Pretoria. The emergence of this new culture in Laudium came with the involvement of its structures of civil society in a broader Pretoria-based non-racial political activity. Ironically, a branch in Laudium therefore had the effect of re-racialising political activity.[63] By establishing a branch in Laudium, political activities were now focusing on the community itself which was in the main of Indian origin instead of maintaining a focus on the broader Pretoria in a non-racial manner. ANC branches were taking the shape of racially and ethnically divided communities instead of breaking these down.

Building ANC structures

Establishing the ANC's PWV region was not easy. The interim leadership was led by Tokyo Sexwale, Winnie Mandela, Barbara Hogan, Paul Mashatile amongst others. The PWV region was a hive of activity, political strife and uncertainty, and we were starting at ground zero. Our experience was in the underground and mass democratic movement structures and not with legal party-political structures. The structures that we were establishing were also different from that of civil society and the MDM. The environment was difficult. In many places, it was hostile and unsafe. There were many no-go areas and a lot of uncertainty and yet many expectations and pressure.

There was a natural push for membership numbers. This was a fundamental shift because membership numbers now depended on the payment of a minimum fee of R12 rather than a mere adherence and belief in a political programme. In the past, we recruited people into the organisation. Now, we enrolled members on the purchase of a membership card.

As a regional coordinator, I had two major tasks: to establish ANC branches in each area and facilitate elections at both branch and regional levels. To achieve this, each regional coordinator was required to attend branch meetings and oversee the formal processes of establishing their executive structures. At these meetings, we also provided reports on regional and national developments, monitored the election of office bearers and provided guidance to the newly established structures. We needed to fill the legal space afforded to us by the changed political conditions. At this stage, there was no strategy to attend to the political education of the branch members. This meant that we were attending to the formal aspects of the ANC's structures without attending to the political dimension.

However, while the ANC was now a legal organisation, we still had to deal with the challenges we faced when we were banned. Our cadres were not safe. Political assassinations and no-go areas were all too common. The playing field was not level. The dreaded 'third force' was active, faceless and very dangerous. There was hardly a township branch that was free from violence.

I recall my visit one evening to Kagiso, facilitating the establishment of the branch structure. Close to the venue and as I turned the last corner, I found a man standing in the middle of the road firing his revolver at someone who was running in the direction from where my car was coming. The person fleeing the scene was spotted firing his weapon into the ANC offices. The officials retaliated. This incident shook me up. Fortunately, no one was hurt but it did give me an understanding of the difficult conditions under which the ANC had to establish legal structures.

Nevertheless, we succeeded in establishing our branches and electing our first regional structures. With branches and regions properly in place, it was now time to elect our national leadership. My attendance of the ANC's 1991 national conference, held in Westville Durban, was a major highlight. The conference was a dramatic affair, the atmosphere exciting. The ANC elected its first leadership in more than 30 years. O.R. Tambo was made chairperson – a new post to honour him for his leadership of the ANC during the organisation's darkest hours and yet to respect his deteriorating health after his stroke in 1989. Nelson Mandela was unanimously elected president and Thabo Mbeki his deputy. Cyril Ramaphosa, who was until then secretary-general of the NUM, was elected secretary-general and Jacob Zuma his deputy.

On 13 November 1991, Madiba announced that the first multi-party constitutional talks would start. Scheduled to officially take place at the World Trade Centre in Kempton Park, this set off a series of preparatory negotiations between the various political parties, also at the same venue. I was approached by the Transvaal Indian Congress (TIC) to join their delegation. I was really excited because it meant that

I was now also able to participate in discussions that would affect the shape of a future democratic South Africa.

Working for the ANC's regional office and participating in the pre-negotiations discussions in Kempton Park, while still being responsible for the Laudium branch of the ANC, was very taxing on my time and gave me little time to spend with the family. By this time, Ruby was registered at a Montessori school and Yusuf was an extremely active toddler. It was also at this time that my father's health took a turn for the worse with the onset of kidney failure. Fortunately for me, my main task of helping the PWV regional office to establish its branches and get the regional leadership elected was attended to.

While we all threw our energies into the establishment of the ANC's branches and regions, little thought was given to the type of organisation that we were building. We became so engrossed in this effort that we no longer considered who became members. A R12 fee was all that was needed to become a member. No consideration was given to the politics of the person. We wanted the numbers and this is what we got. This also made the ANC extremely vulnerable because it did not take long for opportunists to recognise the value of holding ANC membership.

CODESA I

The first plenary session of the Convention for a Democratic South Africa (CODESA) began on 21 December 1991 at the World Trade Centre in Johannesburg, with 228 delegates from 19 political parties attending and pledging their commitment to negotiations by signing the declaration of intent. While most parties were excited at participating, the Pan Africanist Congress (PAC), AZAPO and the Conservative Party boycotted the event.

A management committee of all parties was established to supervise the CODESA process, supported by a daily management committee and a secretariat. While the management committee was chaired by Pravin Gordhan, Mac Maharaj and Fanie van der Merwe, the director general of the Department of Constitutional Development Services, headed the secretariat. Each of these individuals set themselves apart as leaders in the process of negotiations and earned the respect of all. Pravin proved to be an extremely astute chairperson who masterfully managed extremely difficult processes. As for Mac and Fanie, this was a duo that became a critical channel for resolving difficult problems and making sure that the communications between the ANC and the government were unfettered.

The major outcome of CODESA I was the creation of five working groups to deal with specific issues. Working Group 1 was responsible for the creation of an environment for free political participation and the role of the international community. Working Group 2 dealt with constitutional principles and the constitution-making body. Working Group 3 focused on interim government. Working Group 4 considered the future of the homelands. Working Group 5 was given the task of addressing the time frames and responsibility to implement the decisions taken at CODESA I.

On 20 January 1992, the working groups started their work and scheduled meetings twice a week. Each group had almost 80 people, making a negotiated compromise on the various issues quite difficult. Only Working Group 3 produced a compromise that was used in the later negotiating processes. It was also the only group that made use of a technical committee of experts. One of the experts in this Technical committee was Arthur Chaskalson, who very quickly stood out for the masterful manner in which he was able to construct constitutional solutions responding to the debates taking place.

I continued as a delegate of the TIC. There was something grand about holding the negotiations at the World Trade Centre, a sprawling complex with more than enough space and a maze of corridors leading to meeting rooms of many different sizes. The environment helped lend a sense of seriousness to the meetings and I enjoyed my experience here because it placed me at the centre where the future of South Africa was being shaped.

The next plenary session, referred to as CODESA II, was scheduled for March 1992. At this time, I was working with my parents in their shop, giving me an opportunity to spend time with them. Observing De Klerk's call and the eventual holding of the all-white referendum became exciting talking points with my father, who had strong political views. De Klerk was under real pressure after CODESA I. His ruling National Party lost three by-elections to the Conservative Party and was uncertain of the support of white people. He had something to prove and wanted to demonstrate the support he still enjoyed amongst whites for the process of change. He succeeded with this in the referendum called for on 17 March 1992.

Before I was able to get settled in my father's shop, I got a call from Mac Maharaj. He asked if I was interested in applying for the post of national coordinator of the ANC's Negotiations Commission. This was clearly an exciting prospect because it would allow me to be at the centre of the ANC's negotiations effort. Even more exciting was the idea that I could be part of the process that was going to shape the future of the country. This was hardly something I could refuse.

I was so excited that I did not give a thought to the possible impact of this commitment on my young family. I did this before in exile. Without thinking much about it, I applied for the job and started work at the ANC's Negotiations Commission in April 1992.

The ANC's Negotiations Commission

The ANC's 48th National Conference of July 1991 mandated the newly elected NEC 'to take immediate steps to ensure that a comprehensive and representative team comprising all chief negotiators, working groups and researchers, which shall function under the supervision and direction of the NEC, is established. The NEC shall ensure that in all such organs and structures there is adequate and fair participation of women.'

Based on this resolution, the NWC established the Negotiations Commission as a sub-committee on 16 August 1991 with the mandate to direct and manage the ANC's constitutional negotiations. The Negotiations Commission was established with three office bearers.

The chairperson of the commission was the secretary-general of the ANC, Cyril Ramaphosa, while the deputy secretary-general, Jacob Zuma, became the deputy chairperson and Vali Moosa the secretary. The six office-bearers of the ANC were also ex-officio members. In addition, the NWC also appointed Joe Slovo, Joel Netshitenzhe, Thabo Mbeki, Mac Maharaj, Penuell Maduna, Mathews Phosa, Zola Skweyiya, Joe Modise, Joe Nhlanhla, Barbara Masekela, and Baleka Mbete as additional members. The commission reported to the NWC and NEC.

XIV

Negotiating Peace

The Negotiations Commission operated out of the ANC's headquarters at Shell House, which was the most exciting place for a political animal like me to be because it was at the centre of developments that were fast unfolding and the Negotiations Commission was a big part of this.

Managing the ANC's Negotiations Commission

To deliver on its mandate, the commission regularly consulted key stakeholders and role players, engaged experts to advise and help develop negotiating positions which was usually done after considerable debate. As national coordinator, I was responsible for the administration of the commission and all its workings.

This was one of the best jobs in the country to have had at the time. It was a place of great learning and the best exposure I could possibly get. I got to work with some of South Africa's greatest political thinkers, leaders and constitutional experts who shaped the future of our country. I was privy to conversations and discussions which allowed me to understand the fears and concerns of not only each of the political parties, but their leaders too.

My team of administrators consisted of four people. The opposing side – the administration supporting government – was 90-strong, with virtually unlimited resources. Despite this, the negotiating team was never left wanting, with documentation always well organised and preparations meticulous.

Part of my function was to help prepare agendas, put together working documents, issue the invitations and organise the venues for the commission's meetings. I often thought of my job as one that allowed me as an unelected official to convene meetings at which the top six office-bearers of the ANC would attend when available. I especially enjoyed those meetings that Madiba and Sisulu attended. They were always elegantly dressed and prompt, if not early, and brought a sense of decorum to these gatherings. Madiba always made a point of walking to each member of the Commission and greeting them warmly. True to legend, he had a great memory and made a point of remembering names. I will never forget my second meeting with him two weeks after I was first introduced. He greeted me by name as if we knew each other for a very long time. He made me feel very special.

The Top 6 were always very much aware of the weight of their comments and views, but never took advantage of this. They preferred to listen and take studious notes rather than actively participate. I will always remember a meeting towards the end of 1993, when we were discussing electoral matters. Madiba waited for all to speak before he asked for permission to make a point. In carefully measured terms, he paid tribute to the contribution made by the youth, sacrificing their education, and often their lives, for the struggle. He argued that they demonstrated commitment and a maturity that deserved acknowledgement, which could be done by lowering the voting age to below 18. He suggested 16. It was his view that we should start consultations with stakeholders including the religious community to gain their support for this argument. While there was no contest to the merits of his argument, it was not pursued. Looking back, and considering our increasingly discontented youth, I regret that the wisdom of Madiba's arguments was not better understood.

Crafting our peace

While the mandate of the Negotiations Commission was to direct and manage the ANC's constitutional negotiations, the final objective was the election of a democratically constituted body that would draft South Africa's constitution. A precondition to this, however, was first to negotiate a peaceful settlement. The commission therefore became that forum in which South Africa's peace had to be crafted.

In typical ANC style, it involved continuous debates that were usually very robust and animated. We were gifted with some of the finest intellects, who were also great orators, and did not hesitate to show it. Over a period of two years, between April 1992 and the elections in April 1994, the commission organised or took part in more than 200 meetings ranging from internal discussions, consultations of various kinds, and bilateral and multilateral negotiations with different parties. The peace that South Africa enjoys today was engineered and crafted in these meetings.

I had the great fortune to be the only witness (as opposed to being a participant) of this most amazing part of our history. Unfortunately, the only record of these meetings was a journal, which I put together in the form of minutes, in 21 notebooks to assist me in managing the outcomes and following things up.[64] On the very odd occasion, I also had the good sense to take some photographs.

I will never forget some of these experiences. One of my very first bilateral meetings with the apartheid government was an encounter with the most senior commanders of the SADF. The meeting took place at a hotel close to the airport in Johannesburg. This was the first time that I came face to face with some of the very people who were responsible for authorising the attacks on us and the assassination of many of my friends and comrades. The meeting was cordial, but the tension was very real.

The focus of the ANC in these meetings was for the realisation of a non-racial democracy for South Africa, which however was not the approach of the National Party and organs of the apartheid state. The security forces wanted immunity and to keep their positions; so did the public servants. As for the NP politicians, all they focused on was the rights and interests of the constituency they served – the white minority.

The ANC could not ignore the past when considering the future, but could also not consider only the future of any specific constituency. They had to consider the interests of all the people of South Africa. The debates we had never failed to excite. There was sincerity and honesty in the arguments put forward. Here, I also witnessed the mastery of people like Cyril, Slovo, Mac and Thabo in dealing with very difficult issues.

We attended meetings in government buildings, entering spaces where previously people of colour would rarely have been allowed to gather; and, we were treated with respect. The Department of Constitutional Affairs in Walker Street was a venue for many of these meetings. We drank tea and coffee from the same cups and ate with the same cutlery and crockery as they did. This was definitely new!

I learnt that sometimes one is able to make more progress during the tea breaks than in formal meetings. Sometimes, the intractable nature of the disputes came about not because of a difference of view, but because of mistrust. Allowing adversaries to engage each other as people helped ease this mistrust. As the negotiations unfolded, some important developments became noticeable. From a party resisting apartheid, we were now not only engaged in defining what a new society would look like, but how the country should be governed. A new challenge for us was the question of salaries, which came up towards the end of the process, in a meeting discussing the transition with the parliament staff. Till then, ANC members of the National Executive were earning just over R3000 a month. Slovo's immediate response was that he was quite content with the salary he was earning and saw no reason to change this. This view was, however, not shared by others, who wanted to know the current MPs earnings.

I learnt a valuable lesson about the relationship between ministers and their officials in the public service during these bilaterals. While the public servants essentially did the bidding of their ministers, the lines demarcating the roles played by each side were very clear. Ministers were very clear to limit themselves to policy issues and leave matters of the administration to the public servants. Not only was there a division of labour, but there was also respect.

Two of the senior officials that I had contact with and was able to observe were Fanie van der Merwe and Neil Barnard, both director generals. While these officials would generally defer to their political heads and give them total respect, the ministers would also ask their advice when necessary and listened to them attentively. In later negotiations, I carefully observed the role that Fanie played in finding solutions and compromises. While most polite in his dealings with his ministers, he clearly had their respect and they were equally polite with him. More than 20 years after the establishment of a democratic government, I have yet to witness such a relationship between our ministers and state officials. The lines are more blurred with ANC ministers being more willing to interfere in matters of the administration, while officials often think and act politically.

CODESA II

The ANC's Negotiations Commission was a real rollercoaster ride from the moment we started. CODESA II was to be the start of formal negotiations on substantive issues – South Africa's new democratic dispensation, which was the moment the ANC had fought for for 50 years, thirty of which in a violent conflict. In recent times, there has been much criticism that the process of negotiations during this period was elite-driven to the exclusion of the majority.[65] This is not accurate.

The ANC's strategy was to end the conflict and create a climate conducive to the holding of elections. The constitution itself, it argued, could only be negotiated by an elected body. To achieve this, an interim government was necessary to manage the period leading up to the elections in the first instance, and in the second instance govern the country during the period that the constitution was being negotiated.

CODESA II was originally scheduled for March 1992 but only got started in May due to the March 17 all-white referendum. This meant that the Negotiations Commission only started working on developing its negotiating positions, preparing our delegations and planning the process itself once CODESA II was established.

The ANC had hoped to achieve agreement at this meeting on its proposed two-phased interim government. The first phase would secure a climate conducive for holding an election, while the second would be favourable for the constitution to be negotiated. At this point, agreement was reached on having an entrenched provision that there would be a regional dispensation. This meant that the drafters of a new constitution would have no alternative but to include it in a new constitution. In addition, the NP insisted that there be a special majority of regional representatives which effectively gave minorities special protection. The ANC refused, and the talks deadlocked. I learnt a very valuable lesson then that would remain with me forever – the need to constantly consult and take your constituency on board with you. This is especially so in conditions that are fluid and dynamic.

This was one of the first major blocks in the negotiations process and the ANC knew that it was not possible to move forward taking its constituency on board. After consulting with the Patriotic Front,[66] the ANC held its first national negotiations consultative forum on 26 May 1992, which I was tasked to organise – the first of many. Besides holding further national negotiations consultative forums, efforts were made to consult various structures.

We invited all the constitutional structures of the ANC, including its regions, alliance members, structures of the MDM and other allies. It was quite an angry meeting. I remember Barbara Hogan and Tokyo Sexwale reporting quite sharply on the violence in our township, particularly the killings associated with hostel dwellers. I was familiar with this problem because of my work as a PWV regional coordinator. The situation was indeed frightening. The response from this meeting was unanimous – we should take to the streets with a programme of 'rolling mass action'. This was clearly going to raise the temperatures even more, but this was inevitable since it was now evident that there was a direct linkage between the turmoil and conflict in our streets and at the negotiating table.

Our negotiations were just another front of the same struggle. There could be no separation. We needed to find a way out of what was fast becoming a logjam. How was the ANC going to be sure that the demands made on the regime would be met before substantive negotiations could resume? Leadership was required. Risks had to be taken.

These consultations paved the way to the ANC's first major national policy conference at the end of May that year. These issues naturally dominated discussions at the conference, which went on to provide guidelines for the transfer of power that would lead to the transformation of society. The conference further insisted on various conditions to be met before an election for a Constituent Assembly could be held, including the drafting of the 'Transition to Democracy Act' to provide the legal framework to enable the country to manage the transitional period.

When CODESA II failed, it was clear that South Africa was about to enter a new and very dangerous phase – and the Negotiations Commission was at the centre of it. Just a month into the formal negotiations process after CODESA II started, 45 residents of Boipatong were massacred in June 1992 by residents of a nearby hostel, known to be an Inkatha stronghold. This was not the only episode. Violence was becoming endemic in most parts of the country. Government troops were still occupying many townships and the situation was extremely tense. The ANC's NEC held an emergency meeting and resolved that we could not return to the negotiating table until the violence stopped. Madiba was mandated to communicate this to De Klerk, resulting in the famous exchange of memoranda, with Mac drafting for Madiba.

The ANC made a number of demands before negotiations could resume. They called for the termination of covert operations, including hit squad activity; the repeal of repressive legislation; the suspension of security force officials involved in the violence; the phasing out of hostels for migrant workers; and a ban on the carrying of dangerous weapons in public. The last two demands were at the core of rank-and-file ANC frustrations.

Mac roped me in to assist with the drafting, which explained why the violence forced the ANC to withdraw from the negotiations and set out its demands. After Mac consulted the Negotiations Commission, Madiba signed off the memorandum and I delivered it to the Union Buildings. De Klerk replied shortly thereafter with his own. Madiba followed this up with a second memorandum – again drafted by Mac and with me in tow.

The Channel Bilaterals

These were ominous times. The multi-party negotiations had broken down before it really started. The tension was palpable and there was a great deal of nervousness. The exchange of memoranda did not solve the problem. The ANC leadership from both exile and prison were now back home and we were all exposed. Uncertainty permeated the air. The position adopted by all sides had hardened. The ANC was at its militant best and activists were talking of voting with their feet.

This is when Roelf Meyer reached out to Cyril with a request to meet so that they could better understand what a satisfactory response would be for negotiations to resume. It was a novel approach and a shrewd move. Instead of merely responding to the issues that the ANC raised in its memoranda, he asked to meet so that he could properly understand the issues and better formulate their positions. The bait was set, and the ANC was lured into discreet discussions, which effectively continued the negotiations. Madiba was approached and he agreed that it was acceptable for discussions regarding the memoranda to take place. Initially, Cyril met with Roelf alone. Members of the ANC's NEC got to learn of this and took exception. The Tripartite Alliance partners were equally unhappy. They were suspicious of these developments.

Cyril was called into a meeting of the ANC's officials. He was chastised for engaging in negotiations on his own without having a mandate. He tendered an apology for this oversight. It was then agreed that he should only meet with Roelf with mandated delegations. This was the beginning of a most fascinating episode that famously became known as the Channel Bilaterals.

The Channel Bilaterals were a bit of a trap. We were locked into discussions that went well beyond the question of satisfying the ANC's demands. The ANC was sucked into negotiations on substantive matters and entrenched provisions that determined what the final constitution was to look like. Instead of dealing with how best to respond to the demands of the ANC, the negotiations were drawn into dealing with the concerns of the NP. During these negotiations, De Klerk's government pushed for a two-phase transition with an appointed transitional government with a rotating presidency preferably over an extended period. The ANC's position demanded a short transition in a single stage to majority rule. Other sticking points included minority rights, decisions on a unitary or federal state, property rights and indemnity from prosecution for politically motivated crimes.

The outcome of the negotiations during this period, which led to the Record of Understanding being signed on 26 September, essentially captured the most important compromises made during the negotiations process. Herein lay the rub. The ANC broke off negotiations and made various demands on the apartheid government. In return for a commitment to attend to these demands, the ANC made a number of compromises, which included the 32 constitutional principles which were entrenched.

The most important resolution to come out of these talks was an agreement to have a democratically elected constitution-making body. This is what the ANC won. However, this constitution would have to comply with agreed-upon constitutional principles. The Nationalist Party succeeded in securing agreement that there would be an interim government of national unity that will function within an interim constitution, which would also provide for regional governments. It was also agreed that all political prisoners would be released before 15 November 1992.

The next part of the agreement addressed the matter of hostels. Billy Cobbett and I represented the ANC, the only area in the negotiations process I participated in, rather than merely attending in a support function. Government undertook to urgently attend to the problem of those hostels associated with violence, including the public display and carrying of dangerous weapons, which had to be prohibited.

Then, tragedy struck, again. Another massacre. In September 1992, the Ciskei army opened fire on protest marchers killing 29 people. The country was on the verge of collapse. There were open battles and exchanges of gunfire. This brought a new urgency for a political settlement. There was a level of instability, which the country could ill afford, with the potential of spiralling horribly out of control.

On the evening of Friday, 25 September 1992, both the ANC and National Party negotiating teams reported to their principals. The ANC's extended NEC, which included the regional leadership, met. The atmosphere was electric and I got to see Madiba at his best. Chairing the meeting with Walter Sisulu at his side, Madiba opened the meeting and allowed the team led by Cyril to table their report. When the floor was opened for discussion, all the leading firebrands including Winnie Mandela, Peter Mokaba and Pallo Jordan, spoke in support of the proposed Record of Understanding. Madiba then enquired if there were more speakers wishing to express their views. There were several. He then asked if there were any dissenting voices and no one answered. At this point in time, he then asked for permission to speak and handed over the chair to Sisulu. The entire meeting was stunned because they did not know what to expect.

After praising the work done by the negotiators, Madiba reminded people that in his first speech, after his release, he promised that all political prisoners would be released. His problem with the agreement was that this did not happen. Cyril attempted to assure Madiba that the agreement called for a phased release of political prisoners, but Madiba was not impressed. He asked for permission to adjourn the meeting to directly engage with De Klerk on this matter. The meeting could not refuse this.

Madiba called De Klerk and insisted on the immediate release of political prisoners. De Klerk argued that this was not possible because there were courts sentencing people and that the rule of law had to be respected. Madiba was having none of this and threatened that if De Klerk did not change his view, he would have little option but to inform the world, at the summit of leaders the next day, that he had refused to remove obstacles to the negotiations. In the end, De Klerk buckled and conceded. In one night, Madiba managed to secure a critical victory, which we could not over several months of negotiations. He proved his mettle. This also cleared the way to the plenary session at which the resumption of negotiations was announced.

It is worth noting that while many had criticised the Channel Bilaterals, they all supported the outcome without questioning the compromises made. Nobody complained that we had agreed to an interim constitution instead of the Transition to Democracy Act, which the ANC had proposed as a legal framework while the final constitution was being drafted.

The family paid the price

These exciting developments came at a tremendous cost to my family. I was locked into a process that required my full attention and was very often away from home. Barbara had to attend to two growing youngsters largely on her own. Yusuf was still a toddler and Ruby was enrolled at a Montessori school. It was also during this period that Barbara suffered with a slipped disc, which required an operation on her spine. Her health had taken a beating and I was not able to provide the support required of me. I was largely absent and could not attend to important family matters.

I was not even present when Barbara underwent the surgical procedure because I had to support a most critical bilateral with the South African government which took place out of town. I tried my best, but it was simply not enough. When possible, I took Yusuf with me to the World Trade Centre. All of this naturally put further strain on my failing marriage and family life.

Multi-Party Negotiating Forum (MPNF)

The Record of Understanding was hailed as a major victory giving hope and signalled the resumption of negotiations. It did a lot to dissipate the tension that was building up in the country. The reason for hope was the key message being delivered – that the two major parties were prepared to make the necessary compromises to bring about peace and take the country forward. Despite this, it took nearly six months before the multi-party negotiations were to move forward. Much of the time after the Record of Understanding was signed was spent in defining the form and structure of the negotiating forum. The process only got underway by 1 April 1993.

The year 1993 was to also important for our family. Ruby turned six in July. She was exceedingly bright, already reading prolifically and also proficient at writing because of the mentoring she got from Barbara and her experience at the Montessori school. We tried to enrol her at a highly reputed local school. However, after discussing the matter with the school principal, we agreed to delay this to the next year. This meant that the added stimulation would need to be provided at home. By this time, Yusuf's autistic characteristics began to manifest themselves and this demanded a great deal of added attention primarily by Barbara.

At work, the new negotiating structure came to be referred to as the Multiparty Negotiating Forum (MPNF). The MPNF brought about a new confidence, hope and a sense of urgency in the process. This was also reflected in the fact that the white right (the Conservative Party and the Afrikaner Volksunie), the Pan Africanist Congress, and the KwaZulu homeland government decided to participate in the process albeit for only a short period of time.

The excitement generated was reflected in the media frenzy that ensued. I attended most meetings of the management Committee because of its importance. I was fascinated by the media reports. Because these meetings were closed, journalists had to wait outside for information. Always 'looking for an angle' because they were reporting on the same meetings, they each needed to find something unique and different to report on. The articles I read thereafter were often more exciting than the meetings themselves. More often than not, journalists were writing stories full of speculation because they wanted to publish something that was unique.

I mention this because it taught me an important lesson influencing my later experiences. During a break between meetings, I remember having a casual conversation about my observations with Joe Slovo. He was of the same view and we came to the conclusion that the best way to deal with the media was to have total transparency. We agreed then that we should manage our processes in a future Constitutional Assembly in a totally transparent manner. This would take away room for speculation. As it turned out, this was sound advice.

Soon after successfully resuming multi-party negotiations, the country was again shaken by news of the assassination of Chris Hani on 10 April 1993, which brought the country back to the brink of disaster. Ironically enough, it was like a turning point after which the NP became more motivated to find a solution. We could see this from their conduct because they lost a lot of their usual arrogance and condescending attitude.

The key element was Madiba's handling of the situation. This is when he incontrovertibly proved the quality of his statesmanship and leadership. Madiba's intervention on national television calling for calm on the evening after the assassination saved the country and prevented it from descending into total anarchy. Soon after this tragedy, the date for the first democratic elections as 27 April was set. With this, the attention of the country was immediately focused into a more positive direction. Suddenly, there was an end in sight, and it made all the difference.

The tension in the country nevertheless made us nervous. I was convinced that we were on the brink of total collapse. This uneasiness was to be reinforced when negotiations were dramatically interrupted in June 1993. The right-wing Afrikaner WeerstandsBeweging (AWB) stormed the World Trade Centre in Kempton Park, breaking through the glass front of the building with an armoured car and briefly taking over the negotiations chamber. The point was driven home in a frightening way: there was no guarantee of our security. This served to spur on all parties to pick up the pace and urgently find solutions, a task easier said than done.

Relying on political leadership to come to political agreements was only one part of the challenge. It was quite another thing to have the lawyers creatively articulate these into legally acceptable formulations. The ANC relied on several experts, one of whom was Arthur Chaskalson. Arthur very quickly stood out for the masterful manner in which he was able to construct constitutional solutions. His crisp understanding of the issues and sharp legal mind allowed him to craft some very precise legal and constitutional proposals.

It was a real pleasure to get to know Arthur. I developed a deep respect and admiration for his intellect and skills. Outside the technical committees, Arthur provided the ANC with critical constitutional advice and played an enormous role in the ongoing debates and discussions. However, his humility was most endearing. Arthur came to play an incredibly important role in our constitution-making process. It therefore came as no surprise when he was later made president of the Constitutional Court and then chief justice of the country.

The MPNF ratified the interim constitution in the early hours of 18 November 1993. As South Africans, we rarely need an excuse to have a party, but this was extra special. These ground-breaking agreements were reached on Cyril's birthday, 17 November. Our celebrations could not have been timed better.

One of the many benefits of my work was to support some very intricate processes on memorable occasions. One of those tasks was to give support in writing some of Madiba's important speeches. I was privileged for the experience and exposure. After celebrating Cyril's birthday, which ended around midnight, the team assigned the task of drafting Madiba's speech at the plenary session the next morning to Thabo Mbeki. I was to assist.

Despite the late night, I returned to Johannesburg to pick Mbeki up at 5 am. To my surprise, he was ready. My task was simple. Mbeki spoke and I typed. What fascinated me though was how he would think through the issues. I was amazed at Thabo's intellect, wisdom and ability to think on his feet, literally, because he did this while pacing the floor in a most deliberate kind of a way. Without fail, he produced a great speech.

Not long after this, I fielded a telephone call from a journalist from one of the Sunday newspapers. He complained that the ANC had little to celebrate from the agreement reached. He argued that we 'sold out'. I was quite offended, but allowed him time to expound his theory. His argument was that we agreed to increase the size of government sufficiently enough to retain a space for all the current apartheid public representatives. Even if both the National Party and Progressive Federal Party were to attain the low margins that were predicted in an election, they would all still be guaranteed a place. This meant that none of them would lose their jobs. This, as he explained, was the reason why these parties ended up making the compromises they did. There is some merit in this argument.[67]

The next step after negotiating the interim constitution was to oversee its tabling in what was to be the last sitting of the apartheid parliament just before Christmas in December 1993. Ironic as it was, we had to rely on this very institution to bring an end to apartheid and usher in the new constitutional order. This had to done along with other key pieces of legislation that were designed to facilitate the transition to democracy.[68] That Christmas, the dreaded southeaster came with more than the usual amount of rain and strong relentless winds. Despite this, I was spell-bound by the amazing work done by Arthur Chaskalson and Zam Titus who prepared the final legal text. This paved the way to the establishment of the Transitional Executive Council (TEC), which was to oversee the run-up to the first democratic election scheduled for 27 April 1994.

The ANC's Negotiations Commission had effectively completed its mandate. I found employment in the TEC administration, thankfully an easier job, with my office located in Pretoria rather than Johannesburg. I was grateful for this because it allowed me time to prepare the Laudium ANC branch for our elections.

XV

Negotiating the Constitution

Winning the elections

My nomination as a candidate from the Laudium branch on the ANC's list for the Gauteng Provincial Legislature was confirmed by our provincial conference. This was a turning point in my political life. I had never considered this possibility as an activist and soldier of the ANC, and there was nothing that prepared me for political office and how I would continue our struggle to realise the national democratic revolution.

From the perspective of the branch and community, my nomination made our elections effort easier because the community had a candidate they could identify with. A team under Nava's capable leadership led the election campaign and it quickly gained a life of its own. It was a slick and extremely well organised operation. Our fundraising efforts were well received and so was the support structure that was put into place. Nava mobilised a large team of competent and committed activists. Campaigning was hard work. It meant countless formal and information meetings. We covered all community structures and organised many house meetings. On election day, we were fortunate to have Thabo Mbeki who was deployed to cast his vote in our area. I was sufficiently high on the ANC's list to make it to the Gauteng legislature with very little difficulty.

When the election results were announced confirming the ANC's victory, South African politics had irrevocably changed. I was now a

Member of a Provincial Legislature (MPL). It was yet another totally new beginning in my life. On 10 May 1994, Barbara and I were invited to the Union Buildings to witness the inauguration of Nelson Mandela as democratic South Africa's first president. What a proud moment it was for us. We were seated next to Robert McBride and his then wife, Paula.

The Gauteng Provincial Legislature was soon convened and located at Nasrec in Johannesburg. It did not take long for us to get sucked into this new and foreign political terrain. Not so long ago, I was in exile managing an underground machinery successfully launching military operations in the country. And now I was in government. However, before I could find a rhythm in my work as an MPL, I received a call from Cyril's office requesting me to submit an application for the position of executive director of the Constitutional Assembly. Cyril was elected the chairperson of the Constitutional Assembly and Leon Wessels his deputy. The Constitutional Assembly was the sitting of both houses of Parliament as a constitution-making body, the structure identified by Oliver Tambo in the Harare Declaration that was to be mandated with the responsibility of adopting our constitution.

Cyril and Leon Wessels interviewed me, and I was offered the post in Cape Town. This meant that I had to resign as an MPL and move to Cape Town for two years, which I was happy to do even though the MPL job was for five years. Both Barbara and I agreed to this in the hope that Cape Town would offer us a better lifestyle and family life.

Before leaving, the one important matter I had to attend to was the handing over of my political responsibilities in Laudium. I had hardly understood what it meant to hold political office when I had to leave. I had ambitions of grooming younger activists in our community to take over my leadership responsibilities and hopefully also represent the community in the structures of the ANC and possibly government. This however was not to be.

The democratic elections of 1994 changed our political landscape fundamentally. It also opened a host of new opportunities beyond government. While political office was attractive, many young people were looking at greener pastures that were beginning to open up in both the public and private sector. That said, it remains a major regret that I was not able to convince our young activists to commit to a political role.

In the years following the 1994 elections, a most worrying development started unfolding. With the R12 membership fee alone needed to become an ANC member, in Laudium, like many other places, opportunists began to recognise the value of such membership. Soon, membership cards were bought in bulk and distributed to those who opposed to the ANC. We were in unfamiliar territory. We were no longer an underground structure that recruited people.

Membership not only allowed specific candidates to be voted in, but also gave access to decision-makers in our organisation. Sometimes, these were also decisions relating to tenders and contracts issued by government. In hindsight, it is clear that the precursor to state capture, was the capture of our branches; and this took place not so long after the 1994 elections. The irony is that while committed activists who had struggled in the trenches against apartheid found it more useful to leave the fold after 1994, those who were always opposed to the interests of the ANC, now found it opportune to join it. Many comrades were now on the outside of the ANC and those who traditionally opposed it on the inside.

Constitutional Mandate

Ever since our constitution was adopted in October 1996, there has been much animated discussion regarding the origins of the text and the concept of 'sunset clauses'. There has been a tendency of attributing portions of the text to one or the other author. Such an ahistorical approach is misleading.

The constitution is not a product solely of the negotiation in the Constitutional Assembly because many of its provisions, particularly those relating to the Bill of Rights, are the realisation of years of bitter struggle, sacrifice and imbued with a great deal of historical importance. We often forget that while the members of the Constitutional Assembly negotiated the formulation of the text, the essence of it came from mandates and demands developed over many years.

Our history of constitutional development spans over at least 85 years between two major milestones. Each milestone was composed of a peace treaty ending a conflict and giving birth to a new constitutional order. The Treaty of Vereeniging of 28 May 1902 was the first. This treaty ended the Anglo-Boer War and laid the basis for the adoption of South Africa's first constitution. This constitution of 1910 was drafted in an unrepresentative convention. The second was the interim constitution. It too has been described as a peace treaty that ended a conflict. Like the previous peace treaty, it laid the basis for a new constitution; only this time it was to be drafted in a democratically elected convention, the Constitutional Assembly.

The 1910 constitution was seminal in the development of our history because it gave rise to two parallel streams of constitutional thought. While one stream of thought was based on minority rule, the other was shaped by the struggle for a system free of discrimination. The struggle against colonialism, apartheid and racism was against a constitutional dispensation that provided the legal basis for our oppression.[69]

A good example of the influence on the ANC is its views on a bill of rights. It was not new. Since its formation in 1912, the ANC campaigned vigorously for the recognition and protection of human rights. The annual conference of the ANC held in Bloemfontein in May 1923 adopted a resolution on the bill of rights which claimed 'the indisputable right to a place of abode in this land'[70] and the equal treatment of all. Then, in 1941 President F.D. Roosevelt and Prime Minister Winston Churchill signed the Atlantic Charter.

This charter became the basis for the modern United Nations, but also served to inspire Dr A. B. Xuma, an ANC leader who felt that Africans in South Africa needed to respond. The response came in the form of a document entitled African Claims. With this, the ANC sent a delegation to New York to convince the leaders of the world that a just and permanent peace in South Africa will be possible only if the claims of all classes, colours and races for sharing power and for their full participation in the educational, political and economic activities are granted and recognised.

Our history is one in which the process of resistance itself found expression in developing an alternative vision. This was the vision of a democracy and emerging constitutional dispensation. This is what started to emerge in 1955, at the Congress of the People when the Freedom Charter was adopted. This document was arrived at through the participation of many different communities who were consulted. This Freedom Charter effectively articulated the vision of South Africa's majority and contained many provisions that are enshrined in our final constitution today.

As for the call of a national convention, this was made by the ANC President-General Albert Luthuli in May 1957. He argued that the function of the convention was to allow the people's representatives to discuss the ensuing conflict and find common solutions. This appeal was ignored. Then, on 16 December 1960, a consultative conference of African leaders was held in Orlando, Soweto. Forty African leaders met with liberal and progressive whites. This conference rejected the establishment of a republic and made a call to the African leadership to attend an all-in conference. The purpose would be to demand the calling of a national convention. This convention had to be representative of the people of South Africa and consider a new political dispensation and individual fundamental rights.

On 25 March 1961, the all-in conference met and called for the negotiation of a democratic dispensation. At this conference, Mandela's call for a national convention of elected representatives to determine a new non-racial democratic constitution for South Africa was adopted. Despite the banning of all organisations representative of the majority and a protracted armed struggle, the ANC in 1989 lobbied the Organisation of African Unity to adopt the now famous Harare Declaration that set out the basis for the transition of South Africa to democracy. Central to this strategy was the demand that a duly elected and representative body of the people should be mandated to draft South Africa's constitution.

The work that we were called upon to do in the Constitutional Assembly in 1994 therefore had a long history and background.

Understanding the interim constitution

I can find no better an introduction than the last provision of the South African Interim Constitution to provide an understanding of what the interim constitution represented. The provision is aptly titled, 'National Unity and Reconciliation'.

> This Constitution provides a historic bridge between the past of a deeply divided society characterised by strife, conflict, untold suffering and injustice, and a future founded on the recognition of human rights, democracy and peaceful co-existence and development opportunities for all South Africans, irrespective of colour, race, class, belief or sex. The pursuit of national unity, the well-being of all South African citizens and peace require reconciliation between the people of South Africa and the reconstruction of society.
>
> The adoption of this Constitution lays the secure foundation for the people of South Africa to transcend the divisions and strife of the past, which generated gross violations of human rights, the transgression of humanitarian principles in violent conflicts and a legacy of hatred, fear, guilt and revenge.
>
> These can now be addressed on the basis that there is a need for understanding but not for vengeance, a need for reparation but not for retaliation, a need for ubuntu but not for victimisation.
>
> In order to advance such reconciliation and reconstruction, amnesty shall be granted in respect of acts, omissions and offences associated with political objectives and committed in the course of the conflicts of the past. To this end, Parliament under this Constitution shall adopt a law determining a firm cut-off date, which shall be a date after 8 October 1990 and before 6 December 1993, and providing for the mechanisms, criteria and procedures, including tribunals, if any, through which such amnesty shall be dealt with at any time after the law has been passed.
>
> With this Constitution and these commitments we, the people of South Africa, open a new chapter in the history of our country.

This uniquely crafted provision was the product of a collaboration between Mac Maharaj and Fanie van der Merwe. The provision was drafted at the end of the process and provided the basis on which the legislation establishing the Truth and Reconciliation Commission was crafted. With this provision, it is not hard to understand why the interim constitution is regarded as our peace treaty because it set out the basis of the political settlement with the apartheid government and defined the nature of the transition. The document naturally also sets out the compromises made to move beyond the conflicts of the past.

Of these compromises, there are three that I thought could have been dealt with differently. The first is the agreement to have nine provinces. This compromise cost us most dearly because not all nine provinces are economically viable or can sustain themselves. The original position of the ANC to retain the previous four provinces was correct. However, the compromise struck was to establish provinces such as the Western Cape and KwaZulu-Natal to offer the National Party and IFP some opportunity to hold some power.

The second compromise was the number of representatives to be elected to the national and provincial levels of government. At the national level, Parliament has 490 representatives and the nine provinces added 430 more, which comes at a prohibitive cost. We could have done better with fewer. But this would explain why the National Party compromised. They would effectively retain largely the same number of representatives in government as they had before.

The third compromise was the reliance on proportional representation at the expense of allowing for the direct accountability of representatives. This alienation of our representatives from their constituencies has not done us any favours.

Making the constitution

Working in Cape Town was more pleasant than Midrand. The distance to work was much shorter, even if the traffic jams were equally loathsome. Unfortunately, I did not have enough time to enjoy Cape

Town. That said, my work in the Constitutional Assembly was without a doubt the pinnacle of my career. Nothing could get better than this.

As executive director, I was responsible for managing the entire process of constitution making. Fortunately, I was blessed with an executive team that included Marion Sparg and Louisa Zondo, both of whom were consummate professionals and delivered more than what was required. We were an extraordinary team. While the Constitutional Assembly gave birth to our final constitution, my team was effectively the mid-wife responsible for its delivery.

The executive team were appointed in August 1994. We moved really fast to put the rest of the administration together, most of which we did by October. The speed with which we operated was dictated by the mandate of the Constitutional Assembly. We had to adopt the constitution within two years of the first sitting of the Constitutional Assembly, which took place on 8 May 1994. This meant that the administration had less than 19 months within which to ramp up and deliver on our mandate. The real challenge was a budget which allowed for no more than 30 people to be employed. Despite this, the team were phenomenal.

Aside from the tight timeframe and limited budget, the mandate given to us was just about impossible. The mandate was defined in the Constitutional Assembly's first plenary session. Members of Parliament looked at the challenge more as activists than politicians in a government. When the people of South Africa expressed themselves in the 1994 election, they mandated the newly elected leaders with two distinct tasks. These were to govern the new democratic society and to draft the final constitution. The Constitutional Assembly therefore had a legitimate mandate to draft the final constitution. The ANC however thought differently. For them, the mandate they were given was not sufficient to draft the constitution. The wisdom of their decision was to emerge only later.

It was the late Collins Chabane who most profoundly articulated the mandate that they gave my team: 'Our priority is to ensure that the process is not confined to these walls. We need to ensure that the communities along the Limpopo Valley also have their views heard in this Chamber and in our committee rooms. The final draft must reflect the views of our people in the villages, informal settlements, hostels, factories, towns and cities.'[71]

Taking our cue from this, my team crafted our vision and strategy which had as one of its stated objectives the promise that the process of constitution making would be transparent, open and credible. We argued that our final constitution required an enduring quality and had to enjoy the support of all South Africans irrespective of their ideological differences. The history of political conflict and mistrust in our country demanded that the final constitution be credible. We therefore set ourselves the goal of ensuring that the people would be able to claim ownership of the constitution. We believed that it was necessary to placate the fears and concerns of minorities and yet find favour with the majority. In short, the constitutional foundations of democracy had to be placed beyond question.

To respond to this challenge, I developed an ambitious programme for the management of the constitution-making process. To succeed, our first step was to get our programme approved by the Constitutional Committee, which met in December 1994 and proved to be my baptism into the politics of the Constituent Assembly. The committee consisted of 44 members representing all political parties. The meeting took place in the old cabinet room at the Union Buildings in Pretoria. I remember this meeting well for several reasons. The room had wooden panels covering the walls in a most beautiful ornate setting allowing for participants to sit in a circle. The room was very stately. It was obviously a place with a lot of history and where important decisions were taken. This time, however, we were meeting to change the history of the past in a most profound way.

Because we took a decision to make all our meetings open to the public, I thought it a good idea to invite my father along to observe. He would then be able to see the work that I was doing. The meeting started in a most dramatic way. Before we could get our business under way, Walter Felgate of the IFP launched a vicious attack on me complaining that I would not be able to do my work in an objective way because I was a member of the ANC. Pravin Gordhan immediately came to my defence. After a short debate, the meeting confirmed their confidence in me and made me conscious of the importance of my integrity.

The debate however did little to ease my nerves. It was my first public presentation before the most senior leadership of all the political parties, whose respect and support I hoped to earn. Our proposal was a bold one and very different. I therefore had good reason to be nervous. It did not help that my father, who was sat quietly in one of the coves, fell asleep and started blissfully snoring away as he usually would watching TV.

I prepared what I thought to be a slick PowerPoint presentation. I spent several days getting it to be as perfect as I could. In 1994, we did not have powerful projectors as we do today. I had to rely on a contraption placed on the top of an overhead projector. I dimmed the lights in the room and walked over to the laptop to start my presentation. I was so nervous that I stumbled over the cables linking the laptop to the projector. This brought the entire system including my laptop and projector tumbling to the floor with a loud crash. Everyone was stunned. I was devastated.

But, for reasons I cannot explain, I very calmly walked over to my seat and started delivering my presentation as if the technology did not exist. I suspect that people were so disappointed for me that they allowed me a very easy passage and adopted my programme without too much fuss. The programme provided a work plan for both the negotiation of the constitution with an elaborate integrated process of participation by the public. It also included a constitutional education programme. Needless to say, the programme broke new ground in defining a new international best practice; and, which successfully guided us through the entire process.

With the approval of the Constitutional Committee, my big challenge now was to find the money to pay for the programme because the budget given to me paid for little more than the salaries for a few members of staff. There was not enough money to pay for the civic education programme, the public meetings to be organised throughout the country and the many publications we needed produced. I needed to find donors, so I set up meeting with different donor agencies to convince them to support our programme.

In the '90s, constitution making was deemed as a technical matter requiring legal drafting, rather than any participation from the public. The only money donors were prepared to make available was for teams of international experts, which was not needed with kind of experts we had in South Africa. Finally, we received a positive response from the Danish government and with the steady progress we made, especially a positive public profile, other donors soon started taking an interest in what we were doing. It did not take long before donors started approaching us to support our programme. To confirm the success of our public participation programme, we appointed a team of researchers to help us run regular surveys.[72] This was extremely helpful when reporting to the management committee.

Cyril chaired this committee, which consisted of ten multi-party leaders. It was tasked to oversee the day-to-day progress in the process and the work of the administration team. Cyril was a tough taskmaster who made sure that we were professional in our conduct. This training stood me well in my later work.

Our public participation programme started with an intense programme of public hearings. The objective was to afford the public an opportunity to make their views known. Despite the limited time we had, we engaged with 596 organisations during these consultations. In addition, each of the six theme committees we established hosted a series of seminars and workshops. With this, we developed an excellent database, which helped in our later rounds of consultations. We also used several communications tools including radio and television that proved extremely successful.

Based on the surveys carried out, we confirmed that our initial consultations reached at least 10,412 million South Africans each week. It was very popular. The Constitutional Assembly's official newsletter, *Constitutional Talk*, was produced fortnightly and was distributed to 160,000 people – 100 000 copies were distributed nationally through taxi ranks and another 60 000 sent to subscribers. Our newsletter generated a substantial following.

Much to everyone's surprise, we received 1.7 million submissions confirming the success of our strategy. Even if only about 11,000 were substantive and the bulk of these were petitions, these submissions reflected the views of a significant portion of the population and could hardly be ignored. The first draft of the constitutional text that we produced was publicly referred to as a 'Working Draft'. We printed seven million copies for distribution in all 11 languages and launched it during 'National Constitution Week' from 17–21 March 1997. It was extremely successful in catching the attention of the public.

Our meetings were totally open and transparent and afforded journalists little room to speculate. Our minutes were placed on the internet as soon it was prepared. This set a new international benchmark in the design and management of constitution-making processes, from changing the very language of the process – *drafting* of a constitution and the idea of leaving it to lawyers to do, to *making* a constitution with the participation of the population at large. This was novel.

Internationally, we made it popular to engage in public participation processes, which have now become the new measure and standard for constitution making. We demystified legal and constitutional concepts and placed these in the popular domain, explaining them in 'plain language' in terms that all could understand.

Despite having less than 18 months to finalise the constitution, we accomplished the task after engaging the country in the biggest public consultation programme ever. Then too, the constitution was adopted with almost total consensus. The measure of our success was that the process was conducted in a manner that gave the text itself the legitimacy it needed. This became part of the South African miracle, which was made possible only because of sheer determination. We captured the imagination of the people in South Africa and the respect of the world. For two whole years, we were able to hold the public's attention and focus their minds on the shape of a future South Africa. This was made even more special because South Africa had no prior history of constitutionalism.

Even our lawmakers were impressed. When negotiating those provisions relating to access by members of the public to the work of the National Assembly (Sec 59) and National Council of Provinces

(Sec 72), they incorporated the lessons we learnt in the process of constitution making. This influence can also be seen in Sec 57(1), which deals with the power of the National Assembly to make its own rules. MPs agreed to a requirement that obliged future lawmakers to have 'regard to representative and participatory democracy, accountability, transparency and public involvement' when making law. This has meant that no legislation could be approved without passing this test. The reliance of our courts on this provision to strike down legislation for not meeting this test therefore comes with an immense sense of satisfaction. The contribution of my team has become indelible. My involvement in the constitution-making process was a rare privilege. Not only did I have the opportunity to have a ring-side seat witnessing the making of history, but I was also responsible for facilitating the process. What better could one ask for?

This however would not have been possible without my team who went beyond the call of duty because they had a clear sense of the history that they were making. All too often, they would continue to work well after meetings had adjourned in the early hours of the morning to make sure that the documentation was professionally prepared and ready for the next morning's session which happened to be only a few hours later.

To finalise the drafting, we established a technical refinement team (TRT) consisting of technical experts, drafters and party representatives, the inspiration for its establishment coming from the work of Arthur Chaskalson and Zam Titus in finalising the Interim Constitution. The TRT was important because it gave us an opportunity to make sure that there were no inconsistencies, contradictions or gaps and that the constitutional text read in the best manner possible. I had the good fortune to chair this meeting. Each party gave us their full cooperation, undertaking this task as a collective responsibility, all driven by a sense of history.

The final resolution of all issues paving the way to adoption on 8 May 1996 was recognised by all as a victory that each party celebrated in equal measure. There was no scoring of points. We had together reached the finish line after an extremely long and arduous journey. When the moment came, everyone was just as happy and pleased to savour the moment not for the gains made by any party, but by the country as a whole. After all the bickering and gamesmanship, the political players had come of age and grown immeasurably. They were now ready to take the country to the next stage. The Constitutional Assembly plenary scheduled for the adoption of the constitution was as momentous as it was grand.

The management of plenary sessions of parliament had a tradition. Once all MPs were seated, the speaker would walk to Tuinhuis, situated next to the parliamentary chambers, to escort the president into the parliamentary chambers.

On 8 May morning, as per tradition, Cyril, Leon and I waited for all MPs to be seated and then proceeded to Tuinhuis. As usual, Madiba was prompt and waiting for us. A short while later, a tired and weary-looking Thabo Mbeki arrived. Cyril and I approached and greeted him. He had the task of delivering the keynote address. He looked worried. When we enquired, he told us that he decided to do something totally different with his speech and he hoped it would work out. As it turned out, this was his famous 'I am an African' speech, which was extremely well received and is still recognised as one of the great speeches delivered by an African leader.

Immediately after the plenary Session, I arranged for the newly adopted constitution to be submitted to the Constitutional Court for certification as required by the Interim Constitution. The interim constitution required that the adopted text had to be certified for compliance with the agreed 34 constitutional principles.

Arthur Chaskalson, as president of the Constitutional Court, waited for my submission of the documentation and immediately issued a set of special rules for the management of the process. While I knew that there would be some objections to the text, I did not expect it to be as many as were eventually made. We were equally astonished to learn on 6 September 1996 that the Constitutional Court refused to certify the constitution.

The Constitutional Court identified a number of provisions that they believed did not comply with the adopted constitutional principles. The Court identified several critical failures. Most prominent, was the failure to protect the right of employees to engage in collective bargaining. Others were the failure to provide for the constitutional review of ordinary statutes; weakness in the entrenchment of fundamental rights, freedoms and civil liberties; and a failure to sufficiently safeguard the independence of the public protector and auditor-general. Areas of non-compliance also related to local government responsibilities and powers.

The non-certification of the final constitution posed a major challenge. I had to devise a programme of work that would allow the parties to negotiate the changes required. The professional manner in which my team rose to this challenge was remarkable. We completed our work to schedule and the Constitutional Assembly was able to reconvene on 11 October to adopt the amended constitutional text. Not only were we able to address the concerns of the Constitutional Court, but we also attended to the improvement of several other areas. The result was that we were able to return the amended text to the Constitutional Court, which delivered its judgment on 4 December 1996 certifying the text.

The last act in the process of constitution making that I had to apply my mind to was the signing ceremony that would bring the constitution to life. After carefully considering our options, I proposed that we hold this event in Sharpeville. There were several compelling reasons for this. South Africa's constitutional journey started in Vereeniging where the Peace Treaty between the Boers and the British was signed on 31 May 1902. This treaty started the process leading to South Africa's first constitution based on minority rule. The proposal was accepted. Vereeniging was also De Klerk's constituency. Minority rule had come a full circle because it ended where it had all started.

Sharpeville was also the scene of the massacre on 21 March 1960. Today we remember this date as Human Rights Day and our constitution reflects our determination to protect and promote human rights. Holding this ceremony on 10 December here was therefore a most fitting tribute. What made it more perfect was the fact that the UN General Assembly had adopted and proclaimed the Universal Declaration of Human Rights also on this day in 1948.

Because the physical constitutional text was final and needed to stand the test of time, we procured special paper on which to print it that would not yellow with age. Three copies were printed, two of which were beautifully bound and covered. The first copy was the formal record that would be kept by Parliament after being signed off by both the president of the country, Nelson Mandela, and Arthur Chaskalson as president of the Constitutional Court. The second copy was intended for record purposes. The third was an unofficial copy printed for my records. What made this ever so special is the fact that my copy of the constitution was the first copy of the constitution signed by Madiba. While the Constitution was signed by President Mandela on 10 December 1996, and officially published in the Government Gazette on 18 December, it only came into force on 4 February 1997.

With the signing of the constitution behind us, there were a few things that needed attention before the closing of the administration of the Constitutional Assembly. By this time, most members of our staff had fortunately already found other placements. In keeping with our principle of making the constitution accessible, arrangements were made to have it printed in all 11 official languages in small pocket-sized books. We printed eleven million copies and had it distributed to all parts of the country.

Before closing the administration, the team organised, packed and indexed all the material according to the professional standards required of historical records of this nature and handed them over to National Archives. Over the years, however, I have been contacted by people who enquire about a specific record because of the pitiful state of our archives. One of our first projects was to place all our records on a website, which we did in collaboration with the University of Cape Town. A project of great pride, I even raised funds for the maintenance but once the funds ran out the project collapsed, and the university did little to maintain it. I am sure that there must be a lesson somewhere in all these sad experiences.

Leaving a legacy

Already in 1995, recognising that we were custodians of history in the making and were therefore responsible for ensuring that this history was recorded for posterity, I established the Legacy Project. The first aspect of this was the establishment of a database of all information including submissions and technical reports electronically. This information was recorded on CD discs for distribution. The best way to leave our legacy would have been to ensure that school students were taught as part of their curriculum about our constitution. I held several meetings with both the ministers of education and arts and culture to pursue these ideas. Despite many promises, nothing much came of this.

Also, as part of the Legacy Project, I encouraged members of our research staff to write about our history. Here too, I was not successful. Because I was so determined to ensure that this history was recorded, I finally undertook this project myself and started writing up the history. I was fortunately able to complete this before the physical closure of the Constitutional Assembly administration in April 1997. The book, titled *The Soul of a Nation* was published in 1998 and was even nominated as one of six finalists in the Alan Paton Literary Awards for historical works.

A family punished

Cape Town was a great city in which to settle the family. In 1995, housing was still relatively cheap, and we were able to buy a home just off Kromboom Drive in Rondebosch East after selling off our house in Midrand. Our house was very conveniently located and life generally more relaxed than in Gauteng. We settled well and even got Ruby a dog called Sparky. Schooling for both Ruby and Yusuf was also close by.

Work at the Constitutional Assembly was intense and hectic. Most of my time was committed to a process that I had no control over. There was nothing routine or ordinary, which unfortunately meant that I was yet again largely absent. Thus, once the constitution was signed into law, my big focus was to find employment in Cape Town so as to continue living there. I was interviewed for the post of city manager with the Cape Town City Council but was not successful.

I also made a bid for the post of secretary of parliament, which would have been a perfect fit given my stint at the Constitutional Assembly. However, this too was not successful. This is when the reality of the new South African politics struck me. I was told I could not be considered for this post because the speaker of parliament, Frene Ginwala, was also of Indian origin and this would be politically incorrect. I then applied to the Department of Constitutional Development for a senior post in management which I thought would be another natural fit even if it was Pretoria-based. Unfortunately, I was not successful here too. Finally, Dullah Omar, who was Minister of Justice, encouraged me to apply for a post there, and I was successful.

This however placed me in a real predicament. I could not find a job in Cape Town and Barbara was not happy to return to Pretoria. I had no alternative but to take the job, and so moved back to Pretoria in April 1997 without the family. This was not the best of circumstances and only served to put more pressure on an already unhappy state of domestic affairs.

The first five years of my marriage in Botswana was difficult to say the least. The security situation was extremely tense, and I spent most of my time building the Kabwe Machinery. My time was split between my formal employment as a lawyer during the day and ANC work in the evenings. I simply did not give the family enough attention. The next six years after my return home had been even more difficult. Most of my time was consumed by my involvement in the process of constitutional negotiations. This left me with little time to nurture and build the foundations of a happy family. I simply did not and could not do enough. Despite these terrible conditions, Barbara persevered and did her best to make a home for our family. She nurtured the children and tried to create as warm and loving a set of conditions as she could to make ours a happy and loving home. Despite the best of intentions, my marriage was under significant stress already.

Coming back to South Africa did not change matters. It only made things more difficult. Moving back to Pretoria from Cape Town was as painful as going into exile. I was obliged to leave my wife and children to seek employment elsewhere. My continued absence from key moments in the education and life of my children put a severe strain on all of us. The most painful part of moving to Pretoria was my separation from the children. While I was able to travel to Cape Town very often to see the family, it was not enough. I did not cope well and failed. Relocating to Pretoria in April 1997 led to my marriage breaking down irretrievably. I found it easier to go to war for my political beliefs and dealing with difficult matters in an often-violent conflict than to deal with challenges of a personal nature.

Back in Pretoria, my parents insisted that I live with them, a real blessing after a separation of nearly 20 years. My time spent with them was especially important because my father was terminally ill. He was being treated for kidney failure and dependent on regular dialysis and I was fortunate to spend the last two years of his life at home. He passed away in March 1999.

The loss of my father had a profound effect on me. Like him, I too did not take care of my health. Being heavy smokers with bad eating habits and little to no exercise made us perfect candidates for heart and kidney diseases, which we were genetically disposed to anyway. I became paranoid about my health.

Barbara and I got divorced in October 1999. This was a major turning point in my life. As if losing my father and getting divorced were not bad enough, Barbara decided that it would be best for her and the children if they were to relocate to the UK where she had a better support system. I was devastated, but there was little that I could do about it other than take solace in the fact that the British educational system was better geared to providing the institutional support that Yusuf needed.

Then, just when I thought that I had enough, I became a statistic in South Africa's violent crime. This happened when I was visiting Jeets and Shamim one night. As I alighted from the car outside their house, I was confronted by three armed thugs who demanded the keys and forced me into the boot of my car. It was a most terrifying ordeal because

I was close enough to see my friends through the kitchen window but could do nothing as I had a pistol in my face. Being driven around in the boot of my car was frightening. The purpose of this, I gathered, was to be sure that no tracker system was activated. After a while, the hijackers stopped at the side of a road, just outside of Mamelodi, and ordered me to run into the bushes with the threat that they would shoot me if I hesitated. I needed no further prompt and ran for dear life. Fortunately, I suffered no physical injury.

1999 was a year that I would rather forget.

XVI

Joining Justice

The Department of Justice was the institution of the state that was primarily responsible for putting in place the apartheid legal framework, prosecuting those who violated or challenged it, and maintaining the courts that enforced it. The department was of equal strategic importance in the new democracy because it had to usher in the new legal order and implement the constitution. The appointment of Dullah Omar as the first Minister of Justice in 1994 was therefore an inspired choice. His humility, sharp legal mind, deep and abiding sense of justice, and his formidable determination to fight for what was right made him perfect for the post. Besides this, his amiable character helped tremendously.

Because of the strategic role that the department had in the transformation of South Africa into a constitutional democracy, it was not sufficient to merely take over the Department of Justice. Before it could become an instrument of transformation, it too would have to be transformed. To do this, Dullah appointed a team of people that he could trust to help him develop and implement his strategy. This strategy was called Vision 2020. I could not have chosen a better time to come to the department.

I started my political life in the underground as a young freedom fighter, then found myself in the negotiation of peace and thereafter the constitution. We were now at the beginning of a different journey – the building of our constitutional democracy. This was about implementation of our constitution and it is exactly where I wanted to be. It was yet another new beginning. We fought for our freedom, negotiated and designed the constitutional framework for this freedom and now had to build the institutions to give effect to it. I was most fortunate.

I was appointed as a deputy director-general in a newly established post responsible for corporate services. My most senior post in the public service till then, it carried a great deal of responsibilities and a salary to match. My task was to establish a corporate services branch of the department by consolidating a number of smaller administrative and operational structures.

Corporate services, as a branch of the department, was a huge portfolio that included all financial, administrative, information technology and supply-chain management functions. Each of these functions were individually very exciting and there was a lot to learn. The newly established post of chief financial officer also reported through me and I was therefore responsible for the budget of the entire department which amounted to just more than R5 billion.[73] Facilities management was another area of great interest because we were responsible for more than 550 court buildings throughout the country. The most exciting for me, however, was information technology.

The director-general is the accounting officer and responsible for delivering the strategic objectives of the department. This responsibility is carried out with the support of a team of deputy directors-generals (DDG) each of whom would be responsible for a branch which was supported by an organisational structure and budget dedicated to delivering a specific programme of government. DDGs were part of the executive team of the department. Collectively, one of our key responsibilities was the transformation of the Department of Justice.

The first challenge we faced was that we were effectively dealing with 11 departments! Under apartheid, there was a separate department for white South Africa and for each of the Bantustans. The transformation of the department was therefore not possible without first merging all these disparate entities into one. It was only at this point that we were able to start restructuring the department to respond to the new constitutional dispensation which now had nine provinces. This meant that after consolidating the department into one structure, we then had to restructure it to have nine regional offices.

The reality is that most modern democracies were built and evolved over many decades, and sometimes centuries. Democracy in South Africa was not going to exist only because we passed new laws and established institutions to support a constitutional democracy. We could not just wish or legislate apartheid away. Existing institutions of the state and its structures had to be transformed because they were designed and structured for a totally different purpose. The fundamental values and underpinnings of the structures of government had to be transformed so that they were fit for purpose. This is the challenge that we were confronted with.

The transformation process was not just a process of restructuring, but had more to do with the nature of the organisation and the services it was designed to deliver. A simple example of this was the principle of access to justice. This meant that our services had to be accessible to all and not just a minority any longer. We had to be accessible not just in a physical sense of locality, but the type of services that we rendered which had to give effect to the values enshrined in our new constitution.

Another major responsibility of the department was the establishment of Chapter Nine institutions[74] such as the office of the public protector, Gender Commission and the Human Rights Commission. We had to put into place legislation to give effect to the Bill of Rights including matters of affirmative action, administrative justice, land claims, equality and access to information among a host of other critical areas that make ours the vibrant constitutional democracy that it is.

These were exciting times to work in the public service and we were fortunate to have Dullah as our minister. Instrumental in setting up the new prosecutions system headed by the national director of public prosecutions, Dullah also oversaw the establishment of the Truth and Reconciliation Commission (TRC) which he viewed as one of his greatest achievements.

Under his leadership, our new management team was quick to introduce a range of changes. The new department had a national head office with a regional office in each of the nine provinces. This meant a new management structure and it required a huge effort to put this organisation in place. Transformation affected not only our human capital, but also affected the quality of our infrastructure and court buildings. These were no longer the preserve of those areas predominantly serving white people. Justice had to be seen to be accessible to all.

The elaborate process of budgeting and management of the expenditure was part of my portfolio. The public service was a place of learning because there was such a lot that was happening. One of the important developments was the introduction of the Public Finance Management Act (PFMA). I learnt about the importance of developing a clear strategic plan that was supported by programmes and projects, all of which needed to be budgeted for. Very importantly, I learnt about the importance of accountability and the manner in which public finances were to be dealt with. It was also during this period that the Department of Justice assumed the additional responsibility for constitutional development and thereafter became known as the Department of Justice and Constitutional Development.

South Africa set new benchmarks with regard to both the process of drafting a constitution as well as in its substantive constitutional formulations and instantly gained widespread international interest. Unfortunately, this did not mean that our institutions were mature enough to understand the value of deepening constitutional education in the country or promoting our constitution at an international level. Ironically, the very department of government that was mandated to deal with constitutional development did not understand what it meant and preferred to deal with this responsibility technocratically.

Throughout the world, there was a renewed interest in constitution making as part of conflict resolution and the department had a role to play. It was also natural that given my experience in constitution making, I would be called upon to share these experiences on various international platforms and at a number of universities. At first, I was given permission to participate. However, it soon became an irritant and permission was denied. Where possible, I participated in these events when I could take leave because the department did not see it as part of their mandate. Regrettably, the lack of vision and foresight continues to limit government's ability to deal with this responsibility and legacy. It would also serve to explain government's continued failure to pursue constitutional education as a means of deepening our constitutional democracy.

When President Thabo Mbeki was elected, he appointed Dullah as Minister of Transport. This meant that he was not able to oversee the implementation of the strategy that he put in place. Unfortunately, the ministers that followed did not bother to understand or take ownership of the original strategy, each wanting a strategy of their own.

Integrated justice system

The Reconstruction and Development Plan (RDP) with a dedicated ministry was established in the first term of government, and affected most aspects of government, including the Department to Justice. It introduced a novel approach to dealing with the scourge of crime. The RDP introduced the philosophy of an integrated justice system (IJS). The IJS was premised on the critique that the individual components of the criminal justice system (the police, prosecutions, courts and prisons) should not operate in silos. The criminal justice system had to be managed in an integrated manner. The philosophy was that we needed to manage both the case and the person, be it the accused or victim, through the entire system. This meant that the manner in which the case or person was attended to should be the same by each department instead of duplicating processes. A simple manifestation of this would be that there had to be standardisation between the different departments, be it the police, prosecutions, courts or prisons.

A new structure was established to promote and implement IJS – the IJS User Board. Composed of DDGs from the departments of South African police services, justice, prosecutions, prisons, home affairs and social development, I represented justice on this board and chaired it for nearly ten years. As an RDP project, we reported to an inter-ministerial committee of cabinet, or a cluster of departments. We were part of the Justice and Crime Prevention System (JCPS) cluster.

This new approach to dealing with the criminal justice system included the utilisation of common technologies to support common processes. This meant that only one file would be created with all the data from the departments in it, thus increasing efficiency and allowing for effective communications between departments. The idea of having only one file was simple but radical because it changed the way in which each department managed its business – it was standardised.

Another task of the IJS User Board was the development of a common approach to the procurement of required technologies. This was naturally easier said than done, particularly because each department wanted to control the decisions they needed to take. It was a matter of turf and each had a preference based on their experience and training. The decisions were all very subjective.

Penuell Maduna was appointed Minister of Justice in 1999. Typical of new ministers in office, he set about to immediately restructure the department and develop a new strategy without first familiarising himself with developments. There was merely an assumption that the old strategy and structure needed to be changed.

Government took a decision to enter into a partnership with the business community through a structure called Business Against Crime (BAC). This effort worked with mixed results. BAC assisted Maduna to restructure the department. There were two key developments to come out of this exercise. These were the promotion of both the chief financial officer (CFO) and chief information officer (CIO), who was the manager responsible for information technology, to the rank of DDG and therefore part of the executive team. Both these posts were new to the public service. These changes led to my first redeployment as the manager of a newly established branch – information and systems management (ISM) – in 1999. While I held this post until 2005 and greatly enjoyed it, I was removed even further from my grounding in the field of constitutional development.

One of the first lessons we learnt was that we could not continue to manage the department and realise the political objectives by managing in the old way. The department was focused on serving only part of the population and could not cope if the same service was to be rendered to all the people. It became clear that we would need to harness the potential of technology if we were to succeed. It was easier for us because our department was known as effectively being a 'greenfield' site. The most modern piece of technology that we had when we took power was the typewriter. Of the 11,000-odd staff that we had in the more than 550 sites in 1997 when I arrived, only five sites had networks and less than a thousand members of staff were using computers – most of whom were in finance or in the human resources department. We still depended on typing pools to run our business. As will be seen in my experience with the Masters' Office, the system could not cope with the new political demands of a constitutional democracy.

Unfortunately, new managers started purchasing computers only because it was the trendy thing to do. The absence of standards and systems resulted in a number of problems. When typewriters were used, documents were prepared in long hand and sent to a typing pool to complete. This system allowed for a process of quality control over the documents produced and proper records were kept. Email, while being instant, replaced the production of formal letters. The only record of communications now was in the inboxes of individuals. The traditional filing and records system became redundant.

e-Justice

As the CIO for the Department of Justice and Constitutional Development, it was my responsibility to develop an IT strategy for the department. This was exciting especially because our department was soon placed in the forefront of the utilisation of technology in the public service. The strategy I developed had four key aspects to it. The first was to develop a secure virtual private network (VPN) as the foundation on which to build all our IT systems. The second was to provide all officers of the department with connectivity. This meant that everyone had access to a computer terminal that was connected to one secure network. The third aspect was to develop business systems that would be able to transform the way we did our business. This opened the possibility of developing court and case management systems as well as a host of other applications to manage our administration, document management, finances and human resources. The fourth aspect to this strategy was the integration of the Department of Justice into the broader integrated justice system and partner with the other departments in our cluster.

Up until the late 1990s the justice system in South Africa was subject to many business challenges. Systems were manual and transactions were paper-based, labour-intensive and often error prone. Common problems experienced were ineffective scheduling and missing and misplaced dockets in our courts, making it difficult to manage our courts effectively. With weak governance, corruption became easier and more common.

The logical first step in the e-justice programme was the establishment of a digital backbone on which the entire department could communicate with each other. We referred to this as the Digital Nervous System (DNS). The DNS project was initiated in 2000 and within three years we secured the provision of basic connectivity including email and basic office applications to more than 10,000 judges, magistrates and prosecutors. This meant that judges, magistrates and prosecutors could for the first time now efficiently and securely communicate with each other and had electronic access to vital legal research. A value-for-money study on this project was carried out by a major auditing firm and revealed dramatic benefits and value. The uptake in the use of this new technology was phenomenal. Within a year of the project, we were managing more than 30,000 email messages daily. The provision of email dramatically improved the response time in our communications and made us more accessible to the public and other stakeholders. The use of this technology became critical to the business of the department and so commonplace that people very quickly forgot what it was like before. An immediate effect of the project was that our traditional typing pools became irrelevant. We were able to re-deploy this staff to more meaningful tasks.

A key characteristic of the justice system is the management of information, and more importantly knowledge. In fact, the system is dependent on its ability to share that knowledge. Our system of law is based primarily on precedents. The irony of our environment was that our judges provided copies of their judgments free of charge to a profit-making company and we would then buy access to these very judgments, which we issued so that we could use it in our cases. In fact, the references to these judgments are those provided by the company publishing them rather than the department from which it originated. This was not very logical.

The challenge was to promote knowledge sharing within the department. To do this, we developed an intranet providing users with a common work space. This provided for the publication of all documents and information in an easily accessible manner. This meant that we could dramatically improve communication and reduce the cost of manually printing and posting these to our 550 offices countrywide. Notices and circulars were instantly available to all.

One of the most important achievements of the court management solution that was piloted was the routing of dockets to courts. The pilot proved that we could drop the time for the routing of case files from the police to courts from two days down to one hour. Very soon after the system was implemented, we were forced to test it in a real situation when some 200 dockets were stolen from the Durban Central Police Station. As all dockets had been scanned, officials were able to reproduce these without any delay.

The e-Justice Programme very quickly started producing results and captured the imagination of many in government, both inside and outside of South Africa. No other Department of Justice in the world had managed to ramp up a project to provide basic computer technology to so many in such a short time successfully. The work we did was quickly recognised and in 2002, I was nominated as a finalist in the African ICT Achievers Awards for service delivery in the public sector. In 2003, I was elected by peers in both the private and public sector as the public Sector CIO of the year. This is the highest accolade an ICT worker could receive in Africa. And in 2004, I was again nominated by the Government Information Technology Officers (GITO) Council as the departmental GITO representative of the year.

Not long after Thabo Mbeki was elected president, he engaged the World Bank in a unique programme. He argued that much needed to be done to build the core of the South African public service. What came out of this exchange was a fast-tracking joint programme between Wits Business School and Harvard University in which a large number of senior public servants were put through a senior executive programme. In 2003, I was given this opportunity and became a Harvard alumni.

Our minister until 2004 was Penuell Maduna. He was largely absent and allowed us to get on with our work without interfering too much. His usual explanation was that it was 'urgent matters of state' that kept him busy elsewhere. When Brigitte Mabandla was appointed, she decided that she needed to change things in the department. She came to this conclusion without taking the time to understand anything. As would become a pattern with a number of ministers in government, her starting point was to change the DG. Vusi Pikoli was moved out and she appointed Menzi Simelane.

Like Mabandla, Simelane too came into the department with the intention of changing without trying to understand what he was changing. This, he did without any experience in the department and with no prior experience or skill in the management of a large or complex organisation. Unlike Maduna, Mabandla ruled by proxy through Simelane who thought he knew everything and was not open to any advice. He would often issue directives by SMS in the middle of the night without consulting anyone. The results were catastrophic. Morale plummeted.

A turning point

Several different reasons colluded to make 2005 a turning point in my life. This was the year in which I had my first experience with the media. As a rule, I never interacted with the media directly. All media matters were referred to our public relations department. One day I was informed that a journalist from Radio 702 wanted to interview me. The response of our media team was to ask the journalist to put her questions in writing. The enquiry related to a tender for a service provider to support our infrastructure. The tender was still in the process of being adjudicated by our supply-chain management team. The question posed was whether I had issued the contract to a company owned by my brother, a certain Nazeem Ebrahim. The response given in writing confirmed that the tender was still in the process of being adjudicated. It also explained that not only was I not involved in this process, but I also did not have a brother by the name of Nazeem Ebrahim or one that was involved in providing any IT services whatsoever.

Despite the written confirmation, Radio 702 ran with the story the next morning alleging that I had issued a huge contract to my brother's company. I was accused of nepotism and corruption. The news item was withdrawn after a couple of hours, but not without causing me a great deal of pain and embarrassment. I was forced to defend myself against a false and malicious allegation. The source of the allegation was one of the companies who feared that they would not be successful in winning the tender because of their dismal track record. It was their intention to get rid of their potential competitors. Fortunately for me, the department confirmed that the allegations were false.

Then, I was confronted by another challenge. Without notice, explanation or discussion, Menzi unilaterally decided to appoint me as the chief master. This came at the same time when the IT work we were doing was beginning to take off and show incredible promise. I was surely being tested and was forced to take stock of where I was and what I wanted to do. There were several things that I was not happy with and needed to make a break.

At 48 years old in 2015, I started becoming increasingly paranoid about my health. I smoked too much and ate badly. I finally managed to give up my addiction to smoking, which took nearly 15 years to defeat. I also changed my lifestyle by eating better and started running. Before long, I became passionate about running and attempted marathons.

I had stopped practising my religion when I went into exile in 1979 and neither was I working on my spirituality. This created a void, but it was one that I was hardly aware of. At the end of 2005, my mother had disposed of a property and decided to use the money by taking my sister and me on pilgrimage to Mecca in December. I paid no attention to this until we actually set off on the journey. Remarkably, the moment I arrived in Medina I knew that my life was about to change. The experience was phenomenal. The peace of Medina was extraordinary and my spirituality awakened. My pilgrimage turned out to be a defining moment in my life.

The first chief master

The five years that I worked as the department's CIO was a great learning experience. I was able to venture into a new field, do it successfully and even earn the respect and trust of peers and gain several industry and government accolades nationally and internationally along the way.

By October 2005, we had established one of the most sophisticated VPNs in government capable of supporting a workforce of nearly 15,000 people. We had started deploying business solutions that were beginning to yield positive results in work performance and productivity. For these reasons, I moved feeling quite confident that I was leaving behind a solid legacy that could not be reversed. Nothing could have been further from the truth.

I was appointed as the first chief master on 1 October 2005. A new post, the masters of each high court were accountable to the chief master. My first task was to visit all our offices, interviewed the staff and get to know the business of the master's office. I even got to speak to members of the public that we were servicing in each office. The objective was to record a snapshot of the status of the branch at the time of my appointment and provide me with a benchmark against which progress could be measured. I also wanted to review the existing strategy with a view to understanding what my challenges were.

The core business of the master's branch had five areas. We were responsible for the administration of all deceased estates. Related to the deceased estates was the management of the Guardian's Fund into which the pension funds of all deceased public servants are deposited. The masters are also responsible for the administration of all insolvent estates and of Trusts. Finally, the Masters are responsible for the curatorship of mental patients and those who are not able to take decisions on their own.

The branch had a most noble origin and history. Our function was to give effect to the responsibility of the high court, which acts as the upper guardian of all minor children. My investigation into the performance of the branch led me to believe that the masters' branch lost its focus. The approach to delivering our services had been one of complying with legislation rather than functioning as a protector of the vulnerable. This was because of the volume of work we had to deal with.

Of the five services that we rendered, our biggest challenges lay with the administration of the Guardian's Fund and administration of deceased estates. However, it was our Insolvency section that exposed us to negative press coverage because of the large amounts of money involved. Our business was experiencing a growth of between 20% and 30% annually and our organisational capacity had not been able to keep up with the demand. I could see this from the volume of paper we dealt with and the size of our Guardian's Fund account. We simply did not have the capacity to deal with the volume of paper involved in our work. As for the Guardian's Fund, this had grown to more than several billion rand. We were just not coping.

Human resources norms dictated that the workload we had required more than 1100 permanent employees. We had only 600-odd. However, simply adding more people was not going to solve the problem. We needed to fundamentally change the way our business was functioning. The growth of our Guardian's Fund was largely attributed to the increasing number of AIDS-related deaths and the rise in the number of black people in the formal economy. Another challenge that we were confronted with was the demand to make our services more accessible to the ordinary population, especially the rural poor. We needed a bigger footprint, more offices and therefore more people.

The message was consistent and clear. We could not continue doing business in the old way. We were not fit for purpose. Our branch was not designed to serve the people of the democratic republic of South Africa. We urgently needed to leverage the value of technology and streamline our business processes. In our strategic planning, the first thing I focused on was to provide the Masters' Branch leadership with new direction. I rallied the team around a call that we needed to move from mere compliance to compassion – and, from files to faces! Our function was more than complying with the law; we needed to show compassion, especially to the vulnerable and poor. The cases we were dealing with were not just files or numbers, they involved people who had faces. This meant that people deserved respect.

The next step was to build a team spirit around a common vision and plan. This strategy worked and over the next 18 months, we recorded excellent progress such that Minister Mabandla singled out the chief master and masters' branch for special mention in her 2007 budget vote speech. The progress made however was threatened by the prolonged lack of capacity. Nothing came of the consistent pleas to the DG for support. The problems and challenges we were confronted with were not new but the required decisive intervention was not forthcoming.

An example of the nature of the problem was the manner in which deceased estates were to be managed. During apartheid, when a white person died without a will, the estate had to be administered by the master of the high court. However, when a black person died intestate, the estate was administered by a magistrate. This difference was racist and changed by the ground-breaking judgments in Bhe[75] and Moseneke.[76] There were however two problems: all of a sudden, the workload of the masters' offices grew exponentially when it had no capacity in the first place, and secondly, our 14 offices were not accessible to those in rural areas.

In desperation, magistrates courts were designated as 'service points' and the status quo remained. This however only made the problem worse because the function was now relegated to unqualified clerks instead of magistrates. This meant that the rural population, mainly poor black people who did not have access to legal representation now suffered even worse discrimination. The department, remiss in not planning for the new constitutional reality, had failed the plea of the Constitutional Court when it ordered that we provide the required quality of service. The value of these milestone judgements was lost and we remained in contempt of a most important judgment. It was even more regrettable that these were at least 50% of all estate matters.

The problem was extremely serious. I personally surveyed a number of our offices and interviewed officials responsible for service point management. What I discovered was that there was a margin of error of at least 80% on the files attended to at the magistrate's courts. It was even more frustrating that we had no capacity to perform basic quality checks. Even more regrettable was the fact that many of these estates involved minors with very little assets and whose interests were not being taken care of. The threat of mismanagement, fraud and corruption was very real. Our attempts to address this problem came to nought because our capacity did not suffice.[77]

To address problems of mismanagement, fraud and corruption, we automated the Guardian's Fund with great success. This was however only at six of our 14 offices because some did not have the capacity to deliver the service. Some offices were forced to limit services to only part of the day. A sad example was the office in Kimberley, which was traditionally one of the best-managed offices. Despite having a reasonably well established and competent staff and a small population that needed its service, they only had the capacity to operate for half the day. This naturally had a severe impact on staff morale, which in turn affected the quality of services delivered.

Despite our best efforts, we only managed to secure a meeting with Minister Mabandla in May 2007. However, nothing came of an unequivocal undertaking she gave us that special attention will be given to capacitating our offices. That was it! I could go on no more and resigned on 1 October 2007. Before I left, I wrote a letter to Minister Mabandla early in September asking for a meeting to explain my resignation. I got no reply.[78]

I told her in my letter that: 'The solutions to these problems lay in our hands. We don't need clever strategies to make this Branch a success. While we recorded excellent progress thus far, unless there is a radical change in attitude we will fail. I am not prepared to fail and neither am I prepared to deliver the substandard quality of services that we are obliged to under the current circumstances. I therefore find myself in the rather invidious position where resignation appears to be the only defence I have to protect my integrity and dignity as a manager in the public service and a cadre who was part of the struggle for this hard won freedom and democracy we now have.'

Leaving the public service was not easy because I am by nature a public servant and enjoyed working in government. I understood the public service system and it is where I was happiest were it not for the deteriorating political environment. Over the next ten years, I made every effort possible to return to the fold but could find no opening.

XVII

Starting a New Life

Getting married again!

I continued to hope that my children would someday return to South Africa and decided to buy a place for them to come home to. I bought the house only after my father passed on in 1999. Over the years, they visited me regularly and I them as often as I could. No matter how joyous these times were, it did nothing for the emptiness their absence left in me. It was and continues to be very painful.

Over the ten years following my return to Pretoria, both family and friends tried every means possible to convince me to settle down again. I worked long hours, enjoyed my single status and was just not confident enough to make a real effort to meet someone. However, life was changing. I gave up smoking, became healthier and was even running marathons. I was also head-hunted for a job as a senior executive manager in a German multi-national, T-Systems. But I was nearly 50 years old, and still alone. After a nudge from my sister, Hajira, and a push from several friends, I finally relented and decided to take the plunge by agreeing to consider the few options I had.

Hajira recommended that I meet Soraya, a divorced mother of three young adults – Aadil, Zaahid and Luqmaan. Despite being family, I hardly knew her, but hesitatingly, agreed to meet her. Hajira asked Soraya if she would be prepared to meet with me. She did and it was a start of a great relationship. We bonded over basic things and felt very comfortable in each other's company. Before long, we took the decision to settle down. Quite coincidentally, the most convenient date available for this important occasion also happened to be my 50th birthday. To my surprise, Soraya's family decided to hold a proper full-blown wedding reception with all the trimmings that one would normally do for young people getting married. This was most unusual but very welcome. The reception was grand and very memorable. It was certainly a moment of great happiness for us all.

A month before I got married, I started working with T-Systems. What I discovered very quickly is that politics in the private sector organisations is little different to that which I found in the public sector. Sometimes, it was even more ruthless. After some months, I began to feel as if I was little more than a black face making up the required quota for purposes of more favourable tender bids. What made life even more awkward was the fact that I was parachuted into an organisation and required to supervise managers who were unhappy that they were overlooked when filling my post. This made for an unhappy state of affairs and before the year was over, it was mutually agreed that we part ways.

To clear my mind, Soraya and I took our two mothers on a wonderful holiday to India. After a couple of weeks of job hunting, I received a call from Barbara Hogan, recently appointed Minister of Health. She needed an advisor to help her on strategic matters, particularly focusing on the use of information technology in the health sector. In the 40 years since I became politically active, this was the third time that our paths crossed. I always enjoyed working with her and was therefore very pleased to join her team.

e-Health

Barbara appointed me as a member of a team referred to as the Minister's Advisory Committee for Health (MACH). I was to work on the development of a country strategy for strengthening health information systems and to provide general strategic support.

With this brief, I carried out a detailed investigation into the state of affairs in the National Department of Health. It became immediately evident that it was impossible to manage health services effectively without the benefit of accurate information. The collection of accurate data and a proper understanding of the information it revealed was critical. This was not possible manually. For this reason, a National Health Information System Committee (NHIS/SA) was established in 1995 with members from all nine provinces. The NHIS was mandated to conceptualise and design a national health information system for South Africa, ie, an electronic patient record system for the country. Unfortunately, implementation of this system was and continues to be as elusive as the holy grail. Another major project was that of telemedicine, its objective being to deliver health care to the disadvantaged communities in rural areas through technology. This project equally held great promise, but success here was also elusive.

The delivery of health services was a provincial responsibility and was managed as such. This is when I was introduced to some of the unfortunate aspects of our regional dispensation. What I discovered was that provincial became sites of vested interests. Provinces insisted on managing their own projects in the manner that they wished. This made it impossible to have a coherent national strategy and resulted in duplication and misalignment. It also left space for corruption with huge financial implications because of weak governance.

According to a DBSA report 'Roadmap to Reform',[79] there was an evident failure of the system achieving reasonable goals with it functioning poorly and, in some instances, worsening. We were paying more to deliver a worse service. The budget was bigger, but it did not yield better results. The starting point was to put in place a new strategic plan. Further complicating the matter was the government's commitment to a National Health Insurance system.

Barbara Hogan was appointed Minister of Public Enterprises in May 2009, and Aaron Motsoaledi, the new minister, asked me to continue. The only change was that I now was to report to Dr Molefi Paul Sefularo (Paul). Paul's advisor was Dr Confidence Moloko. What a small world indeed! Confi and Paul were core members of the Thami Mnyeli Unit, which was so critical in the formation of the Kabwe Machinery in 1985. Who would have thought that nearly 25 years later we would be working together in the new democratic dispensation? This time, it was me who would be accountable to Paul and not the other way around. I am pleased that we enjoyed a relationship of mutual respect and trust. Paul was extremely supportive and understood the value of information technology in providing health services.

I established an e-health steering committee consisting of senior officials from each of the provinces. A critical agreement was a moratorium on all further IT procurement to ensure that there would be no duplication and wastage. Paul was exceptional in giving executive support to the development of this strategy and in a few short months, we were able to prepare a draft strategy. Sadly, Paul died in a car accident on 5 April 2010 and I lost my executive sponsor. The department saw me as the advisor brought in by Barbara Hogan, my work was viewed with a fair measure of suspicion and things began to unravel very quickly. It did not take long before I was left with little option but to move.

The department worked a further two years after my departure before an e-health strategy was produced. It was satisfying to note the recognition paid by the Minister Aaron Motsoaledi for the work we did when he stated in the foreword of the strategy that:

> In August 2009, the National Health Council (NHC), chaired by myself and comprising of the 9 Provincial MECs for Health, resolved that the acquisition of software solutions which were not interoperable should be halted until the eHealth Strategy for South Africa is finalised. The strategy should provide us with a clear roadmap that guides us from the current status to an integrated and well-functioning national patient-based information system, based on agreed upon scientific standards for interoperability, which improves the efficiency of clinical care, produces the indicators required by management, and facilitates patient mobility. The architecture of this system should also enable an interface with other transversal systems used in the health sector. Such a system is also a critical enabling factor for the implementation of National Health Insurance (NHI). [80]

Office of the Chief Justice

By the time I left the National Department of Health, I was convinced that I needed to get back into the public service. I know no other life. I understand government and its processes, and I developed good managerial skills with a passion for technology. My background in law was an added bonus. For this reason, I scanned the papers for any possible openings in the public sector and diligently applied for all posts that I thought I could fit in. At 52, I was keen to work my remaining years before retirement in the public service. I even applied for the post I held as chief master, which had still not been filled more than two years after my departure. To my utter horror, I was not even shortlisted for this post.

Of all the posts that I applied for, I only had one shortlisting. It was a rather strange experience. I thought the skills and experience I had were needed. After a couple of months, I was very worried. I was therefore very pleased to get a call from Richard Sizani, whom I knew as a PAC MP in the Constitutional Assembly. I enjoyed working with him because of his forthright manner.

I was told by Richard that government accepted the demands made by the judiciary and agreed to establish the Office of the Chief Justice. This was a precursor to its establishment as a separate entity. There was agreement to build capacity in the Office of the Chief Justice to allow him to perform his functions in both the roles of head of the Judiciary as well as the Constitutional Court. Chief Justice Sandile Ngcobo took advantage of the government's new approach by establishing a committee with the task of conceptualising working models for an institution to support the chief justice in both the roles. The committee was also required to take into account best practices, determine the financial implications of each model, and an implementation schedule for each.

The committee consisted of Arthur Chaskalson and Pius Langa as the joint chairs and a number of academics. I was asked to head the secretariat. This was a great opportunity to work with some fine legal minds and to define what the judicial branch of government should look like. It was a continuation of my previous work in the negotiation of both constitutions and the ten years thereafter in the department of justice implementing the constitution. I simply could not pass this up.

From my work in the Department of Justice, I knew that the judges were never happy with the size of the court budgets and wanted greater control over how it was used. Part of the problem was the worsening relationship between the minister and judiciary after Dullah. Chief justices, Ismail Mohammed, Arthur Chaskalson and Pius Langa, were vigorous campaigners for judicial independence and wanted greater authority to decide on their priorities. Chief Justice Sandile Ngcobo however took this argument further. He believed in parity. It was his argument that there should be absolute parity between the three branches of government. The president, the speaker and the chief justice were co-equals and he wanted to see this parity down to the level of budgets on the security detail and entertainment allowances.

The governance of the South African judicial system has always been somewhat opaque. Traditionally, the executive branch was responsible not only for the magistracy but also for the administration of the superior courts.[81] While section 242 of the interim constitution envisaged merely the rationalisation of the courts, the 1996 Constitution was more ambitious and seemed to mandate reform of a far more fundamental kind. A transitional provision contained in item 16(6) of Schedule 6 mandated the Minister of Justice and Constitutional Development with responsibility for the rationalisation of courts, including their structure and functioning, and of the legislation governing them with a view to establishing 'a judicial system suited to the requirements of the new Constitution'.

I have tried to understand why our constitutional negotiations between 1992 and 1996 did not attend to the transformation of the judiciary as we did the structures of the executive and legislature. There is nothing in the records or minutes to explain this. I remember however that we focused our attention on the transformation of executive and legislative branches of government when negotiating both the constitutions. In fact, very little attention was paid to the question of judicial governance and independence of the judiciary, particularly about how it was financed. This is borne out by the fact that this omission warranted a specific amendment of the constitution that would declare the Constitutional Court as our highest court.

While 16(6) of Schedule 6 of the transitional provision in the Constitution mandated the Minister of Justice to attend to the transformation of our courts, it was only on 28 February 2011, some 15 years later, that Minister Jeff Radebe released a discussion document on the transformation of the judicial system and the role of the judiciary in the developmental South African state for comment.[82]

Government did however agree with the judiciary in August 2010 to implement three phases. Phase 1 would lead to the establishment of the Office of the Chief Justice as a national department within the public service. Phase 2 would see the establishment of the Office of the Chief Justice as an independent entity similar to that of the Auditor-General; and finally Phase 3 would see the establishment of a structure to provide judicial-based and -managed court administration.

Consequently, the president issued a proclamation to establish the Office of the Chief Justice as a government department. The committee established by Justice Ngcobo therefore was intended to deal with the next phase giving us a unique opportunity to guide transformation in this branch of government. The report was delivered on 28 September 2011. However, by the time the report was completed there was a change of guard. Sandile Ngcobo's term came to an end and Justice Mogoeng Mogoeng was appointed. Fortunately, he asked the committee to complete its work. The lesson is that while South Africa's constitution laid a sound foundation, building our constitutional democracy is an ongoing project.

Sadly, this report was the last major assignment that legal giants, Pius Langa and Arthur Chaskalson, were to undertake before passing on, and South Africa was so much the poorer for it.[83] This sad loss made me realise just how fortunate I was to work with such great lawyers who helped shape the history of our country.

A change of pace

In June 2011, shortly after we finalised our report, we celebrated Soraya's 50th birthday by going on her dream holiday to Rome, Florence, Venice and Paris. It was every bit as magical as the brochures promised. The holiday was all the more memorable because it reminded me that I too could lead a 'normal' life.

Since joining the ANC in the '70s, my life had been an incredibly intense rollercoaster ride from which it was hard to get off because total commitment was required. It was not an ordinary office job with regular hours. This made it very difficult for a clear divide between working to earn a living and living. I gave it everything I had. It was never just a job.

This is why having Soraya in my life was so special. Soraya made me feel like an ordinary person capable of ordinary pleasures. Ever so gentle and patient, she gave me the space and support I needed. This is why I was even more keen not to make the mistakes of the past. I had to pay attention to my family life. Having a home and a family was important. I changed the way I managed my life. Family time and especially having meals together became important. I started having weekends 'off'. Going to the movies every week and taking time off to eat out became special and a most enjoyable routine. I came to enjoy our regular holidays and time off alone.

Then, my daughter Ruby gave birth to Lily on 23 July 2011. Not long after this, Amina, Aadil's wife also gave birth to a daughter, Imaan, on 28 September. Four years after getting married again, and in the space of a couple of months, I became a grandfather of two wonderful girls. Times were indeed changing.

XVIII

Working Internationally

Unfortunately, most of my work from this time onwards would take me beyond the borders of our country. Despite my best efforts, I was not successful in finding employment in the public sector. The only work I found since 2010 has been with international non-governmental organisations (NGOs) and the United Nations. Working internationally was effectively another period of exile; this time, for economic rather than political reasons.

What I realised is that my work for these international organisations made me visible and approached more often. You had to be on the circuit. This is not really what I wanted even if I enjoyed the work greatly because it took me away from home several weeks at a time, and often not in the safest of environments. This obviously did not help me trying to lead a 'normal' life. Fortunately, Soraya has been, and continues to be, most supportive.

Before concluding my work at the Office of the Chief Justice, I was approached by the United Nations Development Programme (UNDP) for work in Djibouti to help on the Somali Constitution. I was also offered other pieces of work in both North and South Sudan by other organisations. Shortly after, the UNDP in Zimbabwe asked me to provide support to the constitutional negotiations there on a more protracted basis.

Zimbabwe

Political pressure forced the Zimbabwean government in 1999 to undertake comprehensive constitutional reform to address the deficiencies in the Lancaster House political settlement. The exercise was led by Professor Jonathan Moyo and I assisted as an advisor. The draft constitution was subsequently rejected in a referendum.

By the time that Zimbabwe held its presidential and parliamentary elections in March 2008, the country was experiencing a political, economic and social crisis leading to a very polarised political environment. The level of political strife had the potential of leading to violent conflict. In September 2008, after an intervention from the Southern African Development Community (SADC), the main political parties, ZANU-PF, MDC-T and MDC-M signed the Global Political Agreement (GPA). The GPA provided for reform to create the conditions for increased civic participation in the constitution-making process. It was hoped that these reforms would result in the country's democratic transformation and desperately needed economic development. The international community funded a UNDP project to support the process which included a participatory and consultative outreach programme. Government immediately convened a conference of all stakeholders to consult on how best to implement the provisions of the GPA.

As is usual with processes of this nature, there were invariably delays because promises were made to deliver faster than was reasonably possible. I was brought in to help and was fortunate to be the only international expert in the process. The process was led by representatives of the three major parties – Paul Mangwana, Douglas Mwonzora and Edward Mkhosi.

I enjoyed this assignment. The people were great and easy to work with, the country incredibly beautiful and the weather most agreeable. I was grateful to be included in the negotiations between the leaders and was able to participate in finding solutions. I put in a lot of effort to earn their trust. These negotiations took us to some of the most beautiful retreats in the country. The Zimbabwean people welcomed the process and enthusiastically participated in it. There was always pressure to succeed, especially on Paul, Douglas and Edward whose political careers depended on it.

This is where Jonathan Moyo intervened. Jonathan was responsible for the failed 1999 constitution-making process and referendum. After joining and leaving ZANU-PF several times, he became a minister in Mugabe's cabinet and its public spokesperson. To put pressure on the parties, Jonathan decided to attack me personally, and the role I was playing in the process, in the media. He accused me of being a South African spy with ulterior motives. This attack continued over three consecutive weeks on the front pages of their Sunday papers. As with the attack on me in 1994 by Walter Felgate, I had the good fortune of having political support. The three co-chairs felt obliged to jointly defend me publicly and decided to publish this in an advertorial that extolled my virtues and paid general tribute to my contribution.

Despite the challenges, the process was successfully concluded and the constitution enthusiastically supported in a referendum held shortly thereafter. The first election in terms of the new constitution confounded many critics because ZANU-PF trounced its rivals and returned to power.

I also enjoyed Harare for a different reason. I could train for running my marathons. After joining the Jacaranda Athletics Club in Laudium, I took up road running a lot more seriously. The club had great athletes with a tremendous amount of experience, who inspired me to run the 56-kilometre Two Oceans Ultra Marathon in 2012. My successful completion of this race remains one of my great achievements. I will never forget both the thrill and the pain that went with it.

I completed my assignment in June 2012 and returned home to an uncertain future. This was the challenge of freelance consultancies. They were short-termed and tentative, which meant that before a contract came to an end, one had to start looking for the next piece of work. Gratefully, these anxious times never lasted too long.

In a short space of time, I had three exciting prospects. Mac Maharaj drew my attention to a job opening in the UN for a one-year contract working for their Mediation Support Unit (MSU). The UN's

Mediation Support Unit had a standby team of six international experts who they deployed on 72 hours' notice to any one of the hotspots in the world requiring mediation services. I applied. Then, at the same time, I got a call from a manager in National Treasury who wanted to know if I would be interested in serving on the Special Pension's Appeals Board because of my experience both in exile and in law. As if the two opportunities were not enough, I was also approached by the UNDP to provide support in war-torn Somalia.

In the meantime, Ruby got married in August 2012 and I was happy to travel with Soraya to the UK for the occasion. While Yusuf had come home several times after I got married, it was the first time that Soraya was able to meet Ruby and Lily. It was therefore a very happy time for us all.

A month later, the UNDP asked me to report to Mogadishu to support the new speaker of parliament, Mohamed Osman Jawari, as his strategic advisor. Troops from the African Union had just managed to wrest the control, which Al-Shabaab had over Mogadishu, and a transitional government and parliament was installed with the support of the UN. The situation was so tense that the parliament was sworn in on the tarmac of Mogadishu's airport on 20 August 2012. This was the beginning of a new chapter in my life.

Somalia

Somalia is a fascinating case study of the effects of state failure and the difficult journey a country has to make and the challenges faces in trying to transition towards fragility and eventually a constitutional democracy.

Somalia is located in the horn of Africa and has a 3000-kilometre shoreline along the Gulf of Aden. It is positioned strategically because of the busy shipping lines that pass by its shores. There are two other reasons that make up its strategic location. Its waters are one of the world's great sources of tuna and are thought to hold great reserves of oil. Its traditional capital, Mogadishu, is an ancient city that has, over more than 1000 years, absorbed influences from the Chinese, Ottomans, Persian and Indians. Once one of the greatest of African cities referred to as the 'Pearl of Africa', Mogadishu was a great trading city with incredible charm and a rich architecture, which is still evident despite years of intense and unrelenting urban warfare.

Siad Barre, who came to power in a bloodless coup, led Somalia between 1969 and 1991. Barre ran a strong nationalist government with defined policies and programmes. He is even credited with making Somali a written language and ensuring that its people could read and write it over a short period of time. His policies however led to significant internal conflict which eventually led to the fall of his government in 1991 with Barre fleeing the country.

This collapse resulted in the state itself folding in a rather decisive manner with the delivery of all services ending abruptly. Society became riven with mistrust and civil war between clan-based militia. So dramatic was the failure of the state that not even government infrastructure survived. Nothing was safe from the looting. In response, the international community, under the supervision of the UN, sponsored a series of conciliation conferences between the rival clans and warlords held in neighbouring countries. It is during these conferences that they established a series of Transitional Federal Governments (TFG) based on what came to be known as the '4.5 formula'. This meant that the four major clans of Hawiye, Rahanweyn, Dir and Daarood got equal quotas while the half-point was allocated to the 'minority' clans.

Successive transitional governments failed to bring the fighting to an end. A group of religious leaders stepped in to establish what they referred to as the Islamic Courts Union (ICU) to bring about some order. Unlike the TFG which lacked credibility, the ICU were and are extremely successful. This led to a stand-off between the ICU in June 2006. Until then, the Al-Shabaab was a small insignificant component of the ICU. The international community were more concerned about the rise of the ICU, and their reliance on Shariah law, than the competing warlords who they worked with. Ethiopia and Kenya decided to join the fray against the ICU and invaded Somalia. This invasion fuelled resentment against foreign interference among many Somalis who rallied behind an increasingly militant Shabaab who gained in popular support. This is also when Shabaab became the threat that it is today.

The upshot of this conflict is one of the bloodiest and most relentless episodes in African history. The most intense part of this conflict took place between 2006 and 2012, the ferocity which laid waste to Mogadishu is still evident today. The UN initiated a peace process between the rival group but excluding Shabaab. Part of this resulted in an attempt to draft a new constitutional dispensation. Because of the conflict, this process took place outside mainly in Kenya and Djibouti. Despite claims by the UN and international community, Mogadishu is still a war zone.[84]

It is in this context that I was first introduced to the Somali constitution-making process in 2010. My brief was to work with a committee to share best practices and support the drafting of a constitution, and a draft was produced and launched for consultation in August 2010.

While this was taking place, African Union forces made a massive military effort to wrest control over Mogadishu from Shabaab. This made it possible on 1 August 2012 to hold a National Constitutional Assembly, consisting of a broad selection of leaders, to adopt a provisional constitution and establish the ninth Somali parliament on the tarmac of the airport in Mogadishu. The speaker of this parliament was Mohammad Sheikh Osman Jawari whom I worked with in Djibouti. Jawari appointed me as his strategic advisor. Because the parliament building was totally gutted by the conflict and structurally unusable, the VIP garage space was used to conduct parliamentary business.

The first thing I learnt about the UN is that it is risk averse. This is why they used labour brokers to contract my services. Mogadishu was a shock with nothing in my life thus far to prepare me for this experience. I was not even allowed past immigration without bodyguards. The ride to the hotel was short but fascinating. We travelled the two-kilometre journey in an armoured vehicle escorted by two additional vehicles, one in the front and the other at the back, full of private soldiers armed with medium to heavy machine guns. The hotel was a fortified bunker.

As if to initiate me properly into Mogadishu, I witnessed my first gun battle within the first 48 hours of my arrival. It lasted more than 30-odd minutes and took place less than 100 metres from the hotel. I learnt that violent conflict was never far away. We would soon become so used to the sound of gunfire and explosions that it rarely ever mattered what one was doing. I remember continuing with my breakfast after hearing a car bomb exploding not so far away.

Jawari later provided me with accommodation in the presidential compound, Villa Somalia, which was five kilometres from the airport. This came to be my most expensive taxi ride. It would cost between 1500 and 2000 USD per day because I needed a convoy. It was an experience that was straight out of war movies. We never took the same route to and from and whenever we had an unscheduled stop such as a traffic jam, close protection officers would be immediately deployed around the vehicle. Needless to say, a bullet-proof vest and helmet was part of the package. I had to keep reminding myself that my brief was to help establish a constitutional democracy.

Since 1991, no services had been delivered by government. More than 70% of the population were young people who would not have in their lifetime experienced government in any form whatsoever. Government was no more than an idea or rumour that people would have talked about. All basic utilities and services including water, electricity, health and education were privately provided. Not even taxes were collected. When I studied this phenomenon further, I discovered that Al-Shabaab was better at collecting taxes than the government was. Being a tax collector in Mogadishu was quite a dangerous occupation. Between 2012 and 2014, at least 25 tax collectors were murdered, which was 19% of the city's 130 tax-collecting staff.[85] They had four different governments in the first five years. There was no institutional memory and corruption was institutionalised. We even struggled to find copies of old laws. Ironically, for a country that has not had law, order or a functioning government in three decades, Somalis are intensely political.

My brief started with the development of a strategic plan for parliament, which we needed to establish as an institution. This meant policies, rules of procedures and staffing structures had to be established, and members of parliament had to be trained. Very importantly, we needed to ensure that review of the constitution. Despite the fact that I was there to support Jawari in his role as Speaker, I was obliged to provide whatever support I could to various ministers of government, and sometimes even the prime minister. Later, I would also assist the UNDP in the management of their parliamentary support and constitutional review projects.

Changing fortunes

Just as I was getting into my role as a consultant to the speaker in Mogadishu, the UN confirmed in December 2012 my position on the Mediation Standby Unit (MSU). The MSU, which was based in New York, provided mediation support to countries in conflict. This was quite exciting because it was a prestigious appointment. Annually, the UN appointed six internationally recognised experts to serve on the team who sometimes had to be mobilised within 24 hours. I started 2013 off in quite high spirits for several reasons and to celebrate my good fortune, Soraya and I took our parents on a most wonderful holiday in Thailand. It was really special to see the older people enjoy themselves so much.

In February, National Treasury called to enquire as to whether I would be prepared to serve on the Special Pensions Appeals Board.[86] The government decided that it was proper that people who made sacrifices to bring about democracy in the country be entitled to a special pension. This was to be paid to a person who was either imprisoned, exiled and/or in the full-time employ of a liberation movement for more than five years before the cut-off date on 2 February 1990. Treasury did not mind my commitment to the MSU as it was not a full-time post. I was pleased to work in both the MSU and the Appeals Board at the same time. This was also the first time in more than five years that I was offered a full-time contract of one year.

I travelled to New York in early March 2013 to be inducted into the new team. I took Soraya along. Also in February of that year, Soraya and I bought a house. After a few difficult years, I was very grateful to have a run of very good fortune.

Working for the UN

Working for the UN was a great learning experience. Being an international public servant made up for my inability to be a public servant in my own country. The team performed so well that the UN decided to extend our contracts by another year. My first assignment was in West Africa. Both Liberia and Sierra Leone were in the process of undertaking constitution-making exercises and I was asked to carry out a scoping mission and to identify what, if any, support we could give them.

Liberia and Sierra Leone

Liberia was a fascinating start to my career in the UN. The standard operating procedure required me to wade through large amounts of briefing documents to fully understand the context of the assignment. I learnt that between 1847 and 1980 Liberia was governed by a constitution that recognised a special status for Americo-Liberians, who were freed African slaves that came to Liberia as colonisers would, much to the detriment of the indigenous people. It was rather strange that former African slaves behaved like colonialists.

We interviewed a number of different role players and stakeholders and also consulted with the UN mission on the ground. One of the great benefits of the job was that we had access to the most senior political leaders in each country that we were deployed to. We also got to engage with various civil society structures to hear their perspective on political issues and the solutions required. My next mission was Sierra Leone, which had an equally fascinating history.

Libya

I first visited Libya in the early '80s as part of an ANC youth delegation attending a conference in Tripoli. I was therefore keen to see the city 30 years later: after the fall of Gaddafi I was asked to provide support to the constitution-making process.

Libya's constitutional history was limited to the period between 1951 and 1969. Thus, four decades of autocratic rule left the country with profound weaknesses across the entire spectrum of social, political and economic institutions. That said, there was a political centre, the country was stable and the state functional. Gaddafi was overthrown by forces that had no concern for the continued delivery of services. And without a centre, the state collapsed allowing underlying deep schisms and ethnic tensions to surface in an uncontrollable manner.

I quickly learnt that while the MSU had incredible value to offer to countries, our efforts were limited to the extent that we were trusted. I cautioned that it was not possible to merely rely on parachuting experts into a conflict situation in the hope that we could magically solve problems. Your ability to mediate depended on political actors trusting you. Also, people were not looking for theories and clever ideas, but needed practical solutions. I was therefore of the view that our work should rather focus on building capacity and empowering people.

My experience in Libya, as in Somalia, made me aware that I was now working in some of the most dangerous places in the world. Not long before I arrived in Tripoli, Prime Minister Ali Zeidan was kidnapped from the same hotel in which I was accommodated.[87] Like Mogadishu, the sound of gunfire was frequent. The tragic reality of this was made painfully clear when one of the last people I met in Tripoli, Salwa Bouguiguis – feisty and fearless human rights lawyer – was assassinated in June 2014.[88] I was fortunate to leave before it became unsafe for foreigners to work in Tripoli and all UN staff were withdrawn.

My next major assignment was in Yemen – which was also in a state of collapse.

Yemen

I arrived in Yemen's capital city Sanaa on 1 July 2014. I was immediately taken by the incredible architectural beauty of this ancient city of several thousand years. The journey to the hotel was punctuated with frequent stops at checkpoints managed by heavily armed young and very irritable khat-chewing soldiers belonging to different militia groups.

Yemen was one of the early countries leading the Arab Spring. These struggles unleashed a process that potentially promised the transformation of Yemen with sufficient energy to propel it into becoming a modern constitutional democracy. This was an exciting place to be. A national dialogue conference of all role players was successfully convened and produced a set of rather ambitious outcomes in January 2014. With this, Yemen was set to negotiate its constitution. This is the background to my visit as a member of a UN team.

I was brought in to provide expert advice on both process and substantive issues. What became immediately evident was that there were two major areas of tension. These were the North/South historical divide and the tribal conflict that played itself out between the people of the different regions. Unfortunately, the UN was not very successful at mediating an end to the conflict.

The Yemeni interlocutors were a very impressive lot of people who were sophisticated in both their organisational and administrative skills. I gained an immediate respect for them and was very pleased to return several times thereafter. There was much to enjoy in Yemen; its architecture, history and cuisine and the best honey you will find anywhere. There were however also aspects of their culture and traditions that were hard to accept. Young girls were still being married off at tender ages and many rural Yemeni boys received their first gun, sometimes even a Kalashnikov, as a rite of passage in their teenage years. The other challenge I had was that revenge killings and the acceptance of blood money are not uncommon. Also extraordinary was the widespread use of the recreational drug, khat, by most Yemenis, both young and old. Many members of the Constitutional Drafting

Commission (CDC) also enjoyed this habit.

Unfortunately, the constitution-making process took place in a bubble that was isolated from the increasing tensions brewing around the country. There was a sense of hopelessness, especially amongst those who participated in the revolution. Poor communications gave the impression that the process was not accountable to the public. There was little transparency and it did not bode well. To add to our woes, just as we were beginning to make progress, the security situation in Sanaa collapsed. We were evacuated along with the entire CDC and relocated to Abu Dhabi in the United Arab Emirates. It reminded me of what happened to the Somalis who were also forced to continue with their constitution-making outside the borders of their country.

I worked with the presidium of the CDC on the management of the process through its different phases. My mission proved to be most rewarding because of the relationship I enjoyed with both the secretariat and presidium. The rapport and trust I enjoyed assured me that my proposals would be considered seriously. Unfortunately, this came to naught with the armed intervention of the Saudi coalition forces.

Philippines

My work in the Philippines was another great experience that consisted of several missions to different parts of the country, especially the Bangsamoro area during 2014. This history of the conflict was fascinating.

The Moros, most of whom were Muslims, resisted Spanish, American, and then Japanese rule over 400 years. The origin of the war between the Moros and Christian Filipinos started with the colonisation by Spain. In more recent years, under President Ferdinand Marcos' rule, 68 Filipino Muslim military trainees were murdered Filipino soldiers. The Moro National Liberation Front (MNLF) was formed to seek the establishment of a Bangsamoro nation through force of arms. To avoid further conflict, President Corazon Aquino met the MNLF and paved the way for negotiations.

Following this, a comprehensive peace agreement was signed between the government and the Moro Islamic Liberation Front (MILF) in 2014. They requested support from the UN to develop a comprehensive transition strategy. Of importance to them was the transition from a military organisation into a political party and participating in an election. My engagement with them was successful and I followed up on several occasions. As was the case in both Somalia and Yemen, they found it easier to work with someone of the same faith.

My meetings with them took me to the Moro region, including one of their military bases in the jungles, where I had occasion to spend time with both the political and military leadership of the MILF. They fascinated me because they were disciplined, extremely well educated, sophisticated and very knowledgeable. Their structures showed great maturity and were well developed. I regretted that I was not able to witness the conclusion of their negotiations and agreements reached.

XIX

Somalia Revisited

Supporting parliament

My work in Somalia continued intermittently since my first appointment in 2012. I was very fortunate to work with Jawari through his terms as speaker of the ninth (2012 to 2016) and tenth (2017 onwards) parliaments. My contract was extended to include the provision of strategic support to both the UNDP (who paid for my services) and the Minister of Constitutional Affairs, Abdurahman Hosh Jibril, who was appointed in March 2017. In October 2017, I also supported the Office of the Prime Minister for a short period.

Few international experts have spent as much time as I have in Mogadishu. These were extremely difficult years, but not without benefit. I worked with more than five different governments and three parliaments. I was successful in earning the trust of the key role players and made responsible for crafting the strategies and supporting both the constitutional review and the establishment of their most successful parliament in more than thirty years.

A failing strategy

In 2016, Al-Shabaab became the deadliest extremist group in Africa, responsible for the killings of more than 4200 people.[89] The year 2017 was little different.[90] On 14 October 2017, I was working in my shipping container-cum-hotel room when I heard a huge bang. I went out to investigate only to discover a huge plume of black smoke. It was the biggest truck bomb ever exploded in Africa killing nearly 587 people and injuring a further 316 innocent people.[91]

The truck laden with explosives was destined for the compound where we were living. Fortunately for us, it was prematurely detonated when soldiers at a nearby checkpoint attempted to search the vehicle because they were suspicious. The anger of ordinary Somalis seemed not to have deterred Shabaab because they followed this with several other car and truck bombs killing a further 50 people in the same month.

The violence is only getting worse and the strategies of both the international community and the successive Somali governments since 1990 have not been successful. Their steadfast refusal to find a political solution means they continue to rely on military solutions which have thus far failed. Unless it is possible to decisively defeat Shabaab, and there is no evidence of this happening, there is no alternative to exploring political solutions.[92] Mogadishu remains a warzone and there are few institutions of state that deliver any services to the people. Interesting enough, life in Somalia continues despite the absence of the state, trade is exceptionally brisk in well stocked markets, and real estate in Mogadishu is extremely expensive despite the violence.[93]

XX

Time to Come Home

I returned home in 2017 soon after the horrific truck-bomb attack in Mogadishu. It has taken me a while to admit to the trauma it caused because we were the intended victims. I was therefore very pleased to leave shortly thereafter with Soraya for an island getaway in the Maldives. The holiday was fortuitously planned long in advance to celebrate our tenth wedding anniversary and my 60th birthday. We both needed the escape and time together. It was also a time for us to reflect on our lives and count our blessings.

Our trip to the Maldives was a celebration and I focused on this rather than dwell on the tragedy that befell the innocent denizens of Mogadishu. It is at times like this that I am really grateful to have Soraya as a partner in my life. Soraya always found a way of allowing me the space to deal with the difficult questions that I was faced with and yet provided me with her companionship and comforting support in the most loving way. After the holiday, we spent much time on thinking about our options. There was much to think about. The reality that hit home is that life is fragile and can change in an instant. Change is the only constant. It is therefore important for me to spend as much time with Soraya and the family. I need to come back home.

Working in countries trying to wrestle out of the suffocating grasp of conflict, as I have done for so many years, has helped me to understand the nature of so many fragile states. In several of the countries I worked in, such as Yemen, Libya and Somalia, politics was determined more by the power of individuals than ideology, or political or other formations in society. This made matters all the more unpredictable. It was also not possible to apply the quick fixes that the international community often wanted to see. Solutions were always going to be determined more by internal dynamics rather than externally imposed requirements or dates.

My function was to work with the political leaders in their respective countries to find political and constitutional solutions that may take the country forward rather than solve all their problems.[94] Sometimes, as was the case in Zimbabwe and Somalia, progress had to be measured not so much by taking a country out of conflict, but preventing the country from sliding into deeper conflict.

The real challenge I face now upon returning home is gainful employment. While I have enjoyed being an international public servant and working for the United Nations in different fragile and developing countries, it is my fervent hope that I would have the privilege of returning home to serve the people of South Africa. I remain committed to working to make our country a better place. At heart, I remain a public servant and don't know any other life. I have deeply regretted that I was not able to serve the people of the country whose freedom I fought for. I have therefore set myself the goal of finding a way of coming back home and working in the public sector.

Fortunately, the change of leadership in the country has created new possibilities and much hope. One can only hope that the new changes sweeping through the country would also ensure the public sector is less toxic and more open. Home is where I want to be. I suspect that this is what Uncle Reg meant when he referred to the final destination. Thuma Mina. Please.

Endnotes

1 Marius and Jenny were stationed in Botswana as part of the ANC Internal Political and Reconstruction Department (IPRD). Jenny was also a member of the SACTU committee. The Internal Political & Reconstruction Department was established in 1977 by the NEC of the ANC as part of the Revolutionary Council (RC, later replaced by the Politico-Military Council or PMC).

2 Garth Bennyworth: 'Bechuanaland's Aerial Pipeline: Intelligence and Counter Intelligence Operations against the South African Liberation Movements 1960–1965' at https://www.sahistory.org.za/sites/default/files/file%20uploads%20/bechuanaland_s_aerial_pipeline_intelligence_and_counter_intelligence_operations_against_the_south_african_liberation_movements_1960_1965.pdf, accessed on 11 January 2019.

3 Walter Sisulu, 'We Shall Overcome', in Mac Maharaj, ed. *Reflections in Prison*, Zebra Press and Robben Island Museum, 2001, pp. 79–80, 2001.

4 Unfortunately, I was not able to interview as many comrades as I intended because I was out of the country for most of the time it took to write this book.

5 A bullet-proof vest, helmet and two-way radio was standard issue for all who ventured beyond the UN compound.

6 I had to obtain the approval of the UN Special Representative to live outside the 'wire' where all UN officials were accommodated. As with other countries in conflict, a specially protected zone is set usually in the vicinity of the airport to allow for easy evacuation if the need arises.

7 Passenger Indians were essentially migrants who came to South Africa having paid their own fare. This distinguished them from the Indians who arrived earlier as slaves or indentured labourers.

8 'Sonvadi' in Gujarati means 'fields of gold', evidently because of its past

agricultural glory and wealth.

9 Perhaps this explains why Indians who have some wealth are traditionally so passionate about acquiring property? Culturally, this seems to be an important measure of wealth. This would also explain why etched so deeply into my psyche was the desire to have a home of my own.

10 We were required to prominently display our licence to serve African people above the entrance of our shops.

11 'No Middle Road' by Joe Slovo was published in 1976 in Davidson B., Slovo J. and Wilkinson A. R., *Southern Africa: The New Politics of Revolution*, Penguin, 1976.

12 Back then, we used the term 'propaganda', which we were proud of as there were no negative connotations attached to the term.

13 https://omalley.nelsonmandela.org/omalley/index.php/site/q/03lv02424/04lv02730/05lv02918/06lv02950.htm, accessed on 11 October 2019.

14 This is the recent finding of the reopened Inquest hearing into the circumstances of Ahmed Timol's death.

15 Stephen Ellis: 'An official estimate in 1979 was that the formal ANC political underground inside South Africa consisted of between 300 and 500 people located mostly in the cities, but with a larger informal pool of support. An official document on the underground noted in 1983 that 'very few of our units or single operatives work new strategies under what we understand as ANC discipline' and that 'qualitative change' was needed "desperately".' – Stephen Ellis, *External Mission: The ANC in Exile, 1960–1990*, Oxford University Press, 2013.

16 The End Conscription Campaign was only established in 1983 and was successful in mobilising a large number of white students facing this challenge.

17 Records exist on Rocklyn Mark Williams' input at the Truth and Reconciliation Commission. Available at: http://www.justice.gov.za/trc/decisions/2000/ac200020.htm, accessed on 16 October 2019.

18 During those years, all businesses closed for the weekend except for the Saturday morning.

19 Based on records of the TRC, Mfalapitsa was an askari (which is the term used to describe members of the liberation movements who had joined the SAP and were working against their former comrades). Mfalapitsa's defection was a closely guarded secret. He was stationed at Vlakplaas, a secret security police base, at the time. Available at http://www.justice.gov.za/trc/decisions/2001/ac21198.htm, accessed on 14 October 2019.

20 https://www.sahistory.org.za/dated-event/beginning-anglo-zulu-war-

10-january-1879; https://www.sahistory.org.za/article/zulu-kingdom-and-colony-natal, accessed on 11 October 2019.
21 See, Ellis, *External Mission,* p. 123.
22 The Botswana Pula was always a little stronger than the South African Rand.
23 Gavin Cawthra, 'National Security and the Right to Information: The Case Of South Africa', 26 February 2013, p. 4. Available at: http://www.right2info.org/resources/publications/pretoria-finalization-meeting-april-2013-documents/national-security-and-rti-in-south-africa, accessed on 11 October 2019.
24 Mamasela was a notorious askari, who participated in the brutal murder of a number of cadres.
25 On the morning of 30 January 1981, South African troops attacked and killed a number of ANC refugees in Matola, Mozambique. A statement made by Oliver Tambo on 5 February 1981 can be found at: http://www.sahistory.org.za/archive/statement-oliver-tambo-south-african-raid-matola-05-february-1981, accessed on 11 October 2019.
26 On 9 December 1982, the South African Defence Force commandos targeted a cluster of houses on the outskirts of Maseru where members of the ANC were believed to be in hiding. Meeting no opposition from Lesotho's tiny 2000-man paramilitary force, they blasted their way through numerous homes. By morning, 42 people were dead, 30 of them believed to be members of the ANC. The remaining victims were Lesotho residents, including five women and two children. Their mission accomplished, the members of SADF returned across the border to South Africa without incident. Available at: https://maserumetro.com/news/news/the-last-supper/, accessed on 14 October 2019.
27 The 1985 Gaborone Massacre took place on 14 June 1985 when members of the South African Defence Force crossed into Botswana and attacked South Africans and Batswana in Gaborone and neighbouring villages. Twelve people died during the raid. When the South African army raided Maseru, Lesotho, in 1982, there were some fears that Botswana might be the next target. But others believed it unlikely, and one man said, 'Botswana is the darling of the international community. The South Africans would not risk angering the rest of the world by launching an attack on Botswana.' But Pretoria, either insensitive to world opinion, or disregarding it for reasons known to itself, ignored the international outcry and three times during 1985 attacked targets in Gaborone. For more on this, see, pamphlet by Libero Nyelele and Ellen Drake, published on 14 June 1985. Available

at: http://psimg.jstor.org/fsi/img/pdf/t0/10.5555/al.sff.document.bothisp104_final.pdf, accessed on 11 October 2019.

28 Craig Michael Williamson, born in 1949 to English-speaking parents in Johannesburg, used to be a South African police major, who was involved in a series of state-sponsored overseas bombings, burglaries, kidnappings, assassinations and propaganda between 1976 and 1980. In January 1980, Captain Williamson was unmasked as a South African spy. Williamson returned to South Africa and during the turbulent 1980s worked for the foreign section of the South African Police's notorious Security Branch and South Africa's 'super-spy' transformed into a parcel-bomb assassin.

29 Caxito is located close to a town of the same name in the municipality of Dande, a province of Bengo in Angola.

30 Mainstay was infiltrated into the country in or about 1987 and led a very successful unit that was operational in the Pretoria area. Unfortunately, Mainstay lost his life in one of the operations in Sunnyside, Pretoria.

31 With this communication being restored, I had completed my task and we would once again part ways. However, I later learnt from Ronnie Kasrils when I was in London that they once again needed to re-establish contact with Rocky and I was asked to help. I did so but had no further contact with Rocky. The next I learnt of Rocky was that he was arrested in 1986 and charged in the Johannesburg Magistrate's Court with 'furthering the aims of the ANC'. He was sentenced to six years' imprisonment and released on bail pending appeal. He skipped bail and left the country illegally on 31 May 1987. Apparently, Rocky insisted on returning home, this time in an operational capacity. He was armed with a couple of hand grenades and limpet mines. For reasons that I never go to know, Rocky found it necessary to detonate the small arsenal behind Anthea's Club in the Pietersburg Holiday Inn on 27 March 1988 – an incident for which he then made a full confession and obtained immunity.

32 'White Blocks' is the name given to the cheap prefabricated complex of duplex housing provided to the poor in Laudium.

33 Grad-P Light portable rocket system: The complete system comprises a 9P132 single-round man-portable launcher (it can be reloaded and used again), a 9M22M 122 mm high-explosive fragmentation rocket and a fire control panel. See also: https://en.wikipedia.org/wiki/BM-21_Grad, accessed on 14 October 2019

34 http://www.sahistory.org.za/dated-event/bomb-blast-rocks-anc-london-office, accessed on 14 October 2019.

35 R. Williams, 'A brief historical overview of Umkhonto We Sizwe (MK), 1961–1994', *Military History Journal*, Vol 11, No 5 (2000). Available at:

http://samilitaryhistory.org/vol115rw.html, accessed on 14 October 2019.
36. Sir Neil MacCormick (1940–2009) was a world-renowned legal philosopher and prominent Scottish public intellectual who held the Regius Chair in Public Law and the Law of Nature and Nations at Edinburgh University for 36 years.
37. I got to know General Viljoen during the negotiation of our constitution.
38. https://en.wikipedia.org/wiki/Raid_on_Gaborone, accessed on 14 October 2019.
39. In 'The United Democratic Front and Township Report', Mark Swilling argues that since the inception of the UDF, black resistance in South Africa had become increasingly effective, however that the contemporary history of township revolt was not due to strategies formulated and implemented by the UDF's national leadership. Instead, with the exception of the crucially important election boycotts of 1984, the driving force of black resistance that has effectively immobilised the 'coercive and reformist actions of the state has emanated from below as communities responded to their abysmal urban living conditions'. – http://www.sahistory.org.za/sites/default/files/hws-405.pdf, accessed on 11 October 2019.
40. See the Stuart Commission Report: https://www.sahistory.org.za/archive/stuart-commission-report, accessed on 11 October 2019.
41. https://www.marxists.org/archive/lenin/works/1920/lwc/ch09.htm, accessed on 11 October 2019.
42. https://omalley.nelsonmandela.org/omalley/index.php/site/q/03lv03445/04lv04015/05lv04016/06lv04025/07lv04027.htm, accessed on 14 October 2019.
43. Military Combat Work was essentially training in dealing with conspiracy. As explained by Thula Simpson: 'MCW training focused especially on the skills that such political, military and security/intelligence units would need. Trainees were drilled in different methods of covertly organising workers, recruiting agents, disseminating propaganda, conveying and receiving messages, contacting strangers, employing camouflage, and conducting intelligence and counterintelligence work. Above all they were taught about the cell system, involving each member of the underground recruiting three individuals who would each recruit three more, who all would recruit three others, etc. etc., thus enabling the underground to mushroom, but in a way that each member of the network only knew the identities of the individual who had recruited them and the three persons they themselves had recruited, thereby insulating the rest of the structure

from police hostility.' Available at: https://www.tandfonline.com/doi/abs/10.1080/00020184.2011.557579, accessed on 11 October 2019.

44 All of the comrades in my machinery who I interviewed made a point of mentioning this.

45 The youth and students have historically been the lifeblood of South African politics and will likely remain so for the near future. South African Student Organisation (SASO) was formed in 1968 and immediately filled a political void when it represented the interests of black students. However, by February 1973, they started suffering severe restrictions with the banning of eight of their leaders and were finally banned as an organisation in 1977. This left a huge political gap. AZASO was established in 1979 by students from five black universities and one college of education and effectively filled this void.

AZASO initially emerged as a continuation of SASO but later adopted the Freedom Charter and other policies aligned to the ANC over Black Consciousness philosophies. In addition, while SASO called for a total break away from white student structures, AZASO advocated a non-racial policy. AZASO also worked with formations such as the UDF and COSAS. They saw the Education Charter campaign as a rallying point to mobilise students and worked to make student structures more mass-based. Finally, in 1986 it changed its name to the South African National Students Congress (SANSCO). Like COSAS, they too saw a direct relationship between the educational and other (socio-political) struggles. See also: https://www.sahistory.org.za/article/south-african-national-students-congress-sansco, accessed on 14 October 2019.

46 From about 1983 onwards when there was increased interaction between the ANC leadership and operatives in the country, there came to be known what was commonly referred to as 'the line'. 'The line' usually referred the views or direction given by the ANC leadership. This could apply to various political debates or responding to a particular situation. It could be used in different circumstances where it was a view regarding the struggles against the Tricameral Parliament, dealing with the debates with comrades in the Black Consciousness movement, building of the UDF, etc. Back home, comrades would often talk about 'the line' meaning that this was the directive or approach of the ANC leadership. Sometimes, however, 'the line' was also used to bully people into a particular position because no one wanted to be seen to be taking positions that were contrary to the direction of leadership.

47 In the midst of the state of emergency, the South African Youth Congress

Endnotes

(SAYCO) was formed in March 1987 at a secret meeting in Cape Town. Ephraim Nkwe was a member of its first executive committee and the head of political education of the Soweto Youth Congress (SYC) and the SAYCO. In March 1989, four activists, Nkwe, Mpho Lekgoro, Clive Radebe and Job Sithole escaped from their guarded rooms in Johannesburg's Hillbrow Hospital where they were being treated for the after-effects of a hunger strike while in detention. They sought refuge at the West German Embassy in Pretoria to protest against detention without trial. The four left the embassy after three days following the government's promise that they were free and would not be detained.

Nkwe was part of a SAYCO delegation that visited the ANC in exile when the SAYCO leadership secretly crossed the border to meet with the ANC in exile. He was also the political commissar of his MK unit. In 1989, as defiance against the government's oppressive laws spread like wild fire, the government met it with yet further crackdown. A large number of the mass democratic movement leadership was detained. Nevertheless, detentions did not stop the defiance. Banned organisations unbanned themselves. On 20 August 1989, SAYCO unbanned itself. Nkwe declared, 'From this day, the sixth anniversary of the UDF, all restricted organizations will consider themselves to be free to operate and organize within their constituencies.'

After the unbanning of the ANC, the ANCYL was re-launched in 1991 and Nkwe became its first head of political education. Ephraim Nkwe passed away on 5 May 2013. At the time of his death, Nkwe was the chairperson of the Mpete Mosaka ANC branch in Pimville. See more at: http://www.sahistory.org.za/people/ephraim-nkwe#sthash.fagvlDRu.dpuf, accessed on 16 October 2019.

48 http://www.sahistory.org.za/organisations/south-african-youth-congress-sayco#sthash.eiHxAd3b.dpuf, accessed on 11 October 2019.
49 http://www.sahistory.org.za/archive/chapter-9-tactics-talks-tactics-confrontation, accessed on 11 October 2019. Operation Zikomo was a project put together after the Kabwe Conference.
50 This was the feedback that I got from Yogesh amongst others.
51 A point worth noting about this generation of activists which was specific to the struggles of the 1980s was the effort made in training of activists. Training workshops in drama, media, publications and programmes for the political education of activists was commonplace. This culture unfortunately did not continue after the unbanning of the ANC.
52 This was the same room that Jeets used when he was on the run during

the state of emergency.

53 Government Gazette; Vol. 444, No. 23328; 14 June 2002; Regulation Gazette, No. 7374; No. R. 43, 2002

54 I could not help noticing many years later that Ruby managed her daughter Lily's time in much the same way.

55 This type of training in political education has unfortunately not continued after the unbanning of the ANC.

56 However, after his infiltration into the country, he worked with a unit in Bethal but was soon arrested. He served a sentence of six years on Robben Island and was released in 1986.

57 Mike's full names and details are not known.

58 Govindasamy Krishnasamy Thambi Naidoo was born of indentured stock in 1875 and was involved in South African politics, influenced by the struggle for Indian liberation since early 1900s. Gandhi hailed Thambi Naidoo as one of the most important figures in the history of the satyagraha campaign in South Africa. In 1912, he was appointed the chairperson of the Tamil Benefit Society from whose membership the most dedicated passive resisters were drawn. He was elected president of Transvaal Indian Congress (TIC) in 1932. See further details at: http://sahistory.org.za/people/ck-thambi-naidoo, accessed on 4 November 2019.

59 http://www.sahistory.org.za/article/chronology-meetings-between-south-africans-and-anc-exile-1983-2000-michael-savage, accessed on 16 October 2019.

60 At the time of the incident, there was some speculation as to whether the limpets were sabotaged to detonate early. This was done in other instances with sabotaged grenades resulting in many injuries. However, after investigating the incident, it was evident to me that this was not the case. The limpet did not detonate prematurely. The delay in timing was the result of the Unit deciding to relocate the limpet after having primed it.

61 https://en.wikipedia.org/wiki/Speech_at_the_Opening_of_the_Parliament_of_South_Africa,_1990, accessed on 16 October 2019.

62 Josiah Jele was the head of the IPRD.

63 This is a comment made by Nava in an interview in August 2017.

64 These notebooks are currently held at the Nelson Mandela Foundation library.

65 The criticism is that South Africa's negotiated settlement was a secret pact between white and ANC elites, which excluded the black majority who had

sacrificed so much during the struggle for liberation. See: http://www.news24.com/SouthAfrica/News/boesak-the-anc-sold-out-20170820-2, accessed on 11 October 2019.
66 The Patriotic Front (PF) was formed in October 1991 as a loose alliance of parties that held an anti-apartheid position. The PF conference agreed on a joint programme for the negotiated transfer of power.
67 We now have more than 1000 elected representatives in both provisional and national government. Under apartheid, they had a parliament of 200.
68 This included the Independent Broadcast Authority, Independent Electoral Authority and the Transitional Executive Council laws.
69 Some of the key struggles were against disenfranchisement, land dispossession, job reservation, racial discrimination, and segregation. In each instance, the struggle was against particular pieces of legislation.
70 See Thomas Karis and Gwendolen Margaret Carter, *From Protest to Challenge: A Documentary History of the African Politics in South Africa 1882–1964, Volume 3*, Indiana University Press, 1972, 297.
71 Statement at the plenary session of the Constitutional Assembly on 24 January 1995
72 We were most fortunate in working with David Everatt who led a very talented team of researchers.
73 Subsequent to this, the CFO function became a Deputy Director-General level post and part of the executive team.
74 These include the Public Protector (PP), the Auditor-General (AG), the Electoral Commission (IEC), the South African Human Rights Commission (SAHRC), the Commission for Gender Equality (CGE) and lastly, the Commission for the Protection of the Rights of Cultural, Religious and Linguistic Communities. These institutions are independent of government, subject only to the constitution and the law. However, while they report directly annually to parliament, they are supported by the Department of Justice through which their budgets are allocated.
75 https://en.wikipedia.org/wiki/Bhe_v_Magistrate,_Khayelitsha, accessed on 16 October 2019.
76 See: http://www.saflii.org/za/cases/ZACC/2000/27.html, accessed on 16 October 2019. It is important to note that in the case before the Constitutional Court, the Masters Office master opposed the application on grounds based on socio-economic considerations that included: (a) The lack of human resources, infrastructure, training and finance to administer the intestate estates of Blacks. (b) The current workload of the masters of the high court which already provides substantial pressure and

managerial problems. (c) The transferral of intestate Black estates from the magistrate's to the master's office would create chaos. The minister advanced similar reasons and argued that: (a) It is logistically convenient to administer the estates of Black people by magistrates since magistrates are found in every small town; (b) The methods of administration of deceased estates are informal and relatively swift; (c) Magistrates have a better understanding of customary law; and (d) It is cheaper to have the estates of Black people administered by magistrates since master's fees do not have to be paid. See also: http://www.puk.ac.za/opencms/export/PUK/html/fakulteite/regte/per/issuepages/2003Volume6no2/2003x2xrautenb_art.pdf, accessed on 16 October 2019.

77 In response, we established the Sesifikile project, (meaning 'we have arrived', in Xhosa) project which was designed to. However, even this had limited value because we did not have the associated capacity required to deliver the intended services.

78 I called for decisive intervention. Over the previous three months, I addressed six correspondences to the director-general asking for a meeting to address the challenges we were facing. Unfortunately, nothing came of this. I also explained the impact of the lack of capacity and concluded with recommendations as to the way forward. In short, the concern I expressed was that the department's failure to provide the capacity required was resulting in a rapid deterioration in the quality of services being delivered. Finally, I offered to give my support to and assist with a proper handover to the person who would be appointed as the new chief master. Unfortunately, the department showed little interest in dealing with the challenges and only appointed my successor in June 2011 – four years after my resignation.

79 The full report is available at: https://www.dbsa.org/EN/About-Us/Publications/Documents/Health%20Roadmap.pdf, accessed on 11 October 2019.

80 http://www.health-e.org.za/wp-content/uploads/2014/08/South-Africa-eHealth-Strategy-2012-2017.pdf

81 Governance of the judicial system has been dealt with obliquely in successive constitutions and piecemeal in legislation such as the Supreme Court Act 59 of 1959. Certain significant features of governance, such as the chief justice's headship of the judiciary and the nature and extent of his powers in this regard, have not been made explicit but have largely been left to custom and convention.

Endnotes

82 http://www.justice.gov.za/docs/other-docs/20120228-transf-jud.pdf.
83 Arthur Chaskalson passed away on 1 December 2012 and Pius Langa on 24 July 2013.
84 https://www.saferworld.org.uk/resources/news-and-analysis/post/807-somalias-war-cant-be-won-militarily-time-to-give-peace-a-chance.
85 http://www.aljazeera.com/indepth/features/2014/10/gunning-down-taxmen-somalia-2014102052539346950.html
86 The Special Pensions law applied to a South African if they participated in the struggle and were prevented from providing for a pension because they were engaged in the full-time service of a banned political organisation for a total period of at least five years prior to 2 February 1990. This would also apply to a person who was either banned or incarcerated for the same period. The Appeals Board was a quasi-judicial structure responsible for considering the appeals of those whose applications were turned down.
87 See media reports at http://www.theguardian.com/world/2013/oct/10/libyan-prime-minister-kidnapped; and http://www.bbc.com/news/world-africa-24496357, accessed on 11 October 2019.
88 See media reports at http://www.dailymail.co.uk/news/article-2670556/Prominent-female-activist-killed-Libya.htm, accessed 16 October 2019l; and https://www.fidh.org/en/region/north-africa-middle-east/libya/15664-libya-outrage-following-the-assassination-of-prominent-lawyer-and-women, accessed on 11 October 2019.
89 https://www.usatoday.com/story/news/world/2017/06/14/hostages-attack-somalia-restaurant/102865372/, accessed on 11 October 2019.
90 The UN report however suggests that more than 4,500 civilians have been killed or wounded in the conflict in Somalia for the years of 2016 and 2017. See: https://www.voanews.com/a/un-4500-civilians-killed-wounded-since-2016/4157579.html, accessed on 11 October 2019.
91 https://en.wikipedia.org/wiki/14_October_2017_Mogadishu_bombings, accessed on 11 October 2019.
92 https://www.saferworld.org.uk/resources/news-and-analysis/post/807-somalias-war-cant-be-won-militarily-time-to-give-peace-a-chance, accessed on 11 October 2019.
93 Ironically, not only are you able to find the latest mobile technology in Mogadishu, but you will also get it cheaper than in most parts of the world because no taxes are paid.
94 All too often international agencies would dispatch consultants with a particular world view and ideology and who believed that they had all

the answers to the problems being experienced without bothering to understand the history and culture of the environment we were working in.